As an educator in the field of health sciences, I often get asked by my students how I got "here" and how did my motivations and values shape my career trajectory. I have often stressed the need to follow my gut and the challenges in maintaining balance when you literally want to change the world. I have often wished there could be a resource to support their exploration into their own sense of purpose and abilities while filling the need in the "real world" without burning out. This book is the guide I have been looking for, as it encourages curiosity and a holistic approach to service. I will definitely be recommending this book to my students, who are aspiring health professionals, to help them promote their well-being while becoming curious about their own journey to conscious service.

Paola Ardiles, Senior Lecturer, Faculty of Health Sciences, Simon Fraser University

As a social worker, educator, and clinician, I have worked in various aspects of burnout prevention for over twenty-five years. *Conscious Service* offers a fresh and meaningful perspective on what it means to serve others while honoring the self.

Elizabeth Bishop offers a holistic invitation into a deeper understanding of what conscious service truly means and how to achieve it. Her thoughtful storytelling combined with calls to reflection and action is both informative and inspiring. While this is a book about service, it is ultimately a resonating call to helpers to come home to themselves in loving, compassionate, and caring ways.

This work speaks to the mind, body, heart, and spirit of helpers, asking provocative questions that encourage those of service to remember the self. Bishop invites us into a "pilgrimage of self-connection." She asserts that compassion doesn't make us tired; rather, overextension of the self is what exhausts us. If you want to sustain meaning and increase satisfaction in your service work, and you want to avoid patterns of abandoning yourself that can happen easily to those of us who serve the needs of others, this empowering book is for you.

Lynda Monk, MSW, RSW, CPCC,
Director of the International Association for Journal Writing

In an era of unprecedented global pandemic and employee exhaustion and burnout, resignation of health-care service providers is a growing universal phenomenon. Paradoxically, the health-care community all too often serves others at the expense of their own health and welfare. Our natural predilection toward altruism all too often negates care of self, without which we are seriously constrained in our ability to serve others.

Conscious Service provides a way out of this destructive health-care paradox. Brilliantly written, this treatise in how we process thoughts and connect with others fosters what may be a new generation of thought for training our future health-care providers to be knowledgeable, skillful, dutiful, and altruistic. Such physician traits are required for accreditation of all AAMC medical schools and teaching hospitals. *Conscious Service* would be a useful addition to medical humanities, community science, and bedside rounds for all health-care professionals. The future livelihood of the health-care professions may benefit greatly from the contents herein.

Dr. Brian W. Tobin, PhD, Executive Director, Synergy Global Health Foundation, Inc., Washington, D.C., and former Associate Dean, Department Chair, Professor of Medical Education, Biomedical Science, Family and Community Medicine, Pediatrics, and Internal Medicine, USCSOMG, PLFSOM, MUSM, AECOM

Conscious Service

Ten ways to reclaim your calling,
move beyond burnout, and
make a difference
without sacrificing yourself

Elizabeth Bishop

Hazelden Publishing

Hazelden Publishing
Center City, Minnesota 55012
hazelden.org/bookstore

978-1-61649-958-7

CIP data is on file with the Library of Congress.

Editor's note:
This publication is not intended as a substitute for the advice of health-care professionals.
All the stories in this book are based on actual experiences and personal interviews. Some
names and certain facts have been changed to protect the anonymity of the people who so
generously shared their stories for this book.

26   25   24   23   22   1   2   3   4   5

Cover designer: Terri Kinne
Typesetter: Jessica Ess, Hillspring Books
Developmental editor: Marc Olson
Editorial project manager: Betty Christiansen

CONTENTS

Chapter 3: Embrace Full Responsibility 81

An Invitation to Freedom 81

Chapter 4: Connect with Your Self 117

An Invitation to Discovery 117

For Barb
Without any words, my profound teacher

and

To Life
An endless source of mysterious curiosity

ACKNOWLEDGMENTS

My heartfelt gratitude goes out to Andrea Lien, editorial director at Hazelden Publishing, for championing this project and seeing the vision of the work.

To my editor at Hazelden, Marc Olson, without whose wisdom, intuition, keen eye, and commitment to its core message this book would not be what it is. Thank you, Marc, for your patience, kindness, and partnership.

To the entire Hazelden team—especially Betty Christiansen, Carolyn Williams-Noren, Cathy Broberg, and Jill Grindahl—for your expertise, attention to detail, and contributions to this work. I am filled with gratitude.

To those who agreed to share their stories for inclusion in this book, and to those who offered to read and endorse this work, my deep gratitude. And to all my spiritual teachers—past and present—whose wisdom I continually work to integrate. Your collective work has inspired my understanding of spiritual qualities and human connection.

For my loved ones now departed from this world, I am grateful for our relationships and your ongoing presence in my life. The veil is thin, indeed.

To my sisters and brothers through blood or blessing: Margaret and Steve, Sally, Michelle, Silvana, Erika, Greg and Jelena. Thank you for the laughter, tears, and safe place to land.

For the inspiration to be at my best, especially when I lose my place, my children, Taylor and Shino; Melanie and my beautiful grandson, Cohen—I love and appreciate you with all my heart.

I am forever grateful for the learning and growth that's come from each of you whose paths I have crossed in a service relationship, whether I was the provider or the recipient. I have been endowed with the gift of your stories and embraced by your willingness to hear mine.

I have worked with some of the most amazing people over the course of my career, including colleagues, adult learners, and community partners. Our shared journeys have left permanent etches in my heart and are deeply cherished.

To my traveling companions. When and where our challenges overshadowed the love, thank you for walking the thorny path with me.

Sometimes life shows up in unexpected ways and we are forever changed. Thank you, T, for being such a sweet surprise.

And finally, I thank the work of conscious service itself. You came to me and through me like a divine gift—at times embraced, at times rejected. I am humbly aware that your intent was always for my highest good. I'm glad you didn't give up.

And I am deeply grateful.

PREFACE

Because you are holding this book right now, I assume you have some kind of a desire to serve in the world. You might have built a years-long career in health care or education or human services, or maybe you're just starting out. Perhaps your calling is to a healing profession like massage or Reiki, or to some specific work beyond or complementary to what have been called the traditional helping professions. You might be looking for ways to volunteer your time or donate your effort. Or maybe you're caring for a loved one at home and facing facts that might alter your identity as well as affect the way you spend your days and nights. Opportunities to serve are ever present. Sometimes they arise out of the blue. These days they can seem more urgent and apparent than ever.

As the harsh realities of the messes we have created in our relationships with each other and the planet continue to emerge, illuminated and catalyzed by a global pandemic, we're starting to see cracks in the ways we've understood and embodied vocations of service. We've also become more aware of how service providers like you and me seem set up to suffer. Hard as it is, this moment of dawning awareness is a gift. Let's honor this opportunity. Let's decide that the work of service doesn't have to automatically include sacrificing our sanity, health, safety, and soul. Let's build a new way to serve each other from the heart of our humanity.

I heard a call to serve very early in life, and I knew that whatever I chose as a career would involve some kind of service to others. I dove deep, gave all I had, and sought to change the world with the power of my goodwill and my love. When, some years later, I found myself feeling defeated, exhausted, and empty, I didn't know what had happened or why I felt like such a failure. I didn't understand the important relationship between who I was at my core and what I could offer the world.

In the years that followed, I embarked on a journey of spiritual exploration and personal development. Along the way, I began to see that if my desire to serve the world with my gifts and my energy and my time was going to be sustainable for me and accessible to and effective with the people I wanted to serve, I had to get to know and love myself. Through this lens, my view of service expanded. Service's generous power could not be reserved for my career; it also had to matter in my personal relationships—including the way I regarded and treated myself.

I came to imagine service as an energy that can be expressed in long-term relationships with the people I love most as well as in a moment with a stranger. Service isn't simply a career category or a day job. It is a way of life, and it begins with being of service to our own hearts first.

Writing this book has been a personal, spiritual, and evolutionary process for me. I share with you because our vocations of service connect us. My learning has emerged through my traditional career in services, my curiosity about alternative approaches, my commitment to spiritual exploration, and the richness of my personal relationships, not to mention my deep dives into the dark corners of my own soul.

As new principles and insights have emerged, I've made it my mission to determine how they apply in every experience. I want you to be able to use these insights, as I have, to embrace who you are. I want you to be able to integrate this knowledge, which has rippled into nearly every area of my life, into what you do. Life rarely offers wisdom that applies only to a single person or situation. Our calling includes applying what we receive and sharing it with others.

We each have a unique story. I share from the perspective of my experience and what I have learned and grappled with over the years. I hope you feel an affinity with these ideas and the insights they invite. I hope that the call to conscious service resonates with your life and what you've learned and loved and struggled through. And throughout that experience, I pray that you can give voice to your personal story—past, present, and future—and embrace the ways more conscious and self-connected service can add peace and joy to your life and love to your work.

With all my love,
Elizabeth

Conscious Service

Introduction

The COVID-19 pandemic has highlighted the vital importance of first responders, health-care workers, and other service providers—many of whom have been deemed "essential" in policy as well as in popular imagination. This designation has served as a kind of honorific, highlighting the heroic nature of people whose callings expose them to unique hazards. It has also prompted a conversation about how we as a society actually value, care for, and reward those whose daily work is vital to the basic function of public health and safety (as well as to social services, commerce, education, and elder and child care).

The occupational hazards that service providers face are not limited to contagious diseases like the coronavirus. These years of ongoing crisis have also revealed the burden of secondary trauma, demoralization, and burnout that many of these jobs include. These effects, distressingly familiar to many in the service industries, have only been heightened by the relentlessness of the pandemic, by the ways it has been politicized, and by the surge of human need that has been exacerbated by the added demands this global health crisis has placed on every category of human service.

Fueled by fear and a kind of desperation, we have developed a language about service that often includes metaphors borrowed from warfare. We talk about "front lines" and people serving "in the trenches." Solutions to challenges are addressed with "boots on the ground" and "plans of attack." Our words are geared up for battle. It's no wonder that we so often see a challenge as an enemy and a service relationship as a place to win or lose.

Our current situation is a potential catalyst for transformation not only in the ways we structure our public health and social service systems, but also in the words we use to imagine and describe the work

3

itself. We can step away from us-versus-them thinking and learn how to serve each other as a unified human collective.

Service is an energetic force. Service is about reciprocity, fulfillment, and responsiveness. Too often we experience it as tinged with exhaustion, burnout, and social and cultural warfare. Conscious service invites us to access and harness this energy, contribute to the transformation of dysfunctional systems and ways of being, and join in creating vibrant and sustainable communities that are marked by hope instead of fear.

This generation-defining era offers an opportunity for us to think and act differently. We stand in a moment where the faults and shortcomings of our current thinking and organizing in the human service sector can be first noticed and then transformed into healthier and more human-centered models. It's time for a paradigm shift in the way we service providers approach and understand our work, and for a similar shift in the way our society educates, trains, deploys, organizes, and supports those of us who take on callings and careers as service providers.

The emotional and spiritual challenges facing service providers have been of concern since I started in the field over forty years ago. Today the crisis facing service providers has become apparent not only to those of us experiencing it, but also to those who love us, as well as the community at large. This isn't just because nearly everyone depends on or will depend on some kind of service in our lives; beyond the crisis of the coronavirus pandemic, the current state of disharmony, inequity, and marginalization in the world has deepened these concerns and brought them into wider focus.

It's time to make the happiness, health, and joy of service providers as essential as the work we're called to undertake in service to the world. In his wonderful book *A Deep Breath of Life*, Alan Cohen puts this quite simply: "If your vision of service does not include your own happiness, you've left out a very important person."

When we first step on the path of service, few of us really know what we're getting into. We have grand visions of how we can contribute. Often, we're ill-prepared to include our happiness in this vision, and poorly supported when it comes to managing the discrepancy between our ideals and the realities we come to know in our work.

In the professional sector, many service providers go through a process of disillusionment. We wonder how we went from "I'm going to change the world" to simply struggling to get through the day. This personal angst eventually shows up in the quality of our service. Engaged and effective service is next to impossible when the human resources—the people at the heart of every human service effort—are strained, overwhelmed, disconnected, and unsupported. And everyone loses.

I believe we lose because our approaches are based on outdated and often contradictory beliefs about service. These include cultural assumptions about altruism and the self-sustaining nobility of self-sacrifice in service roles, as well as employer-driven directives about the need for compartmentalization and rigid boundaries. As a group, service providers have readily absorbed these contradictory myths and instructions. The result is an unsustainable paradox whose tension our bodies and minds must hold: we try to effectively and compassionately respond to the serious and interrelated needs of others while also obeying ineffective—if well-intentioned—directives about self-care and professional distance.

Many people believe that the solution to what ails us is achieving a thing called work-life balance. To avoid burnout and its related problems, we're told, we need to find a way to separate our lives from our work.

Managing work-life balance has become a kind of holy grail for those who are concerned about worker turnover and employee morale. This interest isn't limited to service industries. The premise assumes that being at work isn't and shouldn't be a part of living our lives.

Behind most prescriptions for creating work-life balance is a suggestion that when we're engaged with our work, we ought to be estranged from other aspects of our lives, and when we go home we should simply reverse that process. Those of us whose vocations involve the emotional, relational, and spiritual energies of service along with the physical and cognitive labor of hands and head need something altogether different.

Most interpretations of work-life balance are based on the false dichotomy of separation. The truth is that our work and our lives are intertwined, no matter how many guidelines and boundaries we build to make them seem separate.

So what can we do?

We can begin with the matter of balance. If you are feeling out of balance when it comes to your work and your life, reorganizing the *shape* of one or the other is like the proverbial rearranging of deck chairs on a sinking ship. Instead, see what you can do about the *substance*.

Conscious service is concerned with the substance.

This approach is based on the radical assumption that the work we do can be a source of joy and fulfillment, and that joy and fulfillment are not merely fringe benefits of service; they're the heart of the matter. Conscious service acknowledges the good intentions behind superficial strategies for self-care, and it moves beyond them to access the power of responsibility, choice, and inspired action with which we can connect to ourselves in respectful, compassionate, and life-giving ways—ways that take seriously the forces that motivated us to pursue a life of service in the first place. Conscious service begins with the premise that service is a form of love and that our ability to authentically and honorably love others must begin with our capacity to respect and care for ourselves with compassion and affection. It recognizes that compassion does not make us tired; overextension of self and lack of self-compassion are what exhaust us.

In a forty-plus-year career in service, I have personally experienced burnout, addiction, recovery, and personal loss alongside the joys of falling in love, being a mom and grandma, connecting to my passions, and achieving many personal and career goals. I've witnessed the impact of tragedy, trauma, healing, and faith. These experiences have led to insight, growth, and expansion as I've made connections between how I live my life personally and how I show up in service. The process is not always pretty. My own journey seems as layered as the proverbial onion. Yet it has shaped the insights I offer here.

This book is for individuals in vocations of service at all stages of career development, from educational preparation through retirement, from direct service provision to management. It speaks to those in both traditional and alternative roles. Even if service isn't the core focus of your vocation, you can discover keys to feeling better as you serve, live on purpose, and contribute with impact.

If you are interested in finding and sustaining meaning in your service, this book and its ten invitations are for you. If you need creative ways to manage stress and burnout, you're welcome here. If you're committed to high-quality service and can't quite figure out where or how that can happen, come on in. Millions of people like you and me are motivated to participate in the betterment of our world and don't know where to begin.

You can start today, right where you are.

How to Get the Most from This Book

This book is built as a series of ten invitations. Imagine each is addressed to you personally. I lined them up with some reasons in mind, but you're welcome to open the book and consider them in any order that suits you or seems right. Each invitation offers a way into the experience of more conscious service. Some of these may seem more attractive to you than others; that's okay. It's actually perfect. Invitations are intended to make you feel welcome and wanted, not obligated. Come as you are.

Beneath the broad banner of each invitation, you'll find a short introduction followed by a handful of brief sections. Each brief section is intended to offer a window on one or more aspects of the main invitation. Some introduce important concepts or follow lines of logic that help make the idea at work come alive or make more sense. Some share stories that illustrate how the invitations to conscious service have been embraced and accepted by people in all kinds of callings. Occasionally I'll share a snapshot from my own experience—some moment that cemented an idea or brought me to a different level of awareness or offered a key insight. Every now and then I'll pipe up with a special word of encouragement or clarification.

As you peruse these invitations and consider what accepting their call might mean for your life as a service provider, I'll challenge you to pay attention to your feelings. You'll come to learn that the conscious service approach takes our intuition seriously. Call it your gut, your instinct, or the voice of your heart. This special human sense is often a reliable guide as we consider something new—whether that's a relationship, a big life decision (a change of jobs, a move), or a new idea or perspective.

The heart's guidance isn't usually as exact as a turn-by-turn GPS. It often emerges through the contrasting feelings of resonance and resistance.

Resonance

Resonance is a lot like recognition. When something resonates with us, we usually have a sense of familiarity and alignment. Bells ring. The lightbulb goes on. It is an "aha" moment. Something old makes a new kind of sense. I hope this happens a lot for you as you read this book. I believe a great many of the experiences you read about will be familiar, sometimes lamentably so.

Resonance might show up in how easy it is for you to read, or how fast you can digest the content. This feeling can also activate the energy of your curiosity. It can make you want to explore more, learn more. It can even lead you to connect dots and loop in ideas that I've not considered or included. This is a gift.

When you feel the deep chime of resonance, when your experience seems affirmed by being seen and reflected, and when the urge to discover more rises up within you, you are on the brink of breakthrough. Follow that.

Resistance

It's not all bells of recognition and flashing lights of heartfelt homecoming, of course. Some of this material may irritate you or make no sense. I may offer an idea or suggest a concept or share a story that leaves you shaking your head and rolling your eyes. But don't worry. This doesn't necessarily mean either of us is right or wrong about anything. It just means you've identified a place of resistance.

Resistance is an indicator. It means we're in uncharted or unfamiliar territory. We can use this feeling as a cue to run back to the places where we feel less exposed and uncertain, or we can stick around long enough to look at things from a new perspective. Put your resistance to work for you. When you notice your inner judge is ready to raise its gavel, pause for a few breaths. Ask clarifying questions. Delve deeper. Investigate the source of your discomfort. You may stumble upon the very nugget of wisdom that you have been waiting for your whole life.

Even though resonance is usually a more enjoyable feeling—it's lighter, clearer, and more exciting—resistance is an equally powerful tool for enlightenment, growth, and expansion. We learn through contrast as well as correspondence, and from people who push our buttons as well as friends we've had forever (who often push our buttons in their own ways).

Self-Abandonment

Self-abandonment describes the experience of repeatedly choosing against one's own needs in the moment. It's the emotional equivalent of walking away from yourself precisely when you need a friend by your side. One of my wise guides, Sensei Christopher Witecki, was the first to teach me about this spiritual and psychological phenomenon. Compared to the active energies of resonance and resistance, self-abandonment is simply an absence. When we abandon ourselves, we step away from the possibility of authentic connection with others as well as new ideas, approaches, or possibilities in our lives.

The risk and lure of self-abandonment, as well as its many self-negating expressions, will be a core theme throughout our shared exploration. As a concept that describes an experience, self-abandonment is especially applicable to service providers.

We service providers often describe ourselves as sensitive souls. Frequently motivated by a desire to do good and make a difference, we can also be quite externally driven. Any time we are more comfortable giving than receiving, we are at risk for self-abandonment and overextension. This often shows up in symptoms like burnout, exhaustion, and disillusionment.

And these feelings really suck.

They lead us to try to soothe our symptoms and escape painful experiences through all sorts of strategies, many of which seem like self-care but end up as self-harm. Too often this leads to substance use disorders or other patterns of addictive behavior. By the time we're engaging in any form of addiction, we've likely been unbalanced, out of alignment, and hurting for a while.

As you make your way through the following pages, you will have an opportunity to explore your own personal escape routes as well as the experiences, both internal and external, that have you looking for those ways out.

You might experience a sense of shame as we take up these topics together. Most of us have been conditioned to hide our pains and traumas, along with any activities we use to manage them. Addictive behaviors carry stigma in many of our callings, and the suggestion that service providers might need assistance is sometimes met with scorn or suspicion. For now, simply be aware of any resonance or resistance you might feel as we discuss substance use and self-destructive behavior and what these might mean for you, both personally and as a service provider.

Also trust that relief and recovery are real and possible. Conscious service begins with the invitation to embrace yourself wholly and with love, no matter what condition you're in at the moment.

Guiding Questions

Before you open whatever initial invitation may have caught your eye when you scanned the table of contents, I've got one more word about how this book works. At the close of many of the sections you will find a question or two. The questions are meant as prompts for your imagination and anchors for applying the ideas at work within each invitation to areas of your life where they can matter. Reflecting on and responding to them is one way you can make reading this book an active process.

You'll note that most of these questions are about you and your experience. Remaining centered in understanding our own path and determining our next step is more productive than seeking answers for or about other people. When the ideas and concepts you're reading lead you to wonder how others might react or respond (or, worse yet, how you think others might want *you* to respond), try to refocus your attention on yourself and what you want to understand more clearly or more fully.

The most powerful guiding questions illuminate a wide range of possibilities for learning and growth. Questions that keep us mired in over-analysis of the past keep us stuck there.

You Are Welcome Here

As you consider the ten invitations to conscious service, pay attention to what resonates with you and what triggers your resistance. Hold your hurts with compassion, and gently set aside any impulses to step away from your own side. Stay tuned in to your feelings; they will help you decide where to focus your energy. Stay curious. Use questions as opportunities to test ideas and experiment with integrating these ways of being into your whole life. Trust that this journey welcomes all of you. Follow the power, the energy, the curiosity, and the whispers of your heart. These things exist to guide you.

CHAPTER 1

Know Why You're Here

An Invitation to Purpose

In a book full of invitations, this first one welcomes you to wonder about why you do what you do, and what makes you *you*.

And if that sounds a little too heady, read the title again. This chapter invites you to consider—and even take a shot at saying—why you're here: on the planet, in your life, at your best. It's an invitation to discover and describe your purpose. *Purpose,* as I'm using the word here, is less to suggest that there's one narrow and specific use for you in the world, and more a way of describing how actions taken *on purpose* are completely different from events that happen by accident.

Knowing why we're here allows us the opportunity to live on purpose.

When we don't know why we're here—when our life and work seem accidental or incidental—we often end up feeling insignificant and lost. It is challenging, in any case, to capture evidence in the external world that the things we do even matter. This is often true in our personal and professional relationships as well as in our service. When we're able to describe our unique reasons for doing what we do, we have a way to find and feel evidence of our impact according to an internal set of measures that align with and reflect what is most important to us.

The invitation to purpose assumes that each of us would rather make choices and invest our energies and do things *intentionally* instead of by accident. It assumes we'd benefit from knowing what we're doing, and why, rather than stumbling along without a clue. It assumes we'd rather understand and enjoy how who we are and what we do is meaningful to others, and how our contributions make a difference in the world. These assumptions apply to our whole lives, by the way, not only our jobs.

Connecting to our purpose can provide a beacon in dark and murky times when we feel lost, adrift, or stuck. On a practical level, being able to articulate our purpose can help us avoid unthinkingly adopting or copying someone else's. It can also help explain why some situations or jobs or relationships seem to baffle or bewilder us, and some feel easy as anything.

This chapter invites you to become more aware of what drives you, what fulfills you, what comes naturally to you, and how you'd like to feel as you pursue your callings. It also tries to point out opportunities to deepen your capacity for service.

Purpose is a benchmark against which you can measure not only the actions of your service, but also your areas of personal contribution and where you want to grow. In exploring the elements that help define and describe your personal purpose, you'll learn how to better align what you do, how you do it, and how it feels to do it in ways that reflect your most treasured values and deepest beliefs.

As you will hear over and over again in the following pages, your human *being*—your unique self—is an integral element of the service you offer in the world. *You* matter. Always. Exploring what matters to you, and why, is a powerful first venture toward conscious service. The self-knowledge you find here will guide you throughout our shared journey of conscious service, even as your motivations, values, and belief systems continue to evolve and transform.

■　■　■

The Call to Service

Many service providers I know have experienced, in some way, a sense of being called into service. Whether it was through the encouragement or example of someone they admire, a book they read, a personal experience of being on the receiving end of care, or an instance of divine timing, there was a voice within that told them, *This is it! Keep going!*

One colleague described her experience of being called as a "deep knowing" that her specific contribution was needed. Another friend says it feels like an unshakable desire to make a difference in the world. Most people who use the language of *call* to describe what they have heard and responded to say something along the lines of "I *just knew.*"

The call in my own life arrived through a book I read as a teenager. In addition to sparking and affirming a lifelong path of service, this experience also revealed the magic way books are able to connect us with life-changing stories of people we'll never meet. The book was called *One Child* by Torey Hayden, and it opened my imagination to how changing the world often starts with making a difference in one other person's life. At the age of fourteen, I *just knew* that answering this call would also make a difference in my own.

I wasn't wrong.

I used to believe that we each receive a single, divine calling and that I had heard mine. This belief, inspired by an amazing story of the resilient power of love, helped me focus my passion and make courageous personal decisions and career moves. It led me to teachers and companions and experiences that changed my life and expanded my mind and heart in profound ways.

My long and winding journey since has given me a broader perspective about the call. I've come to understand that any time our soul desires expansion, a new call is in the works. Each call offers an opportunity to strengthen our commitment, refine our contribution, step more deeply into service, and know ourselves more fully.

Some of these ongoing calls affirm our direction. Others alter our path entirely. The latter usually arrive when we're so wrapped up in a struggle that we require a lightning flash to get our attention.

Years into one career, I found myself standing in the shower on a Tuesday morning preparing for another mundane day at the office. My unconscious mantra at the time was something like "Just let me get through the day."

When had I gone from "I'm going to change the world!" to struggling to survive? I felt myself come awake. I realized how far away I was from the energy and optimism of that original call, and had been for months—maybe even years. In my state of disconnection, I had missed all the signs that were telling me it was time for a shift. Instead, I found myself hiding in the shower, mumbling about making it through a work shift, dreading the moment I'd have to turn off the tap and face the day.

If you'll pardon the pun, that watershed moment marked a divine turning point for me. Prompted by the voice of my discontent and discomfort, the call had spoken again. Having heard, I could pay attention to the guidance it was offering.

In addition to providing us with specific directions, our calls contain a plethora of information that offers direction and detail as we begin to notice and respond to them. Sometimes, the path is very clear. We take a step in a desired direction and another door opens. Feedback and progress keep us moving forward. The more we understand the nuances of this calling, the more clarity we access when it comes to our unique expression of service in the world.

Sometimes trying to understand these nuances is a process of trial and error, attempt and rejection. This can feel like fumbling in the dark, with only our heart's sense of direction as a compass. For me, these more difficult experiences have offered the most powerful opportunities for transformation and brought me to places and people who were ready for my contribution.

Often we have help in hearing and understanding these calls.

I once job-shared a position with a friend and longtime colleague. We worked well together and had a shared vision. Planning our organization's activities a few months at a time, we would focus on specific goals we hoped to achieve. We honed in on the qualities we were striving to encourage and develop in the service provider teams we led. As part of this process, we took time to check in with each other as well.

As we named goals and highlighted the successes and the frustrations related to meeting them, we would ask each other if there was still more for us to contribute. And more powerfully, we asked one another if we still felt inspired to contribute—if we still felt called. When the answer was affirmative, we carried on with a deepened commitment. Eventually, that answer changed. We had the combined sense that our part in the work there was complete, even though there was more that could and would be done. We recognized that the roles we held now required a different energy, not ours but someone else's. It became clear to both of us that it was time to move on.

When something stops calling you, pay attention to that. Don't try to track it down. Sometimes it's time to let go. A new call is emerging.

What Am I Even Talking About?

The idea of a divine call might not resonate with you for any number of reasons.

That's okay.

I've met lots of people over the years who heard very distinctive calls to serve at one point or another, but not everybody has this experience. Some of us simply found ourselves on the path of service and fell in love with it after the fact. Some of us showed up in these callings because we needed to step on a career path somewhere and it looked like service could be an accessible place to begin.

It is possible that you find yourself in a service role and aren't sure how you got there. Maybe you backed into a teaching job or a gig driving a school bus, and now you love it. Maybe you never felt divine clarity or stirrings in your heart to give back or change the world. Maybe you sat down with a guidance counselor in high school and social work or pharmacy tech or law enforcement popped up on the list and looked interesting or easy or like it paid pretty well.

Maybe your family always expected you to go into nursing or neuroscience. Maybe a career in medicine was an unfulfilled dream they had for themselves. Maybe the honor and status associated with one particular career was part of a story you inherited and pursued without question.

Maybe you are both family member and service provider. Maybe you are a parent or child or spouse or sibling of someone with extraordinary needs. Maybe this person's needs require an investment of your time, energy, and love that is greater than you ever expected.

I don't know how you got here, but I know that you're here now. Somehow you've landed in a place where your skills and gifts and presence are positioned to make an impact in somebody else's life. In the next few pages we're going to explore what keeps you going, what can keep you grounded, and what might make whatever service you're uniquely equipped to offer more rewarding and satisfying for you and more whole, human, and helpful for whomever you happen to serve.

Two Types of Motivation

Motivation is what keeps us going along any given road. Think of it as the gasoline in our metaphorical tank. Without enough fuel, we won't get far. With the wrong fuel, we might be able to sputter along for a while, but we risk damaging the engine.

External motivators are those that fuel us from outside ourselves. They're contingent, which means they depend on people or circumstances or events that lie beyond our control. In the metaphor, external motivators are like the gas in the pump, which needs to be regularly replenished by someone whenever it gets low.

And, depending on your mileage or how heavy you are on the pedal, it gets low pretty often, and sometimes fairly fast.

Internal motivators come from inside us. They're unique to each of us and don't depend on the actions of others. They can be affected by other people and external circumstances, but they exist on their own, and they provide energy and direction all by themselves.

This is, of course, where the metaphor of the engine and the gas breaks down. Cars are incapable of internal motivation. They only start and move when the right combination of external forces comes together to make them do so. But people aren't machines. We human beings have the ability to mix the ways we are motivated and to draw power from within ourselves as well as receive and rely on the energy and assistance we get from others.

Both types of motivators have merit and impact in our lives. External motivators can be extremely powerful drivers toward specific outcomes or achievements. They can also lose their effectiveness as what matters to us changes. Internal motivators are usually related to longer-term processes and experiences. They're more likely to offer energy that lasts.

What keeps you showing up in your service vocation?

What parts of your work feel most rewarding?

External Driving Forces

External motivators are easy to recognize. They sometimes even put food on the table or gas in the literal gas tank. But by themselves they will always be insufficient to the task of keeping us going in ways that help us thrive. Most external motivators demonstrate diminishing returns, meaning they require more and more inputs (money, power, recognition) while offering less and less of the energy they once supplied. For a time, they seem to supply something we're seeking; the energy we gain from each reward sustains us and powers us along toward the next. But before long each reward begins to seem lighter, or the work of reaching the next one becomes heavier—or both. As soon as those scales tip—and they always tip—we can find ourselves depleted, confused, and even angry.

Added to this, the more external the motivator, the less effective it is. It might work for a short period of time, and then the bottom falls out. That's why so many New Year's resolutions—promises motivated mainly by the passing of an arbitrary date—have fallen apart by Groundhog Day.

The Almighty Dollar

Money is often seen as the ultimate external motivator. In vocations of service, this basic understanding has become complicated. Many of us have come to equate being of service with low pay and meager benefits. We've been taught that service, unlike selling shoes or trading stocks, ought to occupy a space that is somehow above merely financial matters. We *shouldn't* want to earn a great living as a result of our service. It *should* be an altruistic act that has nothing to do with financial gain.

No matter how often it uses the word *essential,* our culture of productivity has a hard time rewarding service to humanity in tangible ways. Nearly all health-care organizations, educational institutions, and human services systems operate from a position of scarcity. The unrelenting message is *There's not enough.* Not enough workers. Not enough funding. Not enough resources. Nothing left in the budget. This running assumption about scarcity, combined with an unwillingness to value the work of schoolteachers and home health aides as highly as the work of bankers or advertising executives, perpetuates the myth that service requires sacrifice. A system that's based on this foundation both encourages and expects service providers to burn out.

It's not surprising, given this, how so many service providers have come to exclude ourselves and downplay our personal desires in the process of providing service. We might equate the desire for financial abundance or freedom with being greedy or with having ulterior motives. We might feel like we are being shady or selfish if we benefit financially while those who need and rely on our service continue to suffer.

Those working in traditional service roles frequently rely on side jobs and overtime to make ends meet. Facing a public that doesn't always understand how to value their gifts, alternative service providers can have a hard time pricing their services. It can feel tempting to just give away your time or energy. Personal service providers are rarely financially supported in their roles with loved ones and are often required to work full time, provide care for their loved ones, and regularly incur expenses to hire additional supports.

The truth is that your basic needs for health, security, and safety are as important as the needs of those you are hoping to serve. Your having less does not mean someone else will have more. No amount of lack that you accept, identify, or create in your life will automatically provide abundance for someone who has less than you do.

Of course money matters. Financial security and predictability are a cornerstone of stability for everyone, and service providers are no exception. Your work has value and worth, and you deserve to be compensated in ways that correspond to this value and allow you to live comfortably.

**When it comes to money, what would be a fair wage
for the work you do as a service provider?**

As powerful as it is, the "almighty dollar" isn't the only external motivator in town. It shares space with a few common but less obvious forces.

The Impact of Our Contributions

Since we tend to be uncomfortable talking about money, many service providers point to outcomes when we're asked about what motivates us. "We're not in it for the paycheck," we say; it's enough to see the light of learning in a child's eyes, or to be one link in a lifesaving chain that starts with first responders and ends with physical therapists. We want to make a difference in the world, and when we see that happening because of something we did, it feels really good. In the world of service, reports of positive outcomes and anecdotes about success are the currency that gets us noticed and supported, and these things frequently supply energy to keep us going.

And this works pretty well. Until it doesn't.

When we are unable to see or measure or describe the impact of our service, the energy-producing feedback loop between action and effect loses its power to motivate us. If we've relied on this external motivator as a primary driver, we can start to feel defeated or jaded or hopeless.

What specific difference do you want to make in the world?

How will you know when you've accomplished this?

Power

Even when wages are low and money is tight, many service providers find motivation in the authority that comes with our roles. Whether you're a corrections officer or a second-grade teacher, being in charge of situations and people carries rewards as well as specific responsibilities.

In most relationships of service, power and agency are not equally distributed. Even if others have voice and choice, it's usually the service provider who facilitates access to the supports and solutions that affect people's lives in concrete ways. We're often the gatekeepers and decision makers. Some of us even bear the authority of the state from time to time. This can mean the difference between someone obtaining assistance or being denied or delayed. In some cases, it can mean making decisions about someone's freedom. Even alternative service providers have been entrusted with power in service relationships with people who rely on them for help.

I wish I could say every service provider wielded this power well and always respected and responded to the needs and interests of the person seeking service. The sad truth is that we don't. Later in this book, we'll explore misuse of authority and identify ways we can monitor and manage the privilege that comes with power. For now, it's enough to notice that the authority and access that comes with many service roles is part of what keeps some of us in the work, for good or ill. Because it relies on relationships and transactions with others, power is an external motivator.

> **Where does your current calling provide you with power over someone else?**

Status, Strokes, and Other People's Opinions

Some people in vocations of service are motivated by the status that serving others can offer. We like to be recognized by friends and family—and even strangers—as people who put others before ourselves. It's not too hard to get accustomed to the recognition you get for the special qualities you must possess to be able to help people less fortunate. "I don't know how you do it." "I could never do what you do." "It takes a special kind of person to . . ." If you're at all like me, you enjoy the sense of importance that these remarks bestow on you.

And who wouldn't? In lots of ways they're true. Much of the work of service really does require a certain skill set and suit certain types of people. It's a fact that not everybody is cut out for the roles we serve. Part of the long work of changing the way our culture values and compensates service providers will include recognizing the truly essential nature of our work and the sophisticated skills and qualities of character that service requires.

If we have any doubts about our motives or integrity as service providers, getting this kind of praise can feel awkward or undeserved, but external affirmation and recognition, especially when it comes from a trusted colleague or somebody we respect, is usually deeply motivating. The energy we get from being seen and understood by someone who knows what they're talking about is powerful. As we saw earlier, these relationships can be experienced as part of our ongoing call.

But working for the emotional rewards of positive recognition and celebratory feedback can be just as exhausting as chasing a paycheck. Doing anything solely for the sake of getting something or pleasing someone else has a shelf life.

Whose opinion about your work matters most to you?

What are your top two external motivators?

The Million-Dollar Question

Have you ever been asked what you would do if you suddenly became a millionaire? This question comes up sometimes in break rooms or between shifts—usually when everybody's tired. It's sparked by stories about people who win the lottery or receive an unexpected windfall. We all have an answer. Some people know immediately that they would quit their job—or whatever they were doing at the time—and run for the hills (or the beach). Others claim that nothing would change. These people say they would continue doing what they do because they love it so much. Most of us would probably at least make some alterations.

One day, over the backyard fence, my philosophically inclined neighbor asked what I'd do if the big money arrived in my mailbox. I immediately responded that I would keep doing exactly what I was doing. At the time, I was coordinating and teaching in a human services program. I was having the time of my life with a diverse and energized group of learners. I enjoyed the curriculum. I saw the impact of my work.

All this was true.

Even so, following our conversation I went for a walk and kept thinking about the question. I had pondered it before and answered differently at different times. This time I was questioning the suddenness of my response. Would I *really* keep doing what I was doing?

Maybe I spoke too soon.

The million-dollar question became an opportunity to sort out my motivations.

I knew that I loved working with people—in particular, I loved this current group of learners. I loved their energy, their diversity, their creativity. I was blown away by how quickly a sense of community had emerged among us. It was a safe and supportive, energized and dynamic learning situation.

But I could also see that these particular people were an external source of motivation for me. Not every class would be like this one. Pinning my commitment on one specific circumstance, no matter how wonderful, would set me up for disappointment when it turned out to be impossible to replicate or sustain. External motivators can be powerful, but they're usually fleeting.

I have experienced the tipping scales of motivation in my life many times. I have longed for the recognition, rejoiced in the great moments and special groups, clung to positive feedback, waited for specific results and rewards like I was watching a pot come to boil, and simply worked for the weekend and punched in for the paycheck. And way too often this has felt like dying.

To be honest, I'm not energized by many of the tasks associated with my role as a teacher. The paperwork, the assignments, the organizational politics, and the methods for measuring learning often leave me feeling empty. I've fulfilled these expectations and navigated necessary systems in order to do the stuff I really love. I am motivated by the shared experience of teaching and learning. I get lost in my own learning and feel blessed when I witness and participate in an epiphany with others. I love the experience of shared energy and creativity that occurs when there is a meeting of minds and hearts. I love when ideas come alive.

My joy with this group was about *connection*. I deeply valued the experience of connecting with like-minded, spiritually aligned people. It was like food for my soul. As I walked and thought, I was getting closer to the internal, intrinsic motivation at the center of my calling.

Exploring how complex and intertwined my motivations were that day created a touchstone process, one I return to again and again. As I continue to connect more deeply with the essence of what my soul is searching for, it becomes easier to recognize those times when I have set my hope on unsustainable motivators and external benefits. On that walk, as I weighed imaginary millions against the true things my heart was teaching me, I began to claim my power to pay attention to *all* my motivations and choose to act from the ones that reliably lead me to life.

Each of us has a sense of what makes us come alive on the inside. Notice those times when you are acting out of desire or curiosity or enjoyment or love, with no expectation of reward or even attachment to outcome. These experiences will point you toward your internal motivators. This is what often gets described as *altruism*—the act of giving without expectation of anything in return. Connecting to the unconditional power of your internal motivations is priceless. There is nothing more enduring than an organic engine that provides its own fuel.

As you begin to explore what spurs you on, you may discover that you are not in touch with your internal motivation. Perhaps you can identify only a handful of motivators, and they all seem to depend on something that others do to or for you. Probe beneath the surface for what your soul is actually seeking. If money feels like a big motivator, a part of you has a wish list of items or status or agency. But what deeper longing sits beneath that desire? Is it security? Comfort? Is it freedom? This is one way you can use information from your external drives to discover and develop your enduring internal ignition.

Conscious service is never about finding the "right" motivation according to someone else's standards. It's about learning to understand and access the full energy of what propels and sustains you in serving others. This awareness also allows us a front-row seat to the evolution of our internal motivations as they're refined and focused over the course of our lives.

Attending to heart-based, emotionally attuned motivation is also a way to respect yourself. It's a declaration of self-love. In order for altruism to be something other than an excuse for self-sacrifice, it must apply to you as well. We don't have to stop wanting or needing material rewards and security, but placing high value on your sense of joy and enthusiasm in what you do acknowledges your inherent worth, regardless of the external circumstances.

How would you describe the key motivators active in your life right now?

What holds the most power for you?

What Really Matters

Like our internal and external motivators, our values have a role in defining our priorities and directing our choices. If motivation is the energy that drives us, our values are the compass points that guide us. What we value helps establish what we aim for in life. When there is a disconnection between what we claim to value and the quality or character of the things we do, life gets messy and the outcomes we are striving for elude us. If we value something, we are more inclined to make decisions that align with that value. If something isn't a priority for us, we will behave accordingly.

Seems pretty clear-cut, right?

Alas, it is not. See, we aren't always aware of all of our values unless we seek them out. Like all ideas, values are intangible until we live them, until we own and embody them in ways that become evident in our actions.

I once asked participants at a workshop to consider their top five values. It can be a challenge to encapsulate what's most important to you in just words, but naming what you feel are your core values can provide much insight. Even the act of identifying and articulating what matters most to you is a helpful practice. It focuses your attention and sets an intention.

Once the attendees settled on their top values, I challenged them to identify and detail any and all of their daily behaviors that reflected each value in action. Then I asked them to identify which of their regular behaviors did not reflect the value.

The purpose of this exercise isn't to provoke guilt or shame about integrity or consistency. Rather, its goal is to illuminate the exceptions we allow regarding our own rules. We all have these exceptions. For example, I can say that I deeply value respect—and then find myself a moment later struggling to behave respectfully with one particular person who pushes my buttons.

I can claim to value my health and well-being and even demonstrate that through basic self-care. But then stress mounts or I have an upsetting experience, and it's pizza and cigarettes. Every "bad habit" can seem like the best idea in the wrong moment.

As we identify the distance between the direction our values point and the reality that shapes our day-to-day choices, we can start to see what's in the way of living as we'd like to. We may also notice where we have identified with or adopted values that might not be authentically ours, or where we're still oriented to values we have outgrown. This information offers us opportunity for deeper alignment.

One of the participants in this workshop was Kalia, a social worker in the mental health field. Kalia enjoyed her work and felt quite fulfilled when it came to the service she provided and the relationships she had developed. She had a few frustrations about management and the overall leadership of her employer organization, but nothing she felt she couldn't manage.

The values exercise led to several insights for Kalia. Not only was she able to dig more deeply into the essence of the values she had identified in ways that helped her integrate them more fully in all aspects of her life; she was also able to tune in to those areas where her behavior didn't always reflect what she knew mattered to her.

Whenever we are not living according to the authentic values of our hearts and souls, we tend to feel uncomfortable. It can feel like being stuck, or being lost, or just being confused and tired. We're pretty sure we know what we want to experience and how we wish to show up in our lives, and yet we also feel pulled in directions that point us away from that. Sometimes this is a result of competing values: family calls for one thing; work calls for another. Usually it means we've left our personal wellness unattended.

As Kalia listened closely to herself, she started to recognize where some of the values she had identified as centrally important didn't necessarily hold as much power for her as they once had, or as much power as she thought they should. She saw how many of her actions didn't align with what she said was most important.

Having the opportunity to explore how her daily actions were aligned or misaligned with what she claimed as most important was illuminating for Kalia. She became better able to articulate what her values really were at this time in her life. It became easier for her to identify the actions she would take to make her values real.

Where do you suspect your values and actions might be misaligned?

Where in your life do action and value line up well? How does that feel?

Personal Values and Impartial Service

Exploring our values might feel like a worthwhile personal development strategy, but how does it connect to serving others? Aren't we supposed to forgo our values—leave them at the door—to ensure our objectivity? When it comes to helping other people, what does it matter what I value? Don't the other person's values matter the most? These concerns point to a myth associated with service—one that is designed to keep us from imposing our values on other people.

A key problem with this well-intentioned idea is that it asks us to ignore the important role that our personal values play in our own lives. Denying their existence and influence just means our values will appear in our interactions disguised as something else (usually something as impossible and condescending as impartiality). Whenever we're unaware of and disconnected from our value system, we are much more likely to unwittingly impose our own values on others.

On a practical level, it is very difficult to support someone in a personal decision-making or problem-solving process that honors and aligns with their values if we have not taken the time to get to know our own. This doesn't mean packaging and pushing our values as a to-do list or template. It means meeting the people we work with and serve on the same energetic level—as people for whom values have power. As we align with our values, we deepen our sense of integrity.

In their book *The Power of Full Engagement,* Jim Loehr and Tony Schwartz describe "virtues" as values in action. Values are important to our internal grounding and guidance; virtues allow these things to matter to others. A virtue has tangible effects, qualities, and benefits. Virtues are assets we can share. When we live our lives according to our most deeply held values, our actions back up our beliefs. Other people come to know what to expect from us by our behavior. We become reliable as this repeats.

Making values active in our lives in this way helps us earn the trust of others, but first it offers us the gift of trusting ourselves.

Your Guiding Values

What values guide you? I have asked this question many times of many people. "Family" is probably one of the most common answers. I have no doubt that many people value their families very deeply—I do too! Most of us dearly love and value the people who make up our circles of kin and connection. But set aside the particular people who make up your family unit for a moment. What is it about *family*—however you define it—that makes it such a powerful and positive force in your life?

Responding to this question usually includes identifying the valuable traits and characteristics that *family* encompasses for you. Beneath and within the stories and personal experiences of your life in relationship to the circle of people you consider family, what specific qualities are most important for you? Does family mean connection and home? Does it evoke tradition or loyalty? Maybe the word that resonates is *fun* or *love*.

It may be that you value loving and being loved by others in a way that gives you a sense of belonging. Under the broad banner of *family*—a term that people define and describe in a wide variety of ways—are deeper and more transcendent values: belonging and safety and acceptance.

It's worth noting that not everybody is able to associate the word *family* with such positive terms. Family relationships can also be places of conflict, trauma, isolation, and self-doubt. Recall that here we're talking about the values we hope will hold positive power in our lives. If your family of origin seems like a source of negative value, explore the positive values that characterize your chosen family.

When we dig beneath terms like *family* to unearth the more enduring benefits they bear for us, the value of these benefits can become transferable. Your values become places in which you recognize yourself and others can recognize you.

If belonging is a core value for you, you will know when you're being left out, and you'll also be sensitive to the inclusion of others. If you value loving and feeling loved, then love will be evident in your actions and choices. And those times when you don't feel loved by someone else, you'll know how to love yourself enough to speak up, forgive, or get the hell out.

Ideally, our values guide us in how we wish to live. Your values are there as a standard you are striving to live up to in your own life. They need not set the bar for anyone else. This can sometimes be a tripping point for us as we learn to more fully integrate our values with our actions. As we pay more attention to our own internal alignment, it's easy to start monitoring and judging how well others are living up to our values. Nobody else has any obligation to live according to your personal value system. It needs to work for you, and you alone.

Start to notice the connections between what you value and what motivates you. What will it take for those aspects of your being to work better together—to drive and guide your journey of conscious service?

Here's a list of values. It's in no way exhaustive, but it might get the juices flowing as you consider what matters most to you.

love	honesty	communication	confidence
fun	health	justice	excellence
humor	creativity	friendship	perseverance
compassion	collaboration	adventure	discipline
security	inclusion	learning	equality
safety	patience	growth	fairness
belonging	forgiveness	tradition	objectivity
joy	spirituality	excitement	intuition
peace	sexuality	partnerships	achievement
abundance	intimacy	power	success
intelligence	respect	beauty	happiness
balance	honor	freedom	independence
harmony	loyalty	fitness	community
connection	comfort	kindness	self-sufficiency
relationship	efficiency	generosity	faithfulness
trust	effectiveness	humility	

How do you experience connection between your values and your motivations?

What might you select as three top values in your life? Are these three also your top values in your work?

Say Why You're Here

Everyone operates according to some kind of logic—even people we might experience as illogical or erratic or flaky. *Logic* here simply means connection: *y* happens because of *x*. Noticing and getting to know the logic that guides you—the way your drives and beliefs and assumptions and commitments link together and lead to your behavior—is a process of lifelong learning, and it's essential to the journey of conscious service.

I wrote earlier that knowing why we're here allows us the opportunity to live on purpose.

In addition to encouraging you to grab that opportunity with both hands and all your heart, this concluding section expands the invitation from knowing why you're here to saying it out loud. Developing the ability to name our motivations, describe our values, and demonstrate how these forces show up in our actions gives us words with which to share our unique purpose with others.

By identifying and describing what makes us tick, we build a personal philosophy. Some people call this a set of guiding principles or a personal mission statement.

Like any organization's mission statement, a personal philosophy announces our purpose. It helps us explain ourselves to others, and it helps us find and partner with people and organizations who share our values and goals. A personal philosophy can also act as an internal guide for understanding and acting in the moment—for choosing how to show up with integrity in any given situation.

Think of your personal philosophy as a way of describing your response to what calls you into service. It helps you claim and communicate the details of what drives you as well as what shapes your actions and choices. Your personal philosophy provides a logic that connects your values and links them to the places in the world where they can be of use.

Knowing these things will help you answer the question "Why are you here?" This kind of reflection and self-knowledge can also help you discern whether "here" is a good fit, or if it's time to go someplace else, where your deepest commitments, your standout strengths, and your most heart-aligned contributions will be welcomed and supported and valued as fully as possible.

When you are able to say clearly what you value and know how these foundational commitments get demonstrated in your life and behavior, you're getting closer to answering questions about why you're here and what you are supposed to be doing. In grounding yourself with a statement you can stand on, you'll also create a unique-to-you touchstone that can call you back to balance and center again on your purpose. Whenever you are in doubt about how to proceed, consult your personal philosophy. It is an ever-replenishing source of renewal, energy, and focus and will help you take the next step from a place of authenticity and deep inner trust.

In my work as a teacher, I am energized and amazed by the light that appears in the eyes of students who finally see the purpose of an assignment or a course that at first glance seemed disconnected from their goals. As soon as we know why something matters—even if only to us— we can commit.

State your purpose. In one or two sentences, try to say what you're here for.

CHAPTER 2

Show Up Fully

An Invitation to Wholeness

How are you showing up?

Variations of this question have been on my mind lately. I'm watching my actions from a distance and thinking, *Is that how people see me?* and *Is that how I* want *others to experience me?*

This kind of observation offers me the opportunity to notice those moments when I am not acting or living authentically, with the integrity I'd like. And it allows me the chance to change.

Showing up fully is about bringing full presence and engagement to the relationships of service we offer other people. But accepting this invitation has little to do with other people, and absolutely everything to do with us.

We often talk about serving others in a holistic manner. Whole-person approaches to service delivery seek to consider and account for the widest possible range of factors at play in a person's or family's current experience. Many of us are trained to perform 360-degree interviews or comprehensive intake evaluations. We try to understand and appreciate the complexity of others' lives in order to help them make choices or receive interventions that can lead to optimal personal functioning or happiness or healing or wellness.

This chapter invites you to consider a similar journey for yourself.

This exploration and inquiry is not a selfish act. It is the basis of genuine self-care. To avoid this responsibility is to neglect the full measure of our humanity. Doing so will shortchange our service, regardless of the specifics of our role or profession. We owe it to ourselves, those with whom we share relationship, and the communities we seek to serve to treat our personal human resources as the precious and powerful gifts that they are.

In the previous chapter, we explored some of what led you into service. We pondered the inspiration and curiosity you followed in order to arrive on this path in the first place. We focused on what feeds and guides your intention to respond to the needs of others. Now the priority is to explore and embrace the full scope of your human nature by getting familiar with the dimensions of being that are inside of you—what I call your personal human system.

When it comes to conscious service, it is not so much what you *do* as who you *are* that makes the most difference. The invitation to wholeness is about coming to know and value the essence of *you*.

* * *

The Stuff in the Closet

As we've attempted to project strength and demonstrate our competence, most of us have become used to compartmentalizing ourselves and our lives. We tend to treat our humanity like the storage of our seasonal clothes. We have a box of clothes in the closet for the cold months and a vacuum-sealed package we slide under our beds for the hot ones. This can work for a while, but our humanity needs wholeness. Sooner or later, the artificially separated layers of our being seek to be heard and reacquainted. When we've left parts of us on a shelf in some closet, we'll eventually start to notice that something feels off.

I have watched myself put pieces of myself into boxes on that shelf and walk away. I've ignored those boxes while they gathered dust. I've acted as if they didn't exist just because I choose not to look inside.

And of course I've pretended to be surprised when the shelf collapses and I'm in the midst of the mess of my own making.

You don't need to have all your shit together before you can be of service in the world. You do have to be willing to admit, at least to yourself, that you don't. You do have to become aware that parts of you are healing and growing. You do have to become willing to venture into the dark corners of your own soul and accept the weirdness of your own mind.

This might be the scariest part of the journey toward conscious service. As you unpack those closet-boxes or break the seal on those vacuum bags, you might come face-to-face with sides of yourself that were previously unknown or well hidden. There seems to be a universal human impulse to not be found out—to avoid being fully seen. We fear what the neighbors will think.

Most of us are careful that our weak or embarrassing or unruly parts remain hidden from others. When these aspects of our personalities tumble into public view, we scramble to save face, make excuses, backtrack to cover our ass, and end up wasting energy. In more dire situations we bail, burn bridges, move out or move on, and dream about starting again where nobody knows us.

When we deny our full humanity, we set ourselves up for these falls. In striving to appear perfect, we're loading shelves with boxes that will eventually spill their contents and make a mess. When we do this, we're also discounting and diminishing the utility and even the beauty of our flaws, and we're impeding the development of important and powerful gifts.

Which parts of you seem to be on a shelf somewhere?

Five Channels of Human Being

Pursuing wholeness includes accepting the mysterious complexity of your human condition. This will always include the elements of your personality that make you feel proud and strong, as well as the parts of you that seem useless at best and destructive at worst. Let's delve into the states of being that together comprise your unique presence in the world. This will prepare us to show up with our whole selves and walk the path of conscious service with all of our resources awake, alive, and available.

Every human's experience includes different states of being, or aspects of awareness. These elements of being human work together to shape that personal human system I mentioned earlier. It's what makes us unique individuals. Each aspect of this system offers its own type of perception and sensitivity by which we learn about ourselves and the world. I've identified five ways we receive and process information and experiences:

- Through our physical being
- Through our thought process
- Through our capacity to feel emotions
- Through our ability to connect and communicate with others
- Through the unique voice of our spirit

Imagine these five states as distinct channels on a single radio. Each channel corresponds to a specific frequency on the dial. As the elements of awareness that inform and make up who you are, these channels are each responsible for a specific role in your optimal functioning. Showing up fully means that we perceive and act and process through the widest range of channels possible.

Unlike a real radio, the five channels of the human system do not work independently of each other. Wholeness requires integration and communication and balance between them—it's actually how they work best. As each of us integrates our personal channels and tunes in to our unique frequencies, we align with our highest possible expression and presence in the world. On our way to that goal, in the next few sections, we will get to know and explore these channels one at a time.

We're learning to dance with the mystical nature of our humanity. Don't be discouraged! You have everything you need to find your perfect balance.

No. Seriously: Do Not Be Discouraged

You are already whole.

You are not required to compartmentalize. You don't have to be divided, distorted, split, or hidden. You can harness the power of your whole being to experience full presence and conscious engagement.

This is not a path of perfection. I am an idealist by nature, so I am committed to holding a big and positive vision of what could be for myself, for others, and for our world. That said, I often fall short of these ideals, lose my footing, fall back into old traps, even willingly walk head-first into bad-for-me patterns of behavior and belief. When this happens, I can't tune in to *any* frequency; all I get is confusing static.

Expect and accept that you will share this experience from time to time. Learn to immerse yourself in grace as you go, and treat yourself as someone who possesses value beyond price. Even in your darkest moments, grace can save your life, or broaden your vision, or bring you home.

Our shared human nature is mysterious. It is delicate. It is tough. It is quiet. And it is wild. Claim all parts of your humanity without apology. If part of your humanity spills out in ways that hurt others, claiming the wholeness of your being will add authenticity to any amends you might make. Learn to honor every voice in your internal system. Make a decision to tune in regularly and observe. Absorb what emerges.

You and Your Body

Whatever happens to us mentally, emotionally, spiritually, or relationally eventually affects our bodies. The physical is the final frontier. But this exploration starts with the physical because most of us are more in tune with the material aspects of existence. If we can see and touch it, it's real. When we think about showing up, most of us picture arriving someplace, embodied. In school when the teacher took attendance, we raised our hands to indicate our presence. This is the aspect of our selves that most easily interacts with the physical world of objects, others, and the environment.

Most of us gather information through five physical senses: our ability to see, hear, touch, taste, and smell. Of course, some of these senses are stronger than others, and some of us can even manage just fine without one or two, but as a rule, our five sensory functions allow us to navigate the world, express ourselves, obtain what we need, and learn.

We present ourselves to the world through our physical being. Our bodies translate what's going on inside us through our actions and interactions. Our choices, feelings, thoughts, and beliefs all become tangible—and apparent to others—at the level of behavior.

Your body is also the space where you experience sensation as a response to stimuli. We even feel our emotions as sensations in our bodies. We say we *feel* sad, or angry, or joyful. These emotional experiences reside in our bodies. Your intuitive guidance produces a bodily sensation too. A great deal of information swirls into you through your senses!

When it comes to the human system, our bodies are the vessels through which all the other aspects of our being speak and listen. The most effective way to utilize the powers of this amazing vessel and maximize the many gifts of the physical is to create a solid foundation of health and behavior. Tuning in to this channel is about honoring and caring for your body so it can contain and express your whole being.

This is easier said than done, of course.

I recall times when I felt like I was walking through life with my head not quite attached to my body, my feet not quite touching the earth. When people talked about being grounded, I would nod my head like I knew what they meant, but I didn't have a clue. What I did know was that something didn't feel quite right. I felt slow, sluggish, and cloudy.

Many of us are well adept at ignoring our physical being, even though we know that without life force in our system nothing else matters. Distracted by the material circumstances of our world, we can become disconnected from these basic processes of our human nature.

Here are some ways to reconnect with your physical channel and establish presence within your body.

- **Step outdoors.** Getting outside even briefly has a way of connecting us to the physical. It makes sense that being in nature attunes us to our human nature. We are inextricably connected to the world around us. Feeling the breeze on our skin, immersing ourselves in some water, or soaking up the sun grounds us in the physical world and ultimately within our bodies.

- **Get moving.** Physical activity supports reconnection. Walk. Run. Stretch. Do yoga. Swim. Boosted energy, mental clarity, and better sleep are often the result. Sometimes we have to talk ourselves into moving our bodies, but movement is one of our bodies' main functions.

- **Eat with intention.** Try tracking how your body feels when you ingest anything. Start to make choices by considering what feels best to you over the long term. Capitalize on the energizing responses, and limit the stuff that bogs you down. Personally, I avoid all-or-nothing approaches. I find it creates too much pressure and sets me up for failure.

- **Check in.** Bring your attention to the state of your physical condition several times throughout the day. What are your needs for nourishment, for water, for rest, for relief, for stretching, for breathing in that moment? It is so basic and simple and yet, because our bodies can continue to hum along for weeks and months without much attention from us, it is easy to take them for granted. And that eventually catches up with us.

We humans are amazing creatures designed to physically endure the harshest conditions. And the world may be inhospitable at times, but let us try not to create our own dangerous environments. Let us avoid causing damage to the precious resource of our bodies.

Notice for one day how you take your body for granted.
Choose just one moment to give it what it is asking for now.
Then, tomorrow, do it twice.

Yeah, but Who Has the Time?

A few years ago, a social worker was describing the heaviness of his workload and the demands his organization placed on him. It had gotten so bad, he reported, that he didn't have time to pee. I wish this man's experience was an isolated case, but I know it isn't. If you've skipped meals, deferred personal health care, tried to ration bathroom breaks, or scheduled catnaps around the demands of your work in lieu of a full night's sleep, you know how common this is, and how demoralizing it can feel.

These are stark but real examples of how, as service providers, we often ignore our basic personal needs. The no-pee guy also demonstrates a common follow-up move: suggesting that our self-neglect is someone else's fault—in this case the culture or expectations of the organization combined with the demands of the work itself.

Been there, done that.

Even if we're part of healthy organizations that value worker wellness, many of us find it challenging to find the time and energy to care for our bodies. On our list of priorities, physical self-care regularly ends up near the bottom. "I just don't have the space in my calendar to add one more thing." "I don't have the time or money to buy and prepare healthy meals." "I end up finishing work and tasks late into the night because I run out of time during the day." "I'm running on fumes!"

Sound familiar?

When my children were younger, I used to work through my lunch breaks so I could meet them when they returned from school. This left me eating junk food on the go or skipping meals altogether. By the time three-thirty hit, I was usually ready to fill my face with anything in sight or have a nap (or both). My body got accustomed to that pattern. Even today, I often think I want to nap or eat mindlessly around that time each day, whether or not I am actually tired or hungry.

Once I realized that caring for my physical being was something only I could do, the game started to change. Self-induced physical suffering is not heroic; it helps nobody in the long run. I've come to learn that we all have access to incredible power through acts of personal responsibility, and that our responsibility must begin with ourselves.

Vibrant physical health depends upon basic care practices, and these practices take time. They *deserve* time. We thrive when we eat well, rest well, move our bodies, ensure our personal comfort, and respond to our physical needs as they arise. As we do these things, we create the conditions for an inner space that is relaxed, open, and filled with light.

All the dimensions of our being speak through our bodies, and they speak more clearly when the body is well cared for. We hear more distinctly the wisdom of our emotions. We become more keenly aware of the content and nature of our thoughts. The beliefs and patterns constructing our reality become more accessible and apparent.

And we're more able to discern the voice of our intuition when it's not drowned out by the demands of a hungry stomach or a too-full bladder.

Physical self-care is worth the time it takes. It helps us not only manage daily stress, but also more fully enjoy the pleasures of a healthy, high-functioning human system. It's not just about getting by; it's about maximizing our human energy so we can be of use to ourselves as well as the people we serve.

> **How willing are you to stop and rest when your body or mind says "Enough!"?**
>
> **Does caring for your physical self feel like too much work sometimes?**
>
> **How much joy do you feel as you care for your body?**

Listening to and Learning from the Body

Our bodies are digesting all kinds of energy. This includes what we ingest in the form of food or drink, but also what we immerse ourselves in mentally, emotionally, socially, and spiritually. You can include the quality of your relationships, what you watch on TV, the music you listen to, the material you read, the thoughts you lose yourself in, and the emotional oceans you allow yourself to swim. We're taking it all in all the time whether we are aware of it or not, and like the results of any kind of diet, the effects of these inputs appear in physical ways.

I read recently that our stomachs act like a second brain, producing a large portion of the hormones and other biochemicals responsible for many functions in our systems. This article spoke specifically about the production of serotonin and dopamine, chemical messengers that help regulate many of our bodily functions. These messengers, called neurotransmitters, affect sleep and memory as well as metabolism and emotional well-being. Disruption of these chemicals in our bodies is often connected to depression and anxiety. The article made a clear link between our gut health and our emotional and behavioral health.

Caring for our second brain involves the kind of physical self-care we've been exploring. Accessing the intelligence of this central digestive organ starts with listening to the messages it offers. And while physical sensations might not seem as straightforward as our thoughts or as familiar as our emotions, paying attention to them will help us tune in to more gifts from the physical channel.

Start with Attending to Your Energy

See if you can notice the rhythms of your energy. It ebbs and flows, doesn't it? This may correspond to times of the day or days of the week. It may have more to do with what you're doing or who you're with. You will very likely notice moments of strong, focused energy and other periods where your energy stalls out or dissipates. You might be enticed by the idea that you can achieve a constant and consistent energetic flow with little variation—no major highs and no extreme lows—and there are countless articles to be found offering tips and tricks for balancing blood sugar or exercise or eating to reduce spiking energy levels. There's no shortage of advice, and some of it is valuable.

But what if there is wisdom for us in the energetic peaks and valleys?

What if we are meant to learn from our energetic fluctuations? If our physical channel is in the process of digesting and delivering all the time, we can trust that our bodies will provide us with valuable information from our full human system—as long as we know how to pay attention.

Perhaps that spike in energy is the guidance we need to stay the course in a particular direction, grounded in a commitment to what we have already started. Maybe its message is *Keep going; we are on the right track!* Similarly, when the energy bottoms out, perhaps our bodies are telling us simply to stop. Maybe we are getting the exact help we need to let something go because we just don't have the energy to do it anymore.

Habits, Patterns, and Changing Behavior

Over time, you might notice patterns in your physical responses to situations and triggers. *A* happens and you do *B*. This is a habitual response.

Do you reach for the cupcake, cigarette, or drink when you find yourself in a certain emotional state? You notice a knot in your belly and you feel anxiety creeping in. Your thoughts are screaming for you to do something *now* to feel better and get away from the discomfort. Relief is a powerful motivator. Next thing you know, you're four drinks in and half a cake consumed. You've been blindsided. You never saw it coming. It feels completely outside of your control.

When this happens to me, I often try to figure out where I went wrong so it won't happen again. Prevention becomes my main focus. I must have been doing something wrong. I wasn't paying attention. But before you know it, I feel that knot in my belly again.

There is a tiny moment in every situation like this where a wealth of information exists for you to draw upon—a moment of illumination in which you have the power to step out of the pattern and create something entirely new. This is always a little like crossing a bridge. Whenever we step toward a novel approach, we begin to detach from the old one—even if it's a little bit at a time.

Powerful emotions like fear or anxiety can cause us to ignore what our senses are trying to tell us. As soon as you feel that familiar knot (or whatever your physical cue is), connect with it, embrace it, and become curious about what lesson it holds for you. You will find yourself more able to make a conscious decision about how you will respond this time.

Sometimes you will choose the new response, and other times you may choose the old one. It's okay. I don't know anyone who untangled an old habit or pattern in one go. We're talking about a process of dismantling. No pattern was established in a day, so none will be unlearned in that short a time. Be patient with yourself and embrace your progress and learning as you go. It is not about right or wrong, good or bad. It is about your personal evolution and alignment with your highest good. At times, you can see that clearly; other times the view is obscured. But each step of the way offers you the opportunity for renewed commitment and deeper self-compassion.

Change isn't always about breaking unhelpful habits. You may want to establish something new and positive in your life. Tuning in to the physical channel of your system will provide you with information that can bolster your success and even let you know whether or not you're on the best path.

Take the opportunity to strengthen your commitment to any new direction you intend, and the gift of alignment will follow. Your commitment sets the tone and makes it easier to align your actions with your intentions the next time. And when you miss the opportunity and choose the old pattern instead, let yourself off the hook. Focus on how your body felt all the times you showed up, and begin again.

When you embark on any change, seek the guidance of your heart and your gut and even the energy in your muscles. Ask the question "*Is my body on board?*" The simple act of tuning in with curiosity will allow you to honestly identify the directions that are right for you to take now.

And you will see your own motivations and intentions more clearly as well. Whatever we do for the benefit of our own being—with a view to expanding our capacity for feeling good—usually holds the most juice. And it is usually the best for anyone else involved as well.

Identify one behavior or habit that *always* leaves you feeling good. Do it as often as possible.

Thinking about Thinking

The human brain is the most obvious link between the physical channel and the thinking channel. Human beings use our big brains to process everything that comes at us, from within or without. Our cognitive capacity gives us the ability to make sense of events and fit our experiences into our various frames of reference. This is how we navigate life and integrate learning. Most of us like to know the relevance of the situations and ideas we encounter. We're wired to turn information into knowledge, which then becomes understanding and application in our lives.

The thinking channel is responsible for cognition—the brain-based activities of awareness and analysis. This channel is the part of our human system that weighs information, creates stories, discerns patterns and themes, makes comparisons, uses language, and captures life in mental images.

Even though this channel is only one part of our human system, for most of us the thinking function is usually the first thing that comes to mind when we try to articulate how we receive and consider the information our senses gather. How we engage in this process is as important as the material we are processing.

Metacognition refers to thinking about thinking. It involves noticing and exploring not just *what* we are thinking, but *how* we are thinking. Tuning in to the cognitive channel in order to make the most of its contributions will require us to learn the habits, limitations, and power of our unique thought processes. As we develop the skill of metacognition, of monitoring the ways we think, we will improve the quality and clarity of our thoughts.

How might you describe the typical quality of your thought process? Are you clear and open or cloudy and stuck?

Does this seem to change based on where you are, what you're doing, or who you're with?

Meet Joyce

Joyce, in her eighties, was dealing with a cancer diagnosis as well as depression. Ruminating on her thinking had become a full-time job. It was common for her to feel trapped in certain thoughts, endlessly spinning them like a spider spins a web. Each triggered memory led to a cascade of fearful thinking, culminating in feelings of dread.

As she neared the end of her life, Joyce was also knee-deep in a life review. Depleted physically and primed for glass-half-empty thinking, she was soon adding up all the regrets, the remorse, the missed opportunities, the mistakes, and the hard knocks and determining that this narrative was an accurate summary of her life. As one recalled tragedy piled on top of another, it became next to impossible for Joyce to expect anything better. Caught in this sad loop and clouded by its patterns, her thinking channel was playing a self-reinforcing story that was nearly impossible to escape.

Joyce had become convinced she was being punished. She found herself worrying about how she would feel each morning, bracing herself for what she was sure would be the inevitable dark hole of depression she would wake to. Moments of relief were quickly followed by doubt that they could last.

Of course, they rarely did. Our brains seek shortcuts, especially when our systems are stressed. They prefer predictable patterns and self-fulfilling prophecies, even terrible ones.

Things changed for Joyce when she was supported to try thinking about her thinking and expressing her emotions. Through conversation with trusted friends and family members, Joyce found the courage to lighten her burden by giving voice to her shame and guilt. She needed assurance that she would still be loved, no matter what.

This offered Joyce a different way to perceive her story. She became increasingly able to suspend her worry long enough to consider that there could be alternatives to the relentlessly negative thoughts that plagued her. In the moments when her worry quieted, she found she could reflect with expanded perspective on the events of her life and the meaning she had attached along the way. It was Joyce's ability to engage her thoughts in this way, even if only for brief moments, that allowed her to break the pattern and become centered enough to make important decisions from a place of clarity. She found relief.

Where are your clusters of patterned, habitual thinking?

What helps you expand your thought process?

Critical and Creative Thinking

By developing skill in metacognition, we also become more able to think critically and creatively. Whenever we can slow and monitor our thinking enough to push past easy answers, snap judgments, and taken-for-granted patterns, we are in a position to expand our awareness of what's possible and learn—or even create—something new.

Critical thinking requires focus. It is a specific way of looking at things with a view toward solving problems or overcoming obstacles. It can mean deconstructing the familiar to test underlying assumptions. It can mean deeply understanding what already works and building on that. It always requires patience to stick with a process long enough to see beyond what we already know. Critical thinkers take risks and ask questions. They look for connections. They aren't afraid to be wrong and to make mistakes. They will play the fool in order to find the gold.

Creative thinking is linked with imagination and curiosity. Sometimes this is called out-of-the-box thinking. This aspect of the cognitive channel challenges limits and expands the horizon of our vision. One of the greatest gifts of creativity is the ability to daydream, to conjure up ideas and images of things previously unseen, to envision and then articulate strategies and solutions and grand ideas.

Like critical thought, creativity also requires the ability to suspend judgment; to get outside your comfort zone; to consider alternative perspectives; to take risks; and to be willing to consider options and possibilities that don't yet exist.

Creativity is not limited to artistic expression. You are a creative being regardless of whether you can draw, paint, sing, dance, knit, or write poetry. You create your reality as your actions arise from your thoughts. This process is fueled by the essence of your values and beliefs and is energized by your emotional core. You are a powerful creative force, and you can affect these states and transform your experience.

As key elements of the cognitive channel of your human system, creativity and critical thinking keep you on the cutting edge of your own experience. When well developed, these are the tools of master decision makers and problem solvers. Committed, curious, and creative people change the world.

How willing are you to push the limits of your own thinking?

What helps you think creatively?

Conscious Thinking

To gain deeper understanding of the nature of our thoughts and their impact on the quality of our lives, we must first become aware. We have to be able to see and hear our thoughts if we want to make any sense out of the patterns and connections that occur at the intellectual level.

As we noted in Joyce's experience, the mind can trap us—or offer a gateway to liberation. Our thoughts can play tricks. They can play games that offer us no chance of winning. At times, extricating ourselves from mental chatter can seem impossible, but it isn't. Our minds and our thoughts are capable of expansion, growth, and transformation.

Your perspective about your thought process can make all the difference. To create some distance and witness the contents and quality of your thoughts without judgment, take the observer's view. A simple movement into awareness can help you to find the space to shift mental gears.

Notice the connection between what you think and how you feel. Circular thoughts about unsettling things have a purpose: to get your attention. They're giving you a heads-up so you don't miss anything important. There is no ill intent. Acknowledging our thoughts can often be enough to satisfy their desire to be heard.

Experiment with being grateful for the beauty and uniqueness of your mental processes. Remember, it is in the awareness of the processing and analysis that we can appreciate our journey toward clarity. Things don't often become crystal clear until they have first been cloudy and confused. Your mind is doing what it is meant to do. Your job is to direct and filter that processing as opposed to letting it run wild.

I have come to realize that finding liberation in my mind usually has more to do with stillness than it does with actively clearing out the content. Stillness in the mind occurs as you pay attention to the space between your thoughts and experience the peace that comes in that space.

Tune in to the most prominent thought in your awareness right now. What impact does thinking this thought have on your other states of being? What physical sensations arise? What emotional responses emerge?

Emotional Labor

The energy of the thinking channel is largely analytic. Our brains process ideas and images, synthesizing information into knowledge we use to form judgments and make decisions. The mind considers options, devises strategies, and adapts behavior—and all of this usually happens very quickly. Our neural synapses move at an astoundingly high speed.

Emotional energy is different. Our emotional channel is tuned to the mixed and massive frequencies of human experience that aren't always easy to define or describe. Emotions are felt in the body. We feel our own emotions and we sense the emotional experience of others. This is fundamental to the role of service. And because some emotions are neither easy nor comfortable to feel or witness, it's imperative to honor the labor involved in the process.

Calling this *labor* acknowledges the emotional investment that is required to be of service to others. Emotional investment is essential to the creation of any relationship, and relationship is where service occurs. I would suggest that living in our world today is an exercise in emotional labor, and most of us are ill-equipped.

As we take stock of the emotional cost of service, and the ongoing effects of extended and unrelenting trauma on service providers in every industry, the need to honor and develop the emotional channel of our human systems—to harness the resilient power of emotional intelligence and emotional maturity—is more important than ever.

Emotional sensitivity is often interpreted as a liability—especially in professions or situations that involve trauma care or exposure to others' pain and unhappiness. We are often encouraged to protect ourselves from feeling too much—to avoid wearing our hearts on our sleeves. This advice is offered as a way to protect us from unnecessary pain. Our gentle softness has come to be seen as a vulnerability that leaves us exposed to a harsh and cruel world. Many of us have internalized the ideal of toughness and turned our backs on this part of our being. We've been trained to become people who avoid showing others our tenderness, because it's been cast as weakness.

When did feeling become the enemy?

In fact, it's this repression that can weaken us. Denying or disconnecting from the emotional channel's power to encompass and express painful or frightening experiences as well as joyful and pleasant ones is dangerous. When we hold back or shut down our capacity to feel, we destroy our energy and become susceptible to self-abandonment, illness, and despair.

What are some of the emotionally difficult aspects of your service?

Sensitivity Is a Superpower

For service providers, emotional sensitivity is actually a superpower. Tuning in to this aspect of our human system allows us heightened perceptivity, empathy, and enhanced access to its intuitive guidance. Showing up fully will always include the full range of our emotions. The power of our emotional channel to communicate with the messages supplied by our brains and our bodies is integral to the development of intimate and transformative relationships. And that's what service is all about.

In situations or cultures where sensitivity is not encouraged, many of us can feel a lack of security. If we've been taught to be uncomfortable with what we are feeling or what we anticipate feeling, the information available to us through this channel will be muffled.

When we lose connection with our current emotions, it's easy to slip into self-abandonment. This has a devastating impact on service relationships; it also diminishes our capacity for self-connection and responsiveness. This can lead to a sense of emptiness so profound that the impulse to escape and employ quick fixes becomes impossible to resist.

Managing emotional sensitivity in ways that allow its gifts to shine requires us to create our own sense of security. Instead of seeking an escape, we can allow ourselves to listen to our sensitivity when it is present. This can be so uncomfortable that our impulse is to get as far away from our feelings as possible. But in truth, our feelings just require our kind attention. As we create a safe inner space in which to explore our sensitivity, we will become more secure with the experience, and we'll learn what our heightened capacity to feel has to offer. Here, what has for so long been unfairly judged as a liability can become both a treasure and a tool.

Begin to notice your sensitivity levels. What characterizes a highly sensitive day or activity?

What indicates balance in terms of your sensitivity?

Building Emotional Intelligence

Emotions are chemically based. As our feeling channel responds to the information supplied by our senses, our bodies unleash a flood of hormones. These trigger the emotional states we identify as anger, excitement, anxiety, sadness, or ecstasy (to name just a few). The first step in fostering emotional intelligence is to feel whatever arises. When we're hit with feelings that are uncomfortable or unwelcome, our impulse is often to escape, to rationalize, or to fix them. This desire to turn off our feelings, or move beyond them into the more straightforward realm of solutions and sensibility, ignores the power of the emotional channel and cuts us off from the inspiration, insight, energy, focus, or release that our human system needs to function fully.

Emotional intelligence refers to your potential to connect to your emotional experiences without being overwhelmed by them. Emotional energy is fluid. It offers information in the form of feelings, each with a different quality and energetic intensity. Your emotional intelligence is your ability to manage all the energy that flows through the feeling channel. Emotional intelligence fosters expression and maturity. As we learn to express emotions in ways that honor their power, we open a door to healing and guidance.

Emotionally intelligent people have learned how to remain present with their emotional state—no matter what it happens to be. These people are able to create a safe container for the emotion's expression. As we saw earlier with Joyce, it's by feeling, expressing, and releasing our emotions that we're able to make room for the new experience of relief and the expansion and insights that follow.

Emotional intelligence isn't about being able to name every emotion the moment it arises. You don't have to speak in order to express. You are not required to explain how you feel. You don't have to have a reason for feeling. There is no right or wrong way to feel about anything. In fact, how you feel does not need to be understood by anyone. Rather, your feelings need only be experienced and accepted by you.

How do your emotions show up in your body?

For me, anxiety inhabits the pit of my stomach. It resembles a tight little knot that grows and aches and insists on making its presence known. Happiness feels light in my body. Joy shows up as physical effortlessness and increased energy. Sadness shares its voice inside my heart and chest and feels heavy and tired.

Investigate your emotional landscape. Play with the relationship between some of the feelings I describe here to connect with your personal experience of them.

Habits and Emotional Hometowns

The places where we first put down our roots—and the people who were there as we did—can reverberate within us for a lifetime, even long after we leave. The emotional habits we build in those formative places can stay with us just as long.

A few years ago, on a regular visit to my own hometown, I found myself surrounded by familiar faces laden with old memories. Some of the memories were of fun times, but most seemed either painful or embarrassing. But I felt drawn to these old connections, curious about how I would feel this time. Would it be the same old same old, or might I experience something different this time?

Pro tip: Just hoping a situation will feel different, without intentionally showing up in it in a new way, is a recipe for disappointment.

Anyway, after a clash with an old dynamic, I found myself awash in an ocean of familiar emotions—all accompanied by their physical manifestations and sped-up thoughts. I had the hard knot of self-doubt in my belly while my mind scrambled to analyze what everyone involved might be thinking and feeling about me.

I stopped in my tracks. I was able to ask myself these important questions:

- Do I actually feel this way right now, or is this an emotional habit?

- Do I expect to feel this way? Do I conjure up the emotional energy I anticipate even though I don't really care that much anymore?

With a little reflection, I realized that, just as I'd driven the well-worn highway across Canada back to the town I grew up in, my emotional state had also found an old, familiar path. When I was able to stop and examine the route I'd taken, I realized I'd returned to an emotional hometown that I no longer needed to dwell in. Without having taken the time before that moment to be aware of what I had learned—to carry with me the growth and maturity and experience I'd gained—I showed up as an outdated version of my emotional self.

Our bodies remember old emotional states. A memory is triggered and suddenly we find ourselves reliving an old story—including the thoughts, feelings, and other sensations that we experienced the first time around. Some memories are so profound you can smell them. This is especially true of those times in our lives that have been particularly intense, whether traumatic, tragic, or ecstatic. This physical response to intense memories helps us absorb, process, and integrate powerful experiences over time. When it's working well, this response can provide us with a gentle and gracious space within which we contain, explore, and expand our emotional story.

When this part of our emotional channel is working poorly, we can get trapped in old trauma and duped into believing we're unable to change and grow. Emotional habits can be tricky: comforting and destructive at the same time. We need to learn the difference between current emotional experiences and the emotional hometowns we can now leave behind.

What emotional habits are active in your life?

Do you expect to feel a certain way today based on what happened in the past?

Emotional Maturity
(and a Final Word about That Superpower)

Janelle is my dental hygienist. It might be hard to imagine, but we've had more than one amazing conversation while she cleans my teeth. Last time we took up the topic of sensitivity. We discovered that both of us seem to be getting more sensitive—not only emotionally, but also to what we ingest: food, drink, and social media, for example.

I told Janelle how emotional I was as a child. I would cry at songs and commercials. I was born sentimental. I realized a few years ago that I had learned to stifle this quality because I could see how it often made others uncomfortable—and noticing that made me uncomfortable and confused. Now, I am on a mission to embrace my sensitivity as an innate aspect of my human nature. I'm working to help my emotional maturity catch up with the rest of my human system.

Janelle had a similar story. She acknowledged that sometimes her "big heart" led her into escapist behavior, like eating her feelings (or drinking or smoking them), or kept her mired in discomfort, as though her willingness to suffer would make the pain go away. But Janelle was also able to admit how this quality made her good at her job. It helped her connect with and comfort the sometimes-anxious people who showed up in her chair. Janelle's emotional sensitivity is her superpower as a mom and wife too. It's the vehicle that allows her to develop rich and intimate relationships in her life.

Sensitivity means we are noticing the power of our emotional channel. Feeling in real time means we're finely attuned to living. The capacity to respond emotionally is one key to a life filled with mystery and rich adventure. Denying our sensitivity leads to disconnection from ourselves and distance from others. Your sensitive nature makes intimacy possible. When embraced, the gifts of the emotional channel deepen your experience of unconditional love for yourself and for others. They allow you the courage to explore areas of human experience where others fear to tread.

They help you become adept at ensuring your personal safety in that exploration. This makes you ideal for your role in service.

Feelings can be messy sometimes. They aren't always warm and fuzzy. We may run and hide from time to time. We may choose to go numb for a moment. We may have embarrassing outbursts or even lose our shit entirely on occasion.

Love yourself through it all. Be gentle. Be patient. Brief escapes are part of the process. It's only when we lock feelings up, stuff them down, or attempt to abandon our emotional channel altogether that we run into trouble. Emotions don't go away. When we ignore them, old wounds fester and toxicity permeates the entire system.

To be emotionally mature has nothing to do with controlling feelings or presenting as stoic and cut off. It has even less to do with burying our feelings. Emotional maturity is what we develop as we become more willing to engage with our emotional experience.

As we grow in this way, we learn how to stay with our feelings so they can be expressed and released. This is a demonstration of self-trust and self-respect. Emotional maturity honors this process. It allows emotions space and time, understanding that they are fleeting messengers with important information.

Highly developed emotional intelligence will strengthen your capacity for empathy, compassion, and acceptance as a service provider. Because you've learned to honor your personal emotional experience, you will become more able to recognize and connect with others' emotions without losing your sense of self in the process.

How do you access your emotional wisdom and maturity?

What can you do today that will nurture your sensitivity?

Connection and Unity

As we've explored the various channels of the human system, our focus so far has been internal. Noticing and naming how our physical, cognitive, and emotional channels digest and deliver information about our experience has involved paying attention to what's happening inside us. As we continue to accept the invitation to show up fully in all areas of our lives, we'll start to explore the channels that connect us more directly to the other people we encounter and to the cultures and communities that surround us. This includes our coworkers as well as our families, our friends, and the people to whom our service is directed—and even total strangers.

There's a reason we're moving from inside to out in this chapter. Showing up fully within and for yourself improves your ability to do so with others. Knowing and claiming who and where you are helps you find common ground with others where it exists, and it offers space for patience when you feel worlds apart. Our relationships add a new perspective as well. They offer us ways of understanding how we're perceived and experienced, and they often challenge us to grow.

The social channel of our human system is all about relationships. This channel is dialed in to the frequencies of connection and unity. It's the part of us that craves community and belonging. *Social intelligence* describes our capacity to communicate and network and make use of relationships. At the center of all these activities is our ability to establish trust and reliability with others—an ability we use in all of our relationships: parenting, business partnerships, romantic relationships, and the bond between nurse and person in their care, to name a few.

According to the work of Daniel Goleman, socially intelligent people have a keen sense of relationship to others, as well as the ability to value and honor these connections. Our social channel draws on the other states of awareness to inform our relationships with one another, integrating what our senses gather, what we feel, how we think, and the spiritual qualities related to our beliefs and values.

As you build social intelligence, you create space for partnership. You become able to maintain balance among the needs of all involved. You become aware of subtle dynamics in the social context. You pick up more quickly on the spoken and unspoken messages you receive from others. Awareness of the dynamics of social interaction allows you to respond effectively. You take your time formulating and delivering your messages. You decipher what comes at you with greater objectivity. Social intelligence is the foundation for the transformative relationships and creative communities in which healing can happen.

We long to belong. As human beings, we seek our place in the interconnected community of the world. We yearn for the feeling of being at home with the people in our lives. We seek to know how we fit in the grand design. The social channel expresses this longing and works to fill it.

The Purpose of Relationship

Teaching and learning are key functions of relationship. As children we learned by copying what the big people in our life did. We looked for cues and patterns and rewards while avoiding frowns and disappointment. We're still doing this. Some relationships teach us patience, acceptance, and compassion. Sometimes we are learning how to spot and manage conflict or solve problems. Whether we know it or not, we are always also teaching others what they can expect from us, how we expect to be treated, and how far we are willing to go.

Relationships are containers and catalysts for transformation and evolution. They can be places of powerful joy as well as powerful discomfort. In the context of our relationships, we will experience both connection and disconnection, intimacy and distance, synergy and friction. I like to define *synergy* as a powerful and resonant agreement between people that goes deeper than cooperation. The word literally means "together energy."

In states of connection, intimacy, and synergy, we learn what it means to be in harmony and hold a shared vision. The energy of ease and security make it easy to offer our gifts, because we know that we are recognized and received. As we contribute, we reveal who we are and teach others what matters most to us. The safety of such relationships allows us to more easily learn what makes others tick as well. Free from worry, we are naturally curious and interested. The gifts of the exchange are often very subtle because they are so natural.

When we encounter disconnection, distance, and friction, we often disengage or walk away. Just as we want to flee from emotional turbulence, most of us try to avoid relational unrest. Resist this urge. Discomfort is a place where equally magical transformations can occur. Be willing to stay in the struggle long enough to reap the rewards that are ready to emerge. When we rub each other the wrong way, we often initiate powerful opportunities for growth. The friction and disunity in these situations can offer gifts of insight; we can't receive those if we give up too soon.

Socially intelligent people know how to show up and stay present. They are able to stretch beyond their personal perspectives and open their hearts a little wider. Equipped with an inherent respect and appreciation for the power of relationship and connection, the socially intelligent person is able to be patient and discerning. They know how to fight fair—how to wait in a place of personal power for truth to work its way forward. And they also know when stopping, calling a time-out, or reorganizing a boundary is integral to their self-preservation and security.

What relationships come to mind when you think about synergy? How about friction?

What are you learning in these relationships? What are you teaching?

The Mirror

We service providers are usually other-focused. We like to learn about other people, to understand, to find ways to help or give. We tend to leverage the gifts of connection and intimacy to improve others' situations or health or well-being. We're usually careful to make sure that our relationships of service are one-way—we're not supposed to be the receivers.

This discounts the fact that all genuine relationships are two-way. We are always both giving and receiving. This doesn't mean that everyone involved must somehow benefit equally; it just means that relationships are reciprocal. We get something, even as we're focused on giving. As we continue to develop the social channel of our human system, we'll find that one benefit of the reciprocal nature of relationships is the opportunity for us to see ourselves more clearly and to understand ourselves more deeply.

Other people can function as mirrors to us.

I remember when I first learned about this phenomenon from the work of Debbie Ford. The basic premise is that whenever I observe behavior in another that bothers (infuriates) or attracts me, I'm learning more about myself than I am about the other person.

This was a tough pill to swallow, because other people bug me all the time.

Sometimes what we see is a very subtle reflection. Rather than being a literal replication of my behavior, the mirror often shows a deeper current of motivation or desire that's been raging through me unconsciously until that moment.

People show up in our lives with lessons for us, as well as needs and desires and complicated stories of their own. For example, when someone lies to you, it's not necessarily true that they don't respect or care for you. The person's dishonest behavior shows their lack of self-respect or their fear. It has nothing to do with you.

At the same time, the mirror's wisdom has everything to do with you. Your emotional response to being lied to and the story you tell yourself about what it means are opportunities for self-understanding. The guilt locked in the stores of your past personal dishonesty may spur you to choose this moment to seek healing. Resist the urge to bypass a lesson about your integrity because someone else stepped away from theirs. Take the learning and leave the rest.

Likewise, whenever you admire a positive quality or action in another person, know that you are recognizing an aspect of yourself that has the potential to be developed. If this admiration has any tinge of jealousy, remember that the energy of comparison and envy blocks any possibility for connected relationships. And you may be closer to a personal break-through than you thought possible. We can only identify in others what we possess within. Bless this person for showing you what's possible.

Think of two people in your life, one with whom you feel resonance and another with whom you feel resistance. What can you learn about yourself though the mirrors those people offer?

Attending to the Voice of Your Spirit

As we consider the last of the five channels of the human system, the spiritual channel, it's helpful to make a distinction between spirituality and religion. Some people enjoy a clear relationship between a religious tradition and their own spiritual expression, but this is not always the case. Each of us has a spiritual dimension within our being—a channel in our human system tuned to this frequency—but not everybody identifies with a specific religion's beliefs. On the other hand, many people follow religious doctrines without much connection to their spiritual nature.

While the insights of spiritual masters and the wisdom of all the world's religions can help us understand and describe the spiritual aspect of human experience, you do not need to be part of a religion to claim and develop the capacities of your spiritual channel.

The role of spirit is that of creation and vision. Our spiritual channel also makes meaning out of what we experience. It helps us make sense of our lived experience in nonlinear ways. We learn to sense the best choice and course of action available to us in the moment. This sensed knowing sometimes transcends what the available evidence presents and the logical mind expects. Our spiritual capacity integrates the other channels and allows us full expression of our personality in the world. We can't show up fully without this vital aspect of our humanity.

As you grow spiritually, you can expect to be called to utilize your highly developed qualities, your hard-won lessons, and your curiosity. Life will continue to provide opportunities to learn and expand. You will never develop a quality or skill that you won't be called upon to employ. Ultimately, the spiritual journey requires acceptance of and curiosity about our perpetual evolution.

Do you use religious or spiritual language to describe your work?

Consider your definitions of religion and spirituality.
What is the connection between the two in your personal experience and practice?

Inspiration and Intuition

The spiritual channel provides the space inside of you that believes in possibilities, with an unwavering faith in things that haven't been seen yet. This shows up in our lives as inspiration and intuition.

Inspiration often shows up uninvited. Ideas that spring forward from an inspired place have an energetic compass magnetized toward success. Inspiration moves us from our comfort zones and excites us with big ideas and powerful imagination. It is the stuff that miracles are made of.

Following inspiration's lead requires big faith and enduring patience. Stumbling blocks in this process can be seen as unwelcome obstacles. They can also serve to deepen your commitment to your grander vision by helping you dismantle outdated beliefs and self-limiting perspectives. Tuning in to the spiritual channel is a process of sharpening your capacity to receive the spirit's unique type of guidance.

Intuition arises from inside. Some believe intuition is solely a function of the brain, like lateral thinking. Others see intuition as the interplay between our emotions and our guts—a "sixth sense." Still others consider intuition a social sense, the result of a fine ability to read situations and people. I see intuition as a function of the soul. Intuition is the still, small voice within the spiritual channel that continually alerts us to actions and ideas that keep us evolving toward our ultimate purpose. When tended with care, intuition keeps us connected to our place in the larger stories that encompass and affect our lives.

The seeds for intuition reside within all of us, but they will truly flourish only when nurtured. Keep space around your seeds of intuition. Protect them from being choked out by the weeds produced by your mind and ego. Regularly give your intuition what it needs to grow: your attention, your curiosity, your willingness to listen, and your commitment to the connection. Seek its wisdom often, and wait patiently for its response. Shower it with gratitude. And most of all, trust it.

What does the voice of your spirit sound like to you?

Integration, or the Alchemy of Personal Artistry

As we have explored throughout this chapter, the interrelated channels within each human being create a complex and intricate system designed to help us survive and thrive during our journey here on earth. Learning how to tune in to each channel can bring richness to your experience, expand your sense of self, and offer healing to parts of you that have been bruised or broken. Learning how the channels overlap and inform each other adds the profound quality of integration to the mix.

As a service provider, you might be exposed to a great deal of academic information, field-related research, and industry-accepted best practices. These are some of the tools of your professional or personal call to service; they point to tangible tasks and approaches that become part of what you do each day. You could call these the hard skills, or the science behind service.

As the preceding pages suggest, these skills are only part of the recipe. If we want to show up fully, equal value must be given to the artistry of service. It is through the full expression of your unique human system that you demonstrate your signature style as a service provider and find the joy that comes from doing and being what you love.

In the alchemical process of integration, knowledge turns into wisdom. Philosophical constructs guiding service in the world have little value when they are only transmitted through a single channel. Intellectual dissection alone, for example, is not nearly as powerful as the combination of careful thought, active experience, emotional connection, and the realities of relationship.

Take the often-touted examples of compassion, respect, and acceptance. These are value-based principles we expect to incorporate into service. Knowing how you define these qualities is only the first step toward enacting them. By experiencing these principles in other ways—sensing them in your body, emotions, and spirit and seeing them reflected in your connections with others—you enact them fully, with your whole self.

Actively engaging with and integrating the information from all your channels transforms what you know into wisdom you can feel and use to guide your actions. You are able to tell the difference between the moments when you are grounded in the energy of service and those times when you are trudging through the motions.

A nurse in training learns a wide range of skills and theories. Learning how to draw blood is a knowledge-based skill. Multichannel wisdom is demonstrated when that same nurse can approach a needle-phobic individual with genuine compassion and patience as well as technical proficiency. Integrating wisdom from many channels makes the job easier and the person more comfortable.

Make it part of your regular routine to scan your channels. There will be days when some stations come through crisp and clear and perhaps a little louder than the others. And there will be days when there is nothing but static. Just keep scanning. As you find the delicate balance, you become more and more able to tune in to the channel you're looking for, and more equipped for enhanced service in the world.

CHAPTER 3

Embrace Full Responsibility

An Invitation to Freedom

Responsibility has been given a bad rap. As a concept, it's often met with distaste and avoidance. Responsibility gets portrayed as the party pooper, the one who shows up to stop the fun and bring us back to reality.

The word often stirs up images of being burdened, trapped, or confined. Even as I write this, I can feel myself getting overwhelmed and wanting to escape. Too often in our lives, responsibilities have been things we felt saddled with, things we had to bear or tolerate or put up with in order to occasionally get what we really want. Most of us desire *freedom,* not more restrictions.

And, in fact, it is freedom that awaits as we embrace the deepest levels of personal responsibility available to us. This is one of those beautiful mysteries in life—a paradox that leads us to think we are being offered, at first glance, an unappealing experience when really the gem is just beneath the surface. Spiritual teacher and author Iyanla Vanzant calls this a gift in "ugly wrapping paper."

Responsibility is this kind of gift. Rather than being a burden, full responsibility is the key to unlocking limitless personal power and the path to freedom. Don't miss the party because someone once gave you the wrong address. And don't pass up the opportunity to open this gift just because the wrapper seems sketchy.

Every single moment of every single day, we are faced with the opportunity to either respond or react to perceptions and people and situations. And in the difference between these two approaches—responding and reacting—we find the essence of responsibility and, with it, our freedom. Responsibility is the ability to *respond* to all of life's experiences, both external and internal. To react is to move in the world without forethought or presence. To respond is to consciously approach life events with clarity and engagement.

On some level, we can respond to *everything*. We have the opportunity to respond to our internal experiences and to external conditions. We can respond to other people, to their requests, to their expectations, and to our commitments to them. We can become more and more able to respond to our emotions, thoughts, beliefs, ideas, and interpretations, as well as to our own actions. We can intentionally respond to our desires, to our challenges, to our gifts, and to our learning opportunities.

When we shirk these responsibilities, we limit our choices, and we give away our personal power. The ability to respond to all events—internal or external—is a skill that greatly enhances personal power and expands possibilities. This is your freedom. As you increase your ability to perceive and imagine the many choices available to you in any situation, you will become able to affect and alter your experiences.

In this chapter, you will draw on what you've discovered about your many-channeled self as well as the forces that propel you toward service. Exploring and expanding your capacity to respond provides an opportunity to experience the freedom that often seems elusive when we set out to make a difference. You will develop a refreshed way of working with whatever arises to address and overcome obstacles and conflicts as they show up in life and work, and as they are reflected in the many roles you play.

Understanding and working with this fundamental capacity to choose our response to anything is the ultimate freedom.

■ ■ ■

A Word about *Owning It*

There's lots of talk these days about "owning" an action or opinion or statement or standpoint. "Yes, I did that or I said that, but I own it." It feels to me like something is missing in that statement. It almost sounds like an excuse—along the lines of "Well, that's just the way I am." To step fully into personal responsibility, we need to move beyond simply stating ownership. As anyone attached in this way to a house or a car or a project or a program or a dog or a goldfish can attest, owning something is not the end of our commitment and responsibility. When we own something important to us, we treat it with care. We maintain and nurture it.

Just as authentic ownership involves real responsibility, true freedom always includes consequences. Cause and effect are part of the natural laws of the universe. Every action, every movement, creates a reaction and a shift in all related areas. You are interconnected to all that is, so each of your actions has an impact—a ripple effect. The choices you make today contribute to the creation of the experiences you will have tomorrow. Responsibility recognizes and affirms and respects these interconnections.

What is right in front of you? This is what you are responsible for in the present. What is the next step for you in the present moment?

Daily Duty and the Responsibilities of Living

You are practically responsible for everything in your life.

I know. This sounds like a step in the wrong direction. You might feel like running for the hills here. But bear with me.

Practical responsibility refers to the basic activities in daily life: showing up on time and maintaining commitments. You are responsible for what you agree to, and for following through on those commitments. Most of these agreements aren't verbalized every day; they're implicit. These are the activities that make daily life manageable—I call them our practical responsibilities.

Picture your daily personal routines, the care of yourself, your home, and your possessions. Most of us are responsible for feeding ourselves, which includes preparing the meal and buying the groceries. As we collect material things in our lives, we enter a maintenance agreement of sorts. If something we own breaks, we repair it or replace it (or hire someone else to do this for us). Even these responsibilities can feel like a burden, which may be part of the reason that we hear so much about simplicity and decluttering these days.

When it comes to practical responsibilities, you might look at your life right now and think, *Wow! My time is spent getting ready for work, commuting, working all day, and returning home to care for my loved ones and maintain my home. I take care of my stuff and have the lifestyle I've worked and planned for—the life I've wanted.*

Do you still want it?

Maybe you feel like you've taken on too much responsibility. And maybe you have. What does that mean? What is too much responsibility?

Well, I'm not sure if it is *too much* responsibility or if it's more like *misplaced* responsibility.

I'm talking about those times when we find ourselves feeling resentful because we seem to be the only one taking care of the things that many people use and benefit from. These are perfect opportunities to ask yourself what values are guiding your practical responsibilities.

Let's say that it is really important to you to have a clean and tidy home. You especially like to enjoy a clean, uncluttered space when you are home on the weekends, because it helps you feel comfortable. You want to relax and have some me time. So you decide that Thursday is cleaning day. You want to get it out of the way for the weekend—and you want the weekend to start as early as possible on Friday.

You enjoy a sense of accomplishment and relief once you're done cleaning on Thursday. You're tired but happy and head to sleep just knowing how much your family will also appreciate your efforts.

On Friday morning, when you come downstairs to a sink full of dishes and an unswept floor, you can feel your blood start to boil. You walk into the dining room to find that someone has left their hoodie and keys and a stack of papers on the dining room table. Now you're mumbling under your breath and the air is turning blue. By the time you discover the disaster that has become your bathroom, you're ready to blow a gasket. "This is bullshit!" you declare. And thus begins a day full of internal chatter fueled by your feelings of resentment and your sense that you are taken for granted by the people you live with.

You'd think I've had this experience or something.

I can hear some of you now: "Other people should be helping with those tasks. They should be grateful, dammit!" Let's get rid of that word *should* once and for all. I don't usually see too many things as absolutes, but that word really has no place in our exploration of conscious service in general, and certainly not in our discussion of responsibility. More on that later.

Back to *bullshit* and the righteous rage that rises up when we feel like we're being taken for granted.

Let me tell you, I went pretty far down the resentments path around the housecleaning issue. I tried getting angry and freaking out. I tried convening "the conversation"—you know, the one where you are look- ing for common ground and collaboration but you know the buy-in isn't really there. I even tried the old "I'll just stop doing it and we'll see how they like that" approach.

They had more stamina than me.

Finally, I realized that my desire for a clean house on the weekend belonged to me. I hadn't really checked with anyone else to see if it even mattered to them. I had assumed, without thinking much about it, that they wanted it too. Well, you know what they say about assumptions. Who's the ass now?

I had to discover that I was the only one struggling. I was fuming all by myself.

Breakthrough!

I decided that if I was the one who wanted a clean and uncluttered experience on the weekends, then I would respond to that desire—that value—by making it happen. I stopped expecting that my actions and their effects would be appreciated or even acknowledged by anyone else. I stopped losing my cool when something wasn't picked up later. I chilled out about it. I took this responsibility for myself, and I enjoyed the feelings it generated. This was the first time that I started to concretely realize that my values exist to guide *me* in *my* life, not as a standard to which I can hold other people. I valued the clean house. It didn't matter if anyone else did. I was free. It was that simple and that quick. A single moment of clarity. And it happened because of a shift in my perspective about where my responsibility was rightly focused.

The power of responsibility lies within us, even for the practical stuff. We decide what matters to us and how we wish to respond when things don't line up the way we had hoped—when other people don't do what they agreed to do. For me, the choice is between preserving my peace and my relationships and being at war with those around me whose perspectives and priorities differ. There's always room for discussion about shared tasks and fairness, of course. Communicate and negotiate from a place of personal accountability for your values and preferences. Responsibility is not so much about the chores and tasks as it is about your internal state of balance and harmony.

It took my coming to terms with my power in the face of a sink full of dirty dishes to free me from a cycle of resentment that had lasted for years. The profound can be discovered in the profane. What is sacred often reveals itself in the ordinary.

Our Responsibility for Happiness

As the insight provided by my housecleaning epiphany suggests, practical responsibilities are tangled up in how you manage, utilize, and conserve your resources and gifts—your time, your talents, and your energy. Becoming aware of what you have to offer the world, and how and when you wish to contribute, is your responsibility. You may discover this information through communication with others, but the curiosity that begins the exploration must come from you alone.

In the first two chapters, we explored what motivates us as individuals and the multidimensional nature of being human. While the ways you describe your particular motivations and your capacity to connect with your various channels will evolve over time, the *you* at the heart of these things remains constant. This is your core. It is from your core that you will hear and feel the truth of your heart, the wisdom of your mind, and the desires of your soul. These elements will change over time and through experience, but your fundamental wholeness persists throughout your life.

It is your responsibility to get to know this core self, to learn what ignites your heart, where your inspiration comes from, how you wish to feel, what holds meaning for you, and what you'd like to influence or add to or change. You decide how to spend your time and when, where, and with whom to share yourself on an intimate level. It is up to you to decide how you want to expend your energy and to identify your needs at every level of your being every single day. Nobody can do this for you.

I know it might not always seem this way. Believing the lie that we cannot be solely responsible for our own happiness and joy might be one of the most prominent ways that we shirk our responsibilities. The *should* voice of others' expectations, demands, and values is loud and familiar to most of us. You may have spent your life believing that responsibilities are duties assigned to you by others for others. Like many of us, you have likely been taught and trained to completely disregard the responsibilities you hold to yourself.

Responsibility and Role

Consider all the roles that you hold in your life right now. What words do you use to describe yourself in relation to these roles? Which do you identify most closely with? Remember that some roles are really clear and obvious: parent, teacher, volunteer, etc. Some are less concrete and formal, the roles we take on within the other roles. You might be the problem solver, the decision maker, or the peacekeeper. Are you a leader, an organizer, a helper? Try making a two-column list of all your roles, and see how they match or where they rub.

Responsibility to the roles that you hold in your life is very much like the practical responsibility that we just explored. It means that you are more or less aware of what is expected and required of you in a given relational situation, and you do it. Plain and simple.

Regardless of the specifics of your roles in service to others, whether professional or personal, you are often faced with myriad tasks and responsibilities that demand attention and action. For example, in a counselor's role, these tasks and responsibilities could include direct counseling, paperwork, or being responsive to requests. Accepting responsibility on this level means that you know what is expected of you and you follow through. You demonstrate dependability and resourcefulness. You know who you are as a service provider. As you seek guidance from your core, you will be guided as to how you show up in this role. Not so much *what* you are responsible to *do* but *how* you are responsible to *be*.

Of course we hope that our presence and engagement in service to others will be helpful and contribute in some meaningful way. Whether we're taking a blood sample or teaching five-year-olds their letters, it is our responsibility to fulfill the requirements of our roles while respecting the humanity and autonomy of the human being before us. Defining what is helpful or meaningful to another is beyond the scope of what we can be responsible for. It is our responsibility to ask what that is for each person who enters our care, and to accept the answer even when it is radically different from the one we would give based on our own values.

Even when you fulfill your role to the utmost, there is no guarantee that the person on the receiving end of your service or care or love will grow, change, heal, or transform the way you had envisioned. Believing that your responsibility extends to changing others, making them grow, or creating specific outcomes is a setup for disillusionment. With precious few exceptions, thinking that you have to protect people from themselves is a fallacy. Seeing yourself as a gatekeeper to the "right" or "good" way to live is arrogant. We do not have that kind of responsibility in the lives of others.

Let's take decision-making, for example. Your role might require you to assist someone else through a decision-making process. This might mean that you are responsible for providing as much information as you're able to gather for that person to use in reaching a decision. Once you have done that, you are not responsible for the decision that is ultimately reached.

Unless you are a parent of a young child, working in child welfare, or serving someone who has been deemed formally and legally incompetent to make decisions, you are not required to make that final decision. And even when you have been entrusted with responsibility for such decisions, you are not—and cannot be—responsible for their level of happiness once you have made it.

Your role as a parent might include caring for the physical needs of your children, their health, their comfort, and their education. For a few years of their lives, you are utterly responsible for keeping them safe and alive. It is easy to get confused in these close relationships and start to believe that we are responsible for another's happiness, their sense of self-esteem, their overall emotional landscape, and the nature of their thoughts.

No matter how much we love someone, we cannot make them feel anything purely because we will it. We are responsible to create a safe and loving space. We are responsible to show up and be present in our relationships. We are responsible to follow through with our commitments to the people in our lives. And yet, we cannot guarantee that the other person will receive our love, will feel loved, will feel secure, and will trust us to be there.

Ultimately, we are responsible for the actions we take and the energy we bring to any role we are holding, whether personal or professional. We are also responsible for detaching from the outcome we imagine or hope will result from our actions and our investments of energy, love, and commitment.

You have responsibilities that are inherent to the roles you have agreed to take on in your life. Within these roles, you are responsible *to* the commitments you have made with other people, whether you just met them or you birthed them from your body any number of years ago. This is radically different from being responsible *for* other people's roles and commitments. There may be a fine line here, but identifying which side of the line you are on can make all the difference in the world.

What are your primary roles?

Can you name at least one key responsibility that accompanies each role?

Which Baby Will It Be?

Several years ago, my friend Erika found herself at a responsibility crossroads. She was nearing the end of her first pregnancy and was three years into her role as executive director of an after-school program for children in Texas. Erika had always referred to this initiative as her "baby." She had worked diligently to establish and improve the program, hiring the best service providers and supervisors, overseeing development, and raising funds.

One day, weeks before she was due, Erika found herself in the hospital. Complications with her pregnancy now required bed rest until delivery. She was faced with the question "Which baby will it be?" The choice was obvious, of course, but the need to make it had not occurred to Erika until she found herself in crisis.

Up until that watershed moment, Erika had felt totally responsible for the programs and services of the organization that had entrusted her with its direction. It was up to her to keep everything functioning at the highest level. Would the program survive and continue to thrive if Erika couldn't or wouldn't be the responsible party?

What Erika came to realize had to do with the difference between *to* and *for* when it comes to responsibility. She was uniquely responsible *for* her health and *for* the well-being of her unborn baby. Nobody else could fill those roles. She was responsible *to* her role as executive director. In this case, that meant knowing what combination of things needed to happen so that another person could step in and continue in her place, leading an effective and successful program that served an important and useful purpose.

Erika was skilled in her professional role, so she was impeccably organized and on top of all that was going on with the program. She knew her responsibility was to the organization and the children and families who access the services, and that this meant passing the torch to someone else while providing all the information she could to smooth the transition.

When Erika gazed into the eyes of her healthy newborn baby girl a few weeks later, she had no doubts about her decision, and no regrets.

Don't Hide Your Humanity

In those moments when you find yourself unable to fulfill your roles—and it happens to all of us—you are face-to-face with a beautiful opportunity for deep personal responsibility and self-compassion. Sometimes we struggle, as Erika did, with feeling forced into change by circumstances beyond our control. Sometimes we make mistakes or drop the ball and it's nobody's fault but ours. When we feel ourselves boxed in or limited or somehow not at our best, most of us start to hide the very thing we need the most: our humanity.

If the shit is hitting the fan and you try to tap dance your way around it, you will waste valuable energy that could be better spent seeking help and solving practical problems. Getting to the root of the challenges requires honesty. And at the end of the day, you can only tap dance so long before you trip over your own feet.

When you step into a new role as a service provider, there will be a learning curve. When you are faced with life events or personal challenges, there will likely be an impact on your role performance. These are aspects of our shared humanity that we too often try to discount, deny, or keep secret as we pretend everything is okay. The desire to hide so no one will notice you're faltering will not only hurt you; it will ensure that you do not fulfill your responsibilities. It is a very subtle form of self-abandonment that says, "It's not okay for me to struggle." Take a step back, tell the truth in a safe space, and honor yourself first. Feel the relief that comes when you stop pretending. As you accept whatever is impacting you in the moment, you will be able to see more clearly. Then you can return more ready and able to honor your roles.

From Dream Job to Nightmare Burden

Before we go too much further exploring true responsibility and how it moves beyond our roles and into our lives, let's take a moment to explore how false responsibility shows up.

Have you ever found yourself struggling to do all you could to make something happen or avoid a certain outcome? If you're at all like me, you likely felt helpless, hopeless, frustrated, resentful, and angry. At the base of these emotions, you may have recognized a profound sense of fear. And underneath that, you might have become aware of the belief that it was up to you to keep the world spinning.

News flash! It's not.

That's a lie you're telling yourself.

The universe will stay in motion even if you go to sleep for a month.

False responsibility is the lie that tells you that you need to control something beyond yourself. This whopper always comes wrapped in a second lie that makes you believe that you *can*. Whether you're hoping to change the behavior of another person or the perceptions that others have of you, your desire for control often also involves some fear— usually the intense desire to escape a feeling you don't want to feel.

When I was fresh out of college, I landed the job of my dreams (at the time) working with adults who lived with developmental disabilities and who required various levels of support. I was introduced to approximately fifty people to whom I was responsible. At the time, I firmly (and falsely) believed that I was responsible *for* them.

It was the autonomy in this job, combined with the personal and intimate nature of the relationships, that I loved so much. I had opportunities to work with interesting people, navigate social challenges, and connect emotionally with others. This gave me a sense of doing something that mattered. And I was good at it.

Coming up against the constraints of the system, society's prevailing attitude about disability, and the unpredictability of human nature (mine included) added dimensions to my dream job that I wasn't prepared for. This soon left me feeling a bit out of control.

I would lie awake in bed at night, holding my breath and going back and forth in my mind about how I would prevent someone from doing something that I was sure would lead to their demise. I felt it was on me to be available no matter the hour. In some situations, I had even decided to give my personal phone number to a few individuals who I was sure would spontaneously combust if they didn't have access to me when they needed me. I was very important—a legend in my own mind.

Overextension is an expression of self-abandonment. It leads us directly into circumstances that will require us at some point to decompress or let off steam in order to avoid decompensation in our health and our performance. But decompensation can also happen in the decompression process. When the pendulum has swung too far, we are unlikely to approach rebalancing in a kind and gentle manner. Instead we tend to make choices that push just as far in the opposite direction. We get drunk. We sleep with a stranger. We blow our entire paycheck on something we don't need because we believe we deserve it. We utterly disconnect from the basic needs of self in a fruitless attempt to feel better. The intent might be pure, but the action lacks integrity.

You won't be surprised to learn that a few months into my dream job, I awoke one morning in despair. I didn't want to go in. I couldn't do it. I was entirely spent. I had been starting each day already exhausted from the mental and emotional energy I had expended the night before. My face ached as a result of clenching my teeth all night in a subconscious attempt to keep everything together.

I called in sick and then, of course, proceeded to feel guilty because I wasn't really sick.

That uncomfortable day revealed to me one of my biggest fears: appearing incompetent to my supervisors and colleagues. I believed that the behavior of the people I was assigned to support was a direct reflection of the quality of my service. If I were doing a "good" job, then the people I serve would be doing well without any problems or any missteps along the way.

What a crock!

In an attempt to demonstrate my willingness to go above and beyond in my service to others, I had exhausted myself. I was no use to anybody—not the people I was meant to serve, not my colleagues, not my supervisor, and not even myself. I was miserable. I could not avoid the truth that in a few short months my dream job had become my worst nightmare.

My experience that morning was a chance for me to challenge my belief system. I became aware of my opportunity to shift perspectives. I also started to learn that if I am not at my best for providing service to others and bringing positive energy to my roles, it is better for me and everyone around me if I slow down, step back, and even hibernate— *without guilt.*

Many insights later, I have become more familiar with the feelings I experience when I start to step into false responsibility. I know now that my temptation to go too far was usually accompanied by the unfounded and completely condescending belief that the other person wasn't capable and would not be able to manage their own life as well as I could manage it for them.

Did I mention how important I was?

This was not a onetime trip to the land of false responsibility, of course. I've been a frequent flyer. But I'm traveling that way less often now. The antidote to the self-abandonment that comes with believing and acting on the lure of false responsibility lies in our preparedness to respond to the truth about ourselves.

If you struggle with substance use or other addictive tendencies, you already know how powerfully you are impacted by emotional, mental, spiritual, and physical energy shifts. If you also identify as a sensitive soul, consciously navigating an ever-shifting internal landscape can be overwhelming. I still find myself starting to head down the path of self-abandonment when situations have triggered fear inside of me. I have also learned how to pay better attention to the emotional messages I receive when I put that hairy toe over the line into overextension.

The levels and facets of personal responsibility that we'll explore in the rest of this chapter provide a foundation for responding with care and kindness to ourselves. When we stand on the brink of some choice or impulse toward self-abandonment, being awake to our thoughts, sensations, and emotions can help us pause before we engage in behavior that might harm us or others. Embracing our spiritual responsibility allows us to create a sense of safety and security as we navigate any challenging beliefs. Responding to ourselves with love also gives us a greater shot at self-forgiveness—especially if we have recently fumbled.

What are the parts of you that tend to overextend?

What are you afraid might happen if you don't "save the world"?

When the pendulum has swung too far, what are your options for rebalancing?

Responding to Your Thoughts

Thought responsibility moves us further along the path to freedom. Once you are aware of your thoughts and take responsibility for shifting the self-limiting ones, you open up your options. Responsibility, at this level, reminds you of your awesome power to choose your thoughts and to direct your mental energies. You take responsibility by directing your focus.

Recall a time when you found yourself ruminating about something—stuck on the hamster wheel spinning the same rotten ideas over and over again. Your thoughts are running away with you, and you have forgotten that you have the power to get off that merry-go-round.

If you're like me, it might go something like this:

That Jane is a real bitch. She's so self-centered and I hate working with her.

She's never liked me. The first time I met her, I knew it was no good. I could just feel it.

I can't stand the way she talks to people in the program. It's so condescending and judgmental. She really thinks she's above it all. It's just the same thing over and over again. She'll never change.

Somebody's gotta put her in her place. I'm going to tell her what I really think tomorrow.

Suddenly, you realize that your stomach is in knots and your anxiety and frustration are building. You start to tune in to the words of your thoughts and one thing you know for sure is that you don't like what you are hearing. You're so pissed off in this moment that you just throw your hands up in the air exclaiming, "I can't help it! I just can't stop thinking about it!"

Stop. Here's your point of power. You have choices.

I have found that the first step is to actively engage with the thought process I am drowning in. Begin to ask it questions. Get really curious and cultivate a genuine desire to understand what's happening. So much of our thinking occurs on autopilot—it seems to just arise based on knee-jerk reactions and unfounded interpretations. It's like a switch gets flipped and you find yourself on a track you just can't jump off. One thought leads to another, and before you know it you are living a reality inside your mind that has nothing to do with what is actually happening now.

Be responsive. Try telling your thoughts that you can understand what they are going through. You get it. You can see why they would jump to that conclusion and automatically think the worst. It's okay. You will find that this unconditional acceptance and welcoming space provides the opportunity for your thoughts to be heard and acknowledged and, in turn, they will stop begging for your attention. You do not have to agree with them. In fact, this is the perfect time to encourage an attitude adjustment. Acknowledge that the purpose of this pattern of thinking is to protect you and keep you from falling into another unpleasant rendition of an old experience. Remind your thoughts, "That was then, and this is now."

Or engage in the perfect mind game. Offer your thoughts the challenge of reinterpretation. See how many different perspectives you can come up with to give meaning to the current experience. You will be surprised to learn that your imagination has plenty to offer, even if you don't believe that what is offered is possible. Take note of those objections as well. Then, as Jon Kabat-Zinn suggests in his book *Wherever You Go, There You Are,* allow the thoughts to pass through you like clouds float across the sky.

Being responsive to our thoughts can be especially challenging when difficult thought patterns are connected to past unresolved trauma. The responses we experience when trauma is involved are an expression of the autonomic nervous system and are significantly more complex and ingrained within us than the habitual thought patterns we experience in daily life. Quite often, that form of thought responsibility is something we require additional supports to navigate.

What you focus on grows. Be sure you are directing your energy toward what you want to create rather than what you want to avoid. Through responsibility for your thoughts, you have the freedom to choose your interpretation of any event and, in turn, how you act and feel.

That Jane Is a Real Bitch

Let's return to the scenario we just explored. Maybe it could go something like this:

OLD THOUGHT: *That Jane is a real bitch. She's so self-centered and I hate working with her.*

NEW RESPONSE: *Oh boy, you really don't like her! You're pretty pissed off right now.*

OLD THOUGHT: *Well, she's never liked me. The first time I met her, I knew it was no good. I could just feel it.*

NEW RESPONSE: *That could be true—and it could be totally false. Maybe Jane is not feeling confident. Maybe she feels insecure around you. It is possible that Jane's behavior has nothing to do with you. She could have all kinds of things going on in her life that you know nothing about.*

OLD THOUGHT: *Well, maybe. But still, it's no excuse. It's not just me. I can't stand the way she talks to people in the program. It's so condescending and judgmental. She really thinks she's above it all. It's just the same thing over and over again. She'll never change.*

NEW RESPONSE: *Oh, you have really strong feelings about that. I know. And that's okay. You are committed to being respectful in your communication with others. Think about it, though: has there ever been a time when you might have come across as judgmental and condescending? Is it possible that you're judging Jane right now? Is it even remotely possible that Jane could change? Is it possible that you're putting her in a box she'll never get out of?*

OLD THOUGHT: *Yeah, but she doesn't even seem to be aware! Somebody's gotta put her in her place. I'm going to tell her what I really think tomorrow.*

NEW RESPONSE: *Well, that is an option, for sure. You could march in there tomorrow and let her have it. You could tell her what you really think of her. I wonder what that would feel like?*

NEW THOUGHT: *Okay, I get it. If I am so committed to being nonjudgmental and respectful, this is my opportunity to do that. I don't know. I'm still feeling pretty pissed. Maybe I can blow off some more steam and sleep on it. I guess it's possible that I could be kind and try to understand Jane. . . .*

You've changed the game. You have opened the door to a different and deeper understanding. You have shifted from a reactive stance to a responsive one. Just the slightest invitation of a shift in perspective creates space for a magnificent epiphany.

See what happens tomorrow.

You are also beginning the process of discovering how what you think influences how you feel and how you behave. And you are in a prime place to begin a more in-depth exploration of the belief systems that contribute to keeping your thought patterns in place. More on these interconnections later, but for now, open yourself to greater thought awareness.

Thought processes are easily triggered by what's going on around us. Someone might say something that sets us off on a mental expedition. Maybe a song comes on the radio or something happens on TV sparking a memory so vivid it feels like it's happening right now. This takes place all day long. Notice the nature of the thoughts that arise. Are they clean?

What do I mean by *clean*? It's not what it might sound like. Clean thoughts are uplifting, encouraging, energizing thoughts—these are the thoughts that build up your sense of courage, self-esteem, and capability. Clean thoughts lead you to your stores of resilience and hope, and guide you toward the answers that will bring your dreams to fruition.

The quickest assessment of the quality of your thoughts is through your emotions and feelings. Clean thoughts feel good. Unclean thoughts feel heavy and destructive. When you're stuck in a shitty thought process, you will feel . . . well, shitty. When your thoughts are filled with anticipation of all the good that is in your life, you will feel joyful.

Identify some of your recurring patterns of thought. Are there any that you'd like to alter?

How can you begin persuading your thinking to flow in a new direction?

Responding to Your Feelings

Emotional responsibility involves becoming aware of and embracing your emotions. You understand that your emotions act as messengers, carrying very valuable information about your interpretation of what's going on inside and around you. Responding to your emotional state creates emotional intelligence. As you become aware of your emotions, you can name them, acknowledge them, and ultimately accept them. (Notice that I didn't say "like them.")

When we feel emotions that we don't like, acceptance is not usually our initial response. Actually, we are likely to resist unpleasant feelings. Becoming aware of, acknowledging, and accepting our resistance can help us move beyond it. It's amazing to see how quickly our emotional state can shift when we practice loving acceptance toward ourselves.

Being emotionally responsible also provides you with an opportunity to pause before you act. Intense emotions can make you feel out of control and can lead you to act impulsively and out of character. Dealing with the intensity of your emotions can have you turning your back on your heart. Responding to your emotions allows you to see the connection to your thought process as well.

Take our previous dilemma with Jane.

Remember how we noted that the emotional energy intensified as the thoughts spun more and more out of control? When we tried talking to the thoughts, it became apparent that there were a couple of key emotions present: anger and frustration, and maybe a bit of disgust or disapproval when it came to the way we felt about Jane.

Just as we took the opportunity to talk to our thoughts, we can also take a moment to nurture our feelings.

Maybe it would go like this:

RESISTANT THOUGHT: *That Jane is a real bitch. She's so self-centered and I hate working with her.*

EMOTIONAL RESPONSE: *You are sooo pissed off! And that's okay. What would make you feel better right now?*

RESISTANT THOUGHT: *Telling her off would make me feel better.*

EMOTIONAL RESPONSE: *Yes, it can feel so good to just let it all out and vent and blow off steam. You can do that now if you like without Jane even being here. Unless, of course, you really want to hurt her.*

RESISTANT THOUGHT: *I do want to hurt her. I just can't stand her.*

EMOTIONAL RESPONSE: *It's okay—it really is okay. Would it feel better to scream and cry a bit—maybe swear?*

RESISTANT THOUGHT: *Well, she's never liked me. The first time I met her, I knew it was no good. I could just feel it.*

EMOTIONAL RESPONSE: *That's interesting. You don't like Jane, but you also feel like she doesn't like you. Any chance your feelings might be hurt?*

RESISTANT THOUGHT: *Yes. But why do I even care? What do I care if she likes me or not?*

EMOTIONAL RESPONSE: *It's okay that you want to be liked by people, and it's okay to feel bad when you think someone doesn't like you. I don't care how old you are—there's still a little child in there who wants to belong. I wonder if Jane feels the same way.*

RESISTANT THOUGHT: *I never thought of that before. What if I've been making Jane feel bad too?*

EMOTIONAL RESPONSE: *Okay, let's not add guilt to the mix. How about we take care of your feelings first and then we can figure out what to do about Jane?*

NEW THOUGHT: *Okay.*

Emotional energy can be so raw and, at times, scary. And you may feel the urge to resist certain emotions or control them. If we can instead pour our own love over them and create the same nonjudgmental space we would strive for with anyone else, we can find out what these emotions are trying to show us and strengthen our self-compassion muscles all at the same time. There is also an opportunity to connect with other aspects of your awareness and make alterations directed toward how you wish to feel. And when the emotions are light and uplifting, you are blessed with the ability to slow down and actually enjoy the moment.

I believe that emotional energy extends out beyond us. It can move ahead of us into situations we are about to walk into, and it can persist long after we have left an encounter.

What emotional energy would be most constructive for the next interaction with Jane? Explore the question with a frame of responsiveness rather than reactivity.

When it comes to emotional responsibility, remember, whatever happens inside of you belongs to you. It is true that you will be impacted by external events and conditions, and potentially triggered emotionally by other people. And it is also true that whatever arises within is entirely your baby. You are not responsible for the actions of others; that's their baby. However, your emotional response, just like your thought process and interpretation of the event, is yours and yours alone.

Hoping that the other person will stop pissing you off will get you nowhere. Pretending that you aren't bothered isn't going to work, either. Sitting within your emotions and physical sensations with a gentle response will strengthen your emotional intelligence and your propensity to resilience. Practicing emotional intelligence can provide you with valuable information to assist you in similar situations in the future.

To this point, we have focused on situations and interactions that irritate us and trigger uncomfortable emotions. What about the feel-good stuff? We don't often pay attention to the warm and fuzzy feelings like we do the rough and tough ones.

The same process is happening. The other person does something, and your lovey-dovey feelings come to the surface. You feel a surge of joy and excitement. This emotion belongs to you, and you deserve to enjoy and honor it just as much as the less pleasant ones. However, if we make our loving and joyful responses dependent on the actions of others, we run the risk of losing our ability to experience states of love and enjoyment when we are on our own. And it doesn't have to be that way.

Your Emotional Bedrock

At the height of emotional responsibility, you become aware that your emotional terrain can be nurtured and maintained no matter what's happening. During the more traumatic times in our lives, especially times of loss and great struggle, it will not necessarily feel that way.

Here's what I've learned. When I've given energy to strengthening my foundation of joy and peace, I've been more resilient during times of great sadness and despair. When I neglect this foundation, I don't manage those challenging times nearly as well.

Your emotional bedrock is an element of your core identity. When your emotional foundation is composed of the feelings most important to you, there will be a sense of safety in any struggle. It doesn't take the pain away; it reminds you that you have the strength to survive it and to feel better. This is priceless.

So, how do you create a foundation of core emotions and feelings that make your life meaningful and fulfilling?

Pay attention when you are involved in any activity. Tune in to how you feel when you are doing something. Check your emotional state when you are interacting with someone. How do you feel when you are deciding on the next steps to take? Your emotions will speak to you through your physical sensations and tell you all you need to know about every little thing you do and who you do it with.

I practiced this approach during a particularly challenging time in my life. I knew I was going through a transition, and I was caught in a thought vortex trying to figure out what I needed to keep and what I needed to release. I decided to tune in to my emotions and sensations to get to the heart of the matter more quickly. I set the intention that, in everything I did and every interaction I had, I would pay attention to how I felt before, during, and after. I would track what felt good to me and find ways to do more of that. Those things that didn't feel good would be on the chopping block. Part of this process also included getting really clear on how I *wished* to feel in the various situations and relationships I was reviewing—what I wanted my emotional bedrock to consist of.

As I focused on my emotional experience and what it told me about what felt right, clarity came easily, and my commitment to what mattered most went through the roof.

We are here to feel as good as we possibly can. *Good* is subjectively defined. It is your responsibility to determine what that means for you and to respond when the meaning changes. When you are self-connected, you will know when things are shifting and your perspective needs to be altered. This doesn't mean we won't experience the gamut of emotions throughout our lives. Remember, we learn through contrast as well. When something feels wrong or bad to us, we are getting the information we need, and now we have a choice about how we wish to respond.

You cannot pick and choose your emotions, resisting the yucky ones and fully engaging in the fun ones. Whenever we try to shut down one aspect of our emotional reality, we minimize our experience of them all.

Life happens. Shit happens. Emotions happen. They happen in order to be felt and released—perhaps over and over again, but released just the same. We are not meant to stew in and dwell on our emotions. Emotions are messengers. They move through our experience in order to give us the information we need to make our next steps as soon as we feel ready.

When nurtured, your emotional bedrock can become a source of security and stability. It becomes a place from which you can flourish, expand, integrate, and heal. From here, you can receive and trust joy with gratitude. In the depths of despair, you can access strength, courage, and faith. When you miss the mark and step out of alignment (as we all do), your emotional bedrock serves as a safe place to start again.

What is the emotional bedrock of your experience?
Can you rely on it?

Does it support you in your darkest moments?
If not, what might require adjustment?

Acting Responsibly

We have examined our practicalities, our roles, our thoughts, and our emotions. Your capacity for personal responsibility has expanded. Your next step will plant you more firmly within your personal power.

The experience of personal power shows up in moments of self-connection. You do not need to strive to be in a place of personal power all day. It is not a static condition. Rather, your goal is to continually step into your personal power as it presents itself in each moment. Your mission is to recognize when you have disconnected—often signaled by a dip in your energy—and to make the commitment to reconnect and reengage with yourself. Each time you step into personal power, you open the space for clarity and focus in your actions.

It might sound as though this is a lengthy process, that it will take too much time and become cumbersome. It has the potential to be that way if you get stuck in mental overanalysis or emotional resistance. However, in a state of self-connection, the process occurs quite naturally and spontaneously. The mere presence of self-connection indicates that we have aligned in body, mind, heart, and spirit. When these systems are go, the right next step usually emerges naturally and in integrity. Guiding questions and reflective pauses can clarify the journey and help us to consciously slow down enough to allow grace to enter any situation. Just ask to be shown your next step.

Just as no one else makes us feel or think anything, neither do they make us do anything. Remember that once we are triggered, the focus is back on us. You determine the length of time and the amount of energy you will expend in keeping that switch flipped. I remember my mom being angry with me as a teenager; she got so worked up that she dropped the f-bomb. Unheard of back then. And she said to me, "Now, look what you made me say!" We laughed about that many times over the years as we both struggled with the growing pains inherent in learning to be responsible for our choices and actions.

Imagine you are engrossed in an interpersonal drama. You and another person are pushing each other's buttons—either with full consciousness and intent to do so or completely oblivious to the impact of your behavior. Your nostrils are flaring and you are ready to flip your lid any second now. This usually feels like a loss of control and can be the impetus for behaving in impulsive and potentially damaging ways, with the end result being more mess to clean up.

To consciously slow down our internal experience does not necessarily mean moving in slow motion or retreating. The act of bringing presence and awareness to what is happening inside of us affects our energy in a way that only we experience. It's not usually detectable to those around us. What's going on inside slows while everything around us keeps moving. This is not about gaining control over the situation or another person. Rather, it's about establishing a grounded and centered presence within our being which strengthens the sense that we're in control of our state and our experience.

It is in this moment of calm that we can make a choice about how to behave.

Let's take another look at our dilemma with Jane:

In our first kick at it, we had a conversation with our thoughts and uncovered all the assumptions and judgments that were inflaming our emotional state.

In the next phase, we took a few minutes to nurture our feelings, no matter what they were, and created space for them to safely exist. Once our emotional state got the attention it craved, it settled down a little bit and we had the opportunity to take back our power and make a conscious choice about how we wish to engage with Jane next time.

When our behavior reflects how we wish to feel—both in emotional terms and physically within our bodies—and when we can express the purity and clarity of our thoughts, we are in integrity. This is ultimate behavioral responsibility. This is freedom.

And it is powerful.

This kind of alignment has a direct impact on our capacity to trust ourselves. Our behavior is the evidence of our commitment to living out our highest intentions. We learn that we can rely on ourselves to behave in self-supportive ways. We begin to know that we have our own best interests at heart.

Behavioral responsibility has nothing to do with anyone but you. Do not give up your power to choose your actions. Do not let your behavior be dictated by the behavior of another person. When you can stand firmly in your responsibility for how you behave and respond to anything, you will experience freedom. No matter what anyone else does, your power lies in your capacity to choose your response. And this is true on every level: emotionally, mentally, physically, socially, and spiritually. It is in the realm of our actions that we express this deep personal responsibility in the world.

So this means that no matter how aggravating Jane's behavior might look to us, we are still going to behave in ways that align with our own integrity. No matter what she might say or do, we will be true to our own guidance. That is power. That is freedom.

Boxes and Beliefs

Attitudes, beliefs, values, and expectations are shaped by earlier life experiences. As youngsters who were socialized by families and institutions, we tended to take on the belief systems and values of the most prominent people in our lives—family and peers; perhaps a specific authority figure such as a teacher or coach or priest. As we move through life, our experiences either reinforce these inherited or assumed beliefs, or what we encounter challenges the things we've accepted as true or universal. As we pay attention, life offers evidence about the truth and usefulness of these ways of thinking and being. Experiencing this can be a source of freedom and expansion and vitality, or it can feel like a threat, like destabilization, or like limitation and destruction. This choice is yours. What do you choose to believe?

This final aspect of responsibility, which I place in the realm of spirit, gathers and focuses all the previous facets of responsibility in a way that has the potential to shift and transform your experience of reality.

In the realm of spiritual responsibility, you come to understand and appreciate the effects that your beliefs, attitudes, values, and expectations have on your overall experience of life—everything from the practicalities of dirty dishes to the demands of your personal and professional roles, and from your thinking and feeling to the choices you make about your behavior in each moment of the day. Your core belief system is always active within you. Even if you're not paying attention, you will naturally tend to think, feel, and behave in accordance with your deepest beliefs.

What beliefs, values, and expectations were illuminated as we explored the difficulty with our hypothetical Jane? Can she change? Is she capable of that? Is my way the only way—the only right way? Does Jane have to be wrong in order for me to be right?

Take a moment to consider how the energy of these beliefs, values, and expectations impacts future interactions and any possibility for resolution with Jane.

Expectations are a powerful part of the spiritual realm of responsibility. What our belief system expects and supports will come to pass.

She's never liked me.

She'll never change.

She always behaves this way.

It's always easier to notice these patterns in others. You might tend to put that individual in a box, a mental construct that allows you to categorize and label them. We certainly experienced this with Jane.

Once we've locked another person in any particular cage, it can be very difficult to let them out of it—to imagine them differently. We come to expect that the situation will perpetuate. Even if Jane does make changes, we rarely notice, or we mistrust them as tricks. We cannot see what we don't believe is possible. We can come to a point where we don't expect things to change. And this lack of vision will affect our experiences as service providers.

There is no magical formula that can make all irritating people in your life behave differently or disappear. Remember, this part is all about building our personal respond-ability muscles. Jane won't be the only thorn in your side throughout your lifetime. Sometimes we can simply choose to walk away from people who bother or irritate us, and sometimes we make the harder choice to stay engaged.

From the perspective of personal responsibility, what's important is to gain clarity about your capacity to respond to what's happening. It's not about changing things, necessarily, as much as you might want that. Try not to look too far down the road anticipating how you will manage if Jane never changes. How can you respond right now? What will help you manage your experience in this moment? How can you feel better? Do you accept responsibility for your current experience? Consider what you discovered as you explored the previous levels of responsibility. How do you wish to feel? What thoughts and beliefs support that? And what does all this tell you about your next best step?

Acceptance of responsibility at this level plants you firmly in your personal power. In this place, you will be better able to tune in to your intuition and honor your feelings. If it is not time to act, you will find the patience to wait. The first step is restoring your sense of peace and well-being. Communicating with Jane or anyone about Jane when you are out of balance is not likely to bring you the results you are seeking.

Jane's acting like a bitch does not constitute an emergency situation. If something is happening as a result of Jane's behavior that is harmful in any way, then communicate you must. Otherwise, you've got time to work it through.

A final word about Jane: she may never change.

Jane's behavior may continue forever. However, if you embrace personal responsibility at the levels described here, you won't care anymore. You likely won't even notice Jane, so it will seem as though she has changed. Jane's behavior will no longer bug you. You can't be hooked if you don't bite. You won't even notice the bait if you're swimming in a different pond.

What are the "boxes" in your beliefs about others?
How did they get built?

What do you think causes people to change?

Our Responsibility for Hope

Working with others requires the ability to envision change and growth. It is part of your role as a service provider to bring a sense of hopefulness into every interaction. We work with the energies of faith, belief, vision, and support. So much of our labor involves creating safe spaces in which the hopes and dreams of others stay alive and safe.

I recall watching a documentary highlighting the experiences of people living in homelessness. One gentleman talked about his loss of hope. He explained that remaining hopeful was too hard. His experience with hope had always ended in disappointment, so it was simply easier to not hope at all.

Many people you encounter throughout your service—including colleagues like Jane—may no longer be in touch with their ability to dream and believe. Oppression, suffering, victimization, and struggle tend to drain hopeful energy and replace it with bitterness. Part of your role is to stir that spirit again; to believe in things unseen; to see the beauty, the strength, and the wholeness at the core of each being—even if you don't have concrete evidence that it exists.

This part of our responsibility is not so much about being a cheerleader as it is about existing in a state of hopefulness ourselves. We serve hope by trusting that anything is possible. Others don't always want to hear us talk about this, but everyone wants to feel that someone believes it for them.

Do you believe that anything is possible? Really feel that in your heart and soul? If so, you can trust that others will feel it in your presence.

When we're providing service to others, we often ignore the human spirit. When we talk about spirituality, we immediately equate it with religion. If the person we are providing service to doesn't attend a place of worship or speak with recognizably religious language, we usually don't focus on this aspect of their life. This is a missed opportunity.

In my work with people who had sustained brain injuries, I was witness to various levels of healing, rehabilitation, and recovery, but nothing was ever so profound as the healing of the human spirit. This is where acceptance, meaning-making, and the courage to forge ahead into a mysterious new life emerged and grew and flourished. These are facets of the healing process that we all possess, even if we have lost touch with them.

In service to others, we are entrusted with the responsibility of lighting the path, providing the guidance, and preparing for the opportunities. Challenge yourself to believe in the things you wish to create and contribute, even if they are currently elusive. A burning faith in your ability to manifest your desires inspires meaningful action. Explore and love your spirit. It will allow you to recognize and care for the spirit in others. You will step into divine co-creation through your service in the world.

Embracing the fullness of responsibility holds so many benefits. You will know that you have done your part. There will be less temptation to cover your butt or make excuses. All experiences will become opportunities for learning. Soak up the sense of freedom, power, and liberation that accompanies a well-developed ability to respond.

What events or relationships in your life are reasons for hope?

How can you celebrate them today?

CHAPTER 4

Connect with Your Self

An Invitation to Discovery

You have likely noticed by now that this book's approach to service in the world—to responding to the urgency of others' needs—spends a fair number of words inviting and encouraging its readers to focus on themselves. This is absolutely intentional. There's great wisdom in the often-used airplane-safety-talk advice. If we try to help our seatmate put on their oxygen mask before we get our own going, we're likely both in trouble.

No matter the particulars of the calling that shapes our service, each of us wants our participation in others' lives to help rather than hurt. We want to connect with the people we serve in meaningful, supportive, and sustainable ways. In order to have the best chance of that, we need to learn how to do the same thing with ourselves.

Throughout the earlier chapters, we've sought to establish a foundation for conscious service. There has been plenty to think about and feel through. You've worked to build clarity and energy in the motivations and inspirations that keep you connected to your callings. You know that your multichannel human nature requires attention and tuning if you want to show up fully and make a difference in the world. You're increasingly aware of the responsibilities that come with the roles you claim, as well as the deep freedom that comes from the power to choose how you respond to what happens around and inside you.

This chapter invites you to become a traveler on the path of self-awareness and self-discovery as you explore the twists and turns of your life as you've lived it. I'll also introduce, perhaps in a way that's new to you, a skill central to learning from that process: self-reflection. This practice allows you to actively engage and direct your focus and intention so you can unearth the treasure of your own life story and access the power of your distinctive gifts.

And about those oxygen masks: You get to put yours on even if there's nobody sitting beside you. You deserve to live and breathe with peace and joy, even if you're the only person on the whole plane. Like all sacred pilgrimages in almost every spiritual tradition, the journey of self-connection and self-care is an end in itself.

None of us needs to be whole and perfect in order to be healthy and happy, but our joy will flow most easily and be more enduring when we have clear eyes about who we are—when we are able to access and embrace the power of our imperfections and idiosyncrasies as well as our personal greatness. And our vocations of service, which are important parts of the selves we're learning to cultivate and care for, will reflect and involve this joy.

We're on the way.

■　■　■

On Going West

Years ago, I embarked on what I thought would be a pilgrimage. Longing to be closer to my grown children and feeling the need for change, I decided to leave my hometown and go west. This involved resigning my position at the local college and saying goodbye to lifelong friends and family. It felt huge and exciting. I fantasized about how I would re-create my life in a new place; how I would spend time doing what I really loved. I'd finish my master's degree. I'd take care of my body. I'd finally have space and time to write.

I took solace in the fact that my kids would be there to greet me in my new home. However, every other little thing that had helped define my life and lifestyle for decades would no longer be part of my daily reality.

I gave myself a little time to settle in and adjust. This turned into several months of not really doing much of anything. It was almost as if I couldn't quite receive the opportunity to do what I had said for years I longed for. I didn't know how to step into it. I had been so used to surviving under a certain kind of pressure and being lulled by a particular sense of familiarity that I didn't really know what to do with all this freedom. And I was not prepared for the feelings that emerged when my simple securities vanished.

I thought that a new place would automatically make a new me.

In the words of Jon Kabat-Zinn, "Wherever you go, there you are." This simple, penetrating statement could not have been truer for me at that time in my life. I had moved *me* thousands of miles, but I was still right there with myself. I had placed so much importance on shaking up my external surroundings in order to feel renewed that I had overlooked the simple fact that what needed to change was inside me. I hadn't grasped the truth that my geographical journey was not identical to the journey of insight and growth I needed.

This epiphany surprised me. You mean turning my life upside down was not the instant cure for what was missing? This was followed by

"Oh God, what have I done?" and then immediately "What am I going to do now?"

I had nowhere to go but within.

What is notable about so many pilgrimage stories and heroes' journeys is that searchers inevitably come face-to-face with themselves—usually aspects of themselves that were previously unknown or hidden. Walking away from the familiar is only the first step on the path.

The journey into the core of your being does not require changing residence, leaving it all behind, or rearranging anything in the external world. Sometimes these things can help limit distractions or offer focus, of course, but the pilgrimage of self-connection has everything to do with the internal shifts and discoveries that are available to us whenever and wherever we choose to seek them.

Thank God for the compass of the heart. Even though it wasn't as smooth a transition as I had imagined, my heart always trusted that my move was right for me. Accepting this truth without evidence of where it would lead became the first step of a pilgrimage of self-discovery that's still unfolding.

Start where you are; you're always there anyway.

Exit Plans, Escape, and Self-Abandonment

The idea of adventure travel can be exciting. It's fun to read about others' journeys as they travel the world to experience new cultures and new scenery and find new perspective. There is no arguing that shaking up our entire life and leaving behind all we know, even temporarily, is one way to shift perspective and experience something fresh. Even thinking about it can offer a mini vacation from daily stress.

Eric is an early childhood educator in an urban school district. He's an amazing teacher and a great colleague. He loves his work and deeply cares for the children in his classroom and the families his school serves. But sometimes it all feels like too much. His profession is known for rapid turnover. High rates of poverty in his district are coupled with structural racism that keeps some neighborhood schools scrambling for basic supplies. For Eric, work is a source of grief and stress as well as joy and hope. When the pandemic forced him to try teaching five-year-olds via video chat, the discomfort started to outweigh the hope.

One day, while surfing the internet, Eric put a pair of one-way tickets to Tahiti in his shopping cart. He's got a plan, he says, to go there and start a little preschool on the beach.

Eric's exit plan is a fantasy, of course. He knows it too. My friend is staying where he is, and he shows up for his students each day as whole as possible. But those tickets have become a touchstone for his imagination, a small oasis that offers a little relief from the demands of his calling.

In tough times, many of us check the employment ads or daydream about winning the lottery or moving into a cabin in the woods. The desire to easily escape into what we imagine to be a much better situation is part of the human condition and can serve as a psychological reset when we're overwhelmed. Instead of denying it, we can embrace this urge and honor its attempt to soothe our unsettled souls.

We must also differentiate among the desire for discovery, which can lead us to true pilgrimage; temporary flights of fantasy that help us stay grounded; and the urge to escape, which can too often and too easily set us on the path of self-abandonment.

There are no shortcuts to enlightenment, and no path that involves inflicting harm will lead us to respectfully connect with ourselves. In order to reap the benefits of the journey, we must remain present to the process, even when the going is hard and the end seems too far away.

The desire to escape our painful experiences—past or present—can result in the development of substance use disorders or other addictive patterns of behavior. Self-destructive behavior is not the beginning of an imbalance, but rather a symptom of it. By the time we are caught in addictive patterns, we have been out of harmony for a while.

I don't know anyone who stepped into service who did so expecting to be burned out, exhausted, depleted and depressed, or addicted. Most people I know came into service believing that it would be loving, joyful, and fulfilling, an opportunity to experience a sense of connection and meaning in their lives.

And yet so many of us actually find ourselves plagued by self-avoidance and self-abandonment, because somewhere we've taken to heart the false notion that others matter more than we do. We search for evidence of our contribution in the changes we see happening around us; we rarely think to look within to see and appreciate how we are being transformed.

This puts many people who wish to serve on a direct path to burnout and self-harm, solidifying the myth that loss of self and utter exhaustion are inevitable consequences of a life of service. It is a fallacy. The only possible way to actually be fully present for another is to be fully connected to ourselves. One of the most rewarding aspects of this journey is the opportunity to learn to live in a state of unconditional self-love and self-compassion. Without it, we are dead in the water and of no real service to anyone.

Your journey of healing starts when you can breathe again.

We all do it, so let's just accept that reality. What does it look like when you abandon yourself? What trips your desire to escape?

You're Looking through a Lens

You might call it your worldview. I call it your personal lens. It involves the way you see yourself, the way you see others, and how all of it fits together.

The lenses we look through help us make sense of the world and our experiences in it. As the name suggests, your personal lens has a unique and subjective character that has been shaped and polished by the totality of your life experiences, including your relationships, your education and work experience, and your traumas as well as your triumphs.

Your personal lens encapsulates your attitudes, beliefs, and values. Whatever you judge, admire, expect, or assume about the world and everything in it affects the size and shape and quality of your lens. Your cultural identity as well as your gender identity and spiritual self-understanding color the view. Whenever you attach meaning to any event, when you interpret what happens to you or to others, you are doing so through your personal lens. This lens helps you turn what has already happened in your life into a coherent and comprehensible story. It also looks forward, helping you envision what is yet to come.

On any given day, our lenses are also filtered, clouded, or clarified by our emotions, the physical sensations in our bodies, and the chatter of our minds.

Your personal point of view is adjustable. And that is powerful. Shaking things up, reframing and refocusing, removing filters, or simply cleaning away years of gunk requires personal responsibility, a desire for freedom, and a lot of courage. It is a daunting prospect to purposely alter your viewpoint. In doing so you are potentially altering your very approach to living.

Always remember that *you* are in charge of how you engage in this work and how swiftly you move.

An imperfect analogy might help:

Imagine you are watching TV. Whatever is on the tube is annoying you, and you find yourself muttering at the screen and getting more and more annoyed with every passing second. Suddenly, you realize the remote control is in your hand. You hold the power to change the channel, mute the sound, or just turn the thing off.

Please tell me I'm not the only one who gets spellbound this way.

Self-connection turns your attention to the power you've had all along. You can choose how to interpret the events of your life. As you become aware of the lens you're looking through, you can change it, soften its tint, pause and ponder. You can reprogram your belief systems and the values that guide you. You can choose your response when painful memories reemerge in your mind and heart.

Self-reflection allows us to experiment with different perspectives. It lets us challenge the attitudes and expectations that direct our vision away from discovery by keeping us focused on struggle. Self-reflection grounds us in the present so we can more clearly see new possibilities and next steps.

Accessing and adjusting your personal lens is, first and foremost, a gift to yourself. The results can include increased clarity, improved focus, enhanced patience, stimulated curiosity, and a sense of passion. This is not always easy. Be sure to access the support you may need as you do it. We all benefit from wise help and alternative perspectives when we explore and adjust foundational parts of ourselves.

What aspect of your personal lens needs attention?

What can get cleared from this lens so you can see better?

Self-Reflective Practice

Why have we spent all this time exploring the channels of human being and the principle of responsibility? So that those insights can guide you in your self-reflective practice and help you respond to what you discover, and so that you can show up fully and be fully engaged.

Sounds great, right?

Well, it is!

Then, it's not.

Then it is again!

The trouble with any of the temporary states human beings achieve from moment to moment or season to season is that we're prone to slipping in and out of them. Self-connection is no exception. We need predictable ways to keep tuning back in when we realize we have disconnected. Many people find that a habit or established practice is necessary. Most importantly, we need strategies that fit our lives and actually work.

Some self-reflective practices may already be part of your life. These include physical activity, working with a practitioner, journaling, or enjoying music, books, film, and other art. Many people have found meditation and yoga, prayer, and exercises like creative visualization to be effective and enjoyable ways to create self-reflective space. Some of these examples may work beautifully for you, while others may fall flat. Different strategies allow you to exercise different channels of your being—and what appeals to you about any given activity may change over the course of your life. Some strategies are solitary, while others involve groups or teams or partners. Sometimes these categories overlap. For example, you can meditate (ultimately a solitary practice) in a park with a group (adding an element of connection with others and the natural world). Consider your own temperament and preferences as you design a collection of self-reflective practices that resonate with you.

In beginning my own self-connection practice, I experimented with different strategies, making space in my day to engage. I woke up earlier than usual to journal and go for walks. I did more of this at the end of the day. I attended workshops and read books. I was hungry for this kind of personal exploration, so it didn't feel like a burden, but it did involve making choices about how I spent my time.

I initially spent a great deal of time examining the relationships and activities of my life from the outside. I journaled about my challenges and conflicts, but I continued to show up in old ways. I meditated first thing in the morning, and then promptly switched back to autopilot for the rest of the day. It took a bit of time to integrate the insights and the experience of self-connection in my world. Starting from a detached and solitary perspective gave me enough distance to consider what I thought, felt, and believed about the more complicated and crowded parts of my life.

As I began to unearth new insights about myself, my curiosity grew and kept me coming back to self-connection. Gradually, connecting with myself began to feel like a natural—and, before long, necessary—element of my daily life. Self-reflection is not a onetime event or a one-size-fits-all process. It's a skill, and it often occurs not *in* a moment when our sense of self is challenged, but *after* the fact—at least to begin with. Eventually, we find that commitment to our chosen practices yields a more ongoing sense of self-connection. In other words, we need not leave a challenging moment in order to make sense of it; insight replaces hindsight.

Explore different strategies that bring you home to yourself. This is important even when you already have a few tools in your arsenal. Variety is crucial. Having options gives you the ability to reflect according to your mood and the time you have available. Maybe you want to settle in for a long and introspective chat with your heart and you plan a whole day filled with things that bring you there. Maybe you've only got fifteen minutes before your next meeting and you need a shot of self-connected serenity now.

Your challenge is to find what helps you unhook from worrying about the things that are happening around you and start attending to what's going on inside you. The key to identifying what works for you is to experiment. It can be tempting to select a strategy or pursue a practice based on the outcome you are looking for. Don't fall for this. If you expect that emerging from a meditation or returning from your run is going to automatically translate into peace, clarity, or surrender, you might be disappointed. Look for activities that spark your curiosity or interest you for their own sake. Self-reflection begins with attention to the practice, not some hoped-for outcome. Even on those days when I didn't emerge from my practice steeped in peace and vitality, I never felt worse for having spent my time this way.

Just as a fitness routine can plateau if we don't change up our activities, monotony in our self-reflective practices can lead to diminishing results. If you find yourself disenchanted with any given technique or strategy you've adopted, change the game. It doesn't matter what you do to develop your capacity for self-connection. What matters is that you do it.

Any activity that leads you to yourself is an effective one. We are all unique in the ways we get in touch with our core, and what we discover there is purely our own. What we have in common is that we all contain this deeper knowledge, and we all have the ability to gain access to the innate wisdom of our innermost selves. All we need to know is where to look and how to ask. As you step into your own personal practice, be sure to inject a heaping dose of curiosity. It makes it more fun!

When I first began the journey of self-connection, I wasn't aware that simply making the choice to self-reflect was a demonstration of self-respect and self-love, even if only just emerging. As you commit to self-connection, understand that doing so shows you already recognize you are worthy of personal growth. From here, noticing the benefits of your practice will give you the encouragement you need to continue.

Embrace Your Greatness

We rarely take a moment to acknowledge the things we love about ourselves. As a rule, most of us tend to downplay our greatness so we won't appear conceited or self-absorbed. If you're at all like me, you want others to acknowledge your gifts and talents, but on those occasions when they actually do, you're quick to minimize their insight. We struggle to receive personal affirmation. Sometimes we even go so far as to deny or contradict it.

We can get stuck in thinking there is nothing terribly unique about us or about what we offer in service to others. It's time to shake loose that worn-out belief.

Playing small relinquishes our power.

Identifying what makes you great is part of sharing your amazing self in the world.

When you embody your greatness with confidence, you have a jumping-off point from which to expand. Going with what comes naturally and easily opens a path of very little resistance and increases the probability of your success. Success enhances your confidence and provides a benchmark you can return to when you are challenged to grow in other areas.

Your greatness lives deep inside your heart as your natural talents and positive qualities, such as curiosity and passion. We feel alive when we embrace and enhance our inherent gifts. Sharing these gifts only adds to our enthusiasm and joy. Any path you set out on with such joyous energy is destined toward something great!

Identifying personal greatness, even in the privacy of your own heart, can be a daunting process. It is very likely that what makes you amazing has been lost on you to this point. Unless we stop to think about our gifts—or someone we trust calls our attention to a specific event or action—we rarely notice the things that come so naturally and easily.

Start asking yourself what makes you great. Don't be shy about it.

Use joy as a compass in your pursuit. Quite often, what sparks happiness inside is sharing space with your innate talent. See if you can come up with some insights of your own before you start asking others where they think your greatness shines. At this point, use outside opinions only to stimulate your personal discoveries.

You might also be tempted to start making a list of things that you are good at. Be discerning here. We all learn how to do things that have nothing to do with our personal greatness but were fueled instead by our desire for approval, or by the beliefs and values we inherited from others. Sometimes we do these things well. I remember a time when I caught myself exclaiming that a role I was about to accept would "look good on my résumé." It took me a moment to realize that I was building a mental résumé for a job I no longer even wanted!

Embracing your personal greatness can be fun—especially when you don't take yourself too seriously. Seeing yourself as a person of greatness also raises the likelihood that you will experience joy and fulfillment in the process of contributing in the world.

Magnificence might be found in your sense of humor, your ability to see alternative perspectives, your abiding faith in your power to respond, or your capacity for connection. Your greatness may lie in your particular creative expression, or in your ability to inspire or teach. It may show up in the way you speak or solve problems.

Maybe it's your singing voice; you do you, beautiful.

Noticing and owning your greatness can happen with humility and grace. It is an element of self-confidence that has nothing to do with arrogance, because it's just about facts. Humble confidence makes it easier and more enjoyable to simply be who we are and do what we do. Humble, graceful confidence also makes it possible to look with honest and loving eyes at the parts of you that aren't as well developed.

Your greatness is a reliable resource. It can be a source of strength and competence to draw on when you are called to expand or change. Human beings don't grow as well in environments flooded with judgment and punishment, but we flourish when we feel safe and accepted. By celebrating your unique greatness, you provide such a space for yourself.

Learn how to celebrate moments of accomplishment even more deeply than you agonize over moments when you miss the mark. The only way we can offer the best of ourselves to others is to be able, first, to embrace it within ourselves. To present our most natural gifts in the world, we have to know what these gifts are, what gives them strength, and how we intend to contribute with them. And embracing and celebrating your greatness makes you the ideal guide to help others discover their own.

Life is not meant to be so hard. Living in your greatness makes this human experience a little more graceful and adds an element of ease. Take stock of your personal greatness and stand firm in the self-confidence it provides. Without you in the world, something would be missing. When we shy away from this truth, we move toward self-abandonment.

What do you feel when asked to identify what makes you great?

Take a breath. Get over it. Then make a list.

Great Is Different from Perfect

I am a recovering perfectionist. As a child, I engaged in many almost-obsessive behaviors in my attempt to achieve perfection. I rewrote my school notes so there was never a blotch on the page. I challenged myself to Hula-Hoop for ten minutes straight. If I dropped that sucker, I had to start over again. I would almost flip my lid if I wrote a letter to my grandma and made a mistake right at the end. In preparation for tests, I memorized my notes so I could recite the answers verbatim. When it came to personal appearance, no flaw escaped my attention, and my hair, no matter how much I fussed with it, was never just right.

I'm exhausted just thinking about it.

Over the years, I learned to let go of these behaviors. As my life got busier, I had to streamline and simplify my attempts at perfection. At one point, I even stopped thinking about myself as a perfectionist. But old habits die hard. I soon discovered that my perfectionism had just grown up with me, finding subtler and more sophisticated ways to control my life and drive me bonkers.

When I was a young adult, my attitude of perfectionism often put me in a place of judgment. I had developed impossible standards for my own performance, and I often secretly held others to these standards as well. No one ever measured up.

Perfectionism disguised itself as a high level of productivity wearing a pretty mask called organization. And eventually it led to rigidity in my life. I ordered and planned and managed myself into a corner with very little room for escape.

Stuck in that corner, I knew things needed to change, and I turned to personal growth practices, seeking relief. But, at first, I approached those practices with the same perfectionism that had gotten me into that mess. I was constantly in search of the magic remedy that would instantly elevate me to some off-in-the-distance state of peace and enlightenment. I became laser focused in my search for personal perfection.

The irony is I had no idea how I would recognize it when it appeared.

Somewhere along the way, my positive motivation for doing things well (to move myself toward better health and more enlightened self-understanding) had been hijacked by an external motivation to prove that I had already achieved enlightenment—or at least the parts of it that would look good on a résumé. When the desire for perfection is the copilot in this kind of mission, you are doomed. *Doing* in order to *become* is not what self-reflection is about.

As my initial burst of self-help-perfectionist energy wore off, I became more focused on how far I had to go and what would actually help me as I went.

The only way to experience a deeper sense of myself lay in my willingness to surrender and simply be. In that unhurried and goal-less space I was finally free to notice what emerged and how that could inspire my next steps.

I had to trust that my personal gifts and distinctive greatness would emerge if I opened myself to them. The peace I sought couldn't be chased down by an idealized version of myself, nor could it be grasped by pretending I was perfect. I had to grow.

When we focus on fixing or flee from admitting what we perceive as shortcomings, faults, or limitations in ourselves, we get nowhere. No amount of striving will perfect us. Our efforts will never be enough, because what's needed is love—love and acceptance. When we are able to look with love upon all we imagine is wrong with us, the story starts to change.

Just as identifying your natural greatness can guide you toward the places where you are meant to share what you have to offer, recognizing your vulnerabilities is an invitation to expansion. We are not here to remain stagnant. We are ever-evolving creatures who are meant to develop, to innovate, and to show the world what we've got.

Sometimes our limitations are spaces for real growth. There will always be stuff we haven't learned yet and skills we wish to master. These discomforts push us out of complacency and into growth. And they are usually areas that our hearts really wish to explore.

Don't let yourself make excuses because you want to avoid discomfort. Your greatest gift may lie at the bottom of your deepest vulnerability. Your magnificence may reveal itself to you on the other side of what seems like an insurmountable limitation.

When you buoy your vulnerability with awareness and gratitude for your precious natural resources—your personal greatness—you become your own best teacher. You become able to apply these gifts to your learning process and create a safe space for growth and development. Don't let your limitations hijack your aspirations.

At the same time, trust that your limitations are honorable and that they have messages for you. Respect yourself when the motivation to grow in a given area isn't there. This may come as a shock to you, but you don't have to excel at everything. You will never know it all. Sometimes, you will make mistakes. You may not always have the strength to push yourself into spaces where your ego wants to go but your heart does not. Remember the teaching power of resistance. That information will help you to navigate toward the "perfect" place for you.

Perfectionism is a matter of perspective—about adjusting our lenses. We can choose to evaluate ourselves through the eyes of ego and always come up short. Or we can look through the eyes of love and spirit, which recognize our inherent value and potential. In this state of graceful vision, all our human imperfections can be embraced as opportunities for transcendence and active engagement in our personal evolution.

When we keep coming up against a familiar vulnerability that seems to always get us into trouble or limit our progress, we're on to something. What personal growth lessons show up as recurring themes for you?

Your Point of Power

The more you are aware of and connected to what makes you tick, your unique way of seeing things, and the private sacred spaces of your being, the more access you have to personal power. This is an energy that flows through all the channels of your human system. It emanates from within and doesn't depend on external conditions or other people for motivation or validation. It is peaceful. It is contained. Self-reflective practice makes it renewable.

And it is formidable.

Many service providers struggle with claiming and expressing personal power. You may find yourself forgetting that confidence can be humble, playing small because you don't want to appear full of yourself or make other people uncomfortable. In other circumstances you might also feel the urge to present a falsely inflated front, to gloss over your perceived limitations and overcompensate so others won't notice them. These are common human responses to what often feels like dangerous territory.

There is always risk when power is involved. There's also opportunity. Expect to encounter the freedom that comes with embracing your uniqueness. You may find it easier to see and speak truth in each moment.

Helen was my colleague at a community-based rehabilitation agency. During the years we worked together, Helen and I completed annual performance appraisals with each other. Part of this undertaking involved identifying the year's personal achievements, highlighting areas of strength as well as career accomplishments. The process provided opportunities to detail concrete examples of personal skills used in service. It also asked us to identify areas for personal and professional growth.

Helen and I did this many times. We had a collegial relationship, worked well together, and had developed a friendship. As we made our way through each year's appraisal, Helen often included one- or two-word phrases to identify her strengths. She often felt stuck on the question about how she wanted to expand her contribution moving forward.

Sometimes she'd say, "Well, you know me—what can I put down that you don't already know?"

I did know her. Helen had a great deal of talent and commitment to service and the people she supported. She had an interest in what she was doing and wanted to learn more about new cutting-edge approaches. But she struggled to articulate these things, both in the formal process and in our informal conversations throughout the year.

Helen struggled to speak candidly and assertively about where she felt she excelled in her role. She had a hard time providing concrete examples of how and where and why she could be proud of the service she offered.

When I asked how Helen wished to contribute or how she could find deeper meaning in her work, she struggled with that as well. And that would have been okay—we're not always good at identifying or articulating these things. But, in the course of our conversations, Helen revealed to me that she was quite dissatisfied with her experience at the agency. Her inability to speak up and self-advocate was becoming more and more of a crisis.

Helen felt overlooked in the agency. She told me she often felt excluded and even disliked by some of our colleagues. When opportunities to advance came up, she was not considered. Helen expressed having a feeling of not being taken seriously by her colleagues. She felt stuck, and she stayed silent.

Though it felt like a dead end, this admission of stuckness started Helen's journey toward her power. I encouraged her to start with the small act of naming the parts of her job that she really loved. What was it about those particular aspects that energized her and felt fulfilling?

Where else might she experience that fulfillment in her current role, or how might a similar feeling be created in a new and different way? I suggested that Helen start thinking about what she was really good at and how her specific skills could be utilized more fully within the organization. Was it possible that once she started to acknowledge and embrace her unique contribution, others might begin to take notice as well?

Even though I knew Helen pretty well and I could see her strengths and talent, Helen herself had been unable or unwilling to fully embrace her greatness and advocate for its recognition and reward. My cheerleading was strong and supportive, but it was nowhere near as powerful as Helen's own voice when she was finally able to step into her own sense of self and speak from her point of power.

Waiting for others to recognize what you have to offer so you don't have to speak up for yourself is a slow and unreliable way to create the experiences you deserve. Of course, there's no guarantee that other people will respond when you say what you want and need, but it is more likely that they will.

And purely due to the fact that you have stood in the powerful place between your strengths and your vulnerabilities and named your desires out loud, you will begin to travel toward them, even if it means moving out of your current position.

This was true for Helen. Her self-advocacy helped her create changes in her role within the organization, and she realized a newfound sense of enjoyment in her work. And eventually the time came for Helen to spread her wings beyond our agency in a new position at a different place.

As she became more comfortable speaking in detail about her personal curiosities, the areas of herself she wished to develop, and what felt most fulfilling in her work and life, Helen's confidence grew, and her career path clarified. As she connected with herself and honored her heart, doors began to open and she took concrete steps in her personal and professional development.

As you develop a larger and clearer sense of your personal greatness as well as your vulnerabilities, you are poised to make these discoveries start working for you. The information you gain from your efforts at self-reflection and self-connection is powerful. Combined with caring support from people you trust, this information helps you respond to the needs of each moment equipped with self-compassion and self-acceptance. This translates into confidence and transparency as you step into service more fully conscious of what you have to offer and where you need to grow.

Love yourself enough to let those around you know what matters to you. Show others how you wish to contribute and where your powers reside. You are the only one who can discover this information for yourself and share it. Don't hide under a rock expecting others to coax you out.

Do those around you know what lights your fire?

Do they know what you are seeking to learn?

Personal Traps, Self-Esteem, and Your Shadow

We frequently think of our self-destructive tendencies as flaws. We're usually taught to see these aspects of our personality as defects that leave us vulnerable. We might even consider our less-than-healthy habits to be deliberate acts of self-sabotage that prove how little we think of ourselves. There is some truth in that cycle of shame. We act out and then feel bad. Soon, we feel bad about feeling bad, so we fight and resist it. Eventually, we get tired of fighting and give in to some quick relief, and we end up feeling bad again, and even more deeply ashamed.

And then the cycle repeats.

Part of connecting with yourself is connecting with your patterns—even the ones you feel stuck in. Self-reflection can help you identify your personal traps and slippery slopes. We do this not only to avoid them, but to more deeply understand the nature of their message and more fully grasp the opportunity for healing they offer.

The twentieth-century Swiss psychiatrist Carl Jung studied human personality. He wrote about the forbidden impulses and unacceptable feelings and behaviors each of us experience as part of being human. He described this aspect of human personality as the "shadow." Jung suggested that, as individuals and as societies, we have shadows that contain all the destructive stuff that has the power to blow up relationships, break trust, and sow confusion.

Since Jung, many people have written about this concept and put their own spin on the shadow. Maybe you've heard or read about this side of human personality. Perhaps you've even found the idea useful as you recognize and name parts of yourself that feel uncomfortable or unpredictable and chaotic. I like to think of this aspect of me as an unruly sister.

At first glance, my shadow side rarely seems to have my best interests at heart. She seems to show up at the worst possible times. My shadow takes full advantage of my soft spots and vulnerabilities. She taps the parts of me I like the least, the parts I'd most like to keep others from noticing or dealing with: my envy and greed, my prejudices, my aggression, my self-centeredness, my insecurities.

It feels like when what I need most is a megadose of self-love and compassion, my shadow pipes up from the back of the room to point out (in detail) all the reasons I don't deserve it.

When things fall apart, it's tempting to think we had it coming. When things come together, some part of us doubts we deserve it. In either state, we run the risk of running away from opportunities to learn and grow. Knowing what our personal hot spots are—where our fears and denials get the better of us—is one part of the process of learning how to communicate with our shadows.

Garnering the insights of your personal pilgrimage requires the full participation of your whole self. This is where the invitation we explored earlier—to show up fully—applies to every aspect of our personalities, even the wild and weird ones. Even our shadow sides.

What good is our shadow side? It's not always easy to see, but like water that somehow flows through cracks in stone, self-esteem and self-worth are resilient and persistent. They can even thrive in the face of adversity. Sometimes the walls our shadows try to set up around our hearts become the riverbanks that concentrate and strengthen our capacity to believe in and value ourselves.

Recently, I decided to consult my shadow. I wanted to learn more about the parts of her that were really quite admirable. Maybe she even had qualities I wish I more consciously embodied. So, I asked her.

I found there is a part of my shadow that longs to feel free, to indulge in pleasure, to experience the wildness of my personality, to live without inhibition. I'm willing to bet many of you can relate to these desires. Instead of feeling ashamed of these realizations or frightened by their unstable energy, what if we celebrated them? What if we could look at those urges as a completely acceptable part of our nature that we can learn to embody in ways that feel more aligned and hurt less?

If I suddenly want to go out for drinks when I'm feeling uncomfortable in my life, what is that telling me? Is that my shadow saying that I need some relief or emotional release? Is there another way to respond?

This takes practice. Our quick-fix responses are deeply ingrained and often tied to the shadowy places where our unhealed traumas are stored. A self-connected moment provides the opportunity to consider other options.

We don't get to choose what urges and impulses lurk within us, but we do have the power to redefine and repurpose what our shadow selves hand us. There is no part of us that is bad and undeserving—no part that requires punishment. There is no aspect of self that won't evolve when fully immersed in love.

As you continue to explore what it means to love yourself, and how this translates into how you connect with and care for yourself, don't leave your shadow out of it. In fact, bring that interesting, dangerous, and disruptive part of you directly into the conversation. Recognize that extending this particular invitation might be one of the most self-loving acts you will ever do.

This is how we take back our power to choose. And when we're standing at the crossroads between a pilgrimage of self-discovery and a path to self-abandonment, there is nothing more important than having the power to choose.

> **When your shadow drops in unannounced, how might you welcome it?**
>
> **What strategies are available to you?**

Elyse Runs Home

Elyse first began running because she wanted to tone her body and become stronger. At the time she had no idea how valuable it would be as a meditative tool when her life started to slide off the rails.

Elyse was a counselor. She had worked for many years in the field of behavioral health and addiction. She was fascinated and inspired by the stories shared by those she served, and also at times frustrated by the struggles and suffering she witnessed day after day. She often felt a heavy sadness and, lately, even a loss of hope. Elyse had begun to worry that she was burning out. She could feel apathy setting in as she tried to connect with the people who came to her for help, and she often had a hard time getting out of bed in the morning.

Elyse had also started drinking a few glasses of wine each evening. She used this time to relax and let go of her day. She told herself that she didn't need to worry about her drinking because she was a professional. She knew she would "never end up like that." Before too long, however, Elyse began to fear that she was losing control. She noticed that she struggled to get up and run on mornings after she had a few too many. She noticed how early in the day she began to think about those glasses of wine.

Elyse was hurting. She thought that numbing her pain and trying to protect her heart from the challenges she witnessed during the workday was an act of self-love. She thought that detaching from the emotional investments of her service to others was a form of self-compassion. But these things weren't working like she thought they would.

The stories we tell ourselves can become matters of belief. Our beliefs are mutable, of course—they're elements of the personal lens we've discussed. However, it's only possible to alter our belief systems if we are willing to acknowledge them—if we're willing to see where they stop working for us and start working against us.

The mind dislikes admitting mistakes. It's reluctant to reevaluate. All by itself, our thinking channel rarely encourages us toward change.

Elyse was motivated by her discomfort. She became dedicated to examining her life in the moment. How satisfied was she with the current state of affairs? What was beneath the pain she felt she needed to numb with wine? Which of her beliefs were keeping her from moving beyond her struggles?

Elyse brought this exploration to her running practice.

Running, Elyse noticed that she was feeling shameful and guilty about her drinking. She noticed that her drinking also scared the crap out of her. She knew she had begun to negotiate with it, and no matter how hard she tried, she always seemed to be on the short end of the stick.

Elyse's professional role as an addiction counselor made her wary of asking for help. So did her belief that she needed to be above the struggles of depression and addiction. She worried she would be stigmatized or pitied, or even lose her job.

Elyse continued to engage in mindful running. She created a space in which she could be present to her emotions as well as her belief systems without judgment. As her self-reflective practice evolved, Elyse continued to ask herself questions to illuminate the beliefs that were active in all the areas of her life. She often noticed themes.

Elyse learned that she judged herself harshly, even as she feared the judgment of others. She had always believed that it was her role to help others and that it was not okay for her to have any personal struggles of her own. She noticed that one of her core messages had always been that it wasn't okay for her to seek help.

Elyse started every run by simply allowing things to bubble to the surface. Mile after mile, she probed for further understanding, and she gently challenged certain structures to fall away—including beliefs that were keeping her from doing what she knew she needed to do.

Elyse eventually reached out for help. Talk therapy offered a way to address the emotions behind her impulses to escape. She put more focus on reflection and running and less on wine. Hitting the pavement became a sacred practice, a physical action that prompted her to be fearless in the pursuit of her own truth and undaunted by the prospect of shedding beliefs and behaviors that had outlived their usefulness.

Elyse's desire to feel better was an expression of self-love. With honesty and courage, she was able to express self-compassion and soothe the difficult emotions of shame and guilt. Her experience of self-connection and self-reflection made the specifics of Elyse's self-care plan very clear. She knew it would always include running.

As she emerged from her brush with burnout, Elyse also became keenly aware of what needed to change within her expression of service. She felt a renewed sense of commitment to the work she was already doing and found her curiosity returning. She sensed that something within her painful experience would benefit her service to others. And she remained open to allowing that wisdom to surface in ways that would enhance her contribution.

Identify a time when you felt burned out.

What were the key characteristics of that experience for you?

What helped you move through this time?

Self-Compassion

Most of us would agree that we love ourselves. I mean, we have ensured our personal survival at the basic level this far, so we must care on some level, right? We might even be able to say that we like ourselves. We like certain qualities and characteristics we possess. We love everything about us that's lovable.

How many of us can say that we love ourselves unconditionally?

You spent time earlier in this chapter getting in touch with your greatness and your opportunities for growth and expansion. Armed with this knowledge, you considered how to declare your contributions. You primed yourself for learning. You spent time with your shadow. You're getting in touch with the story of you and your life.

You have begun a pilgrimage of discovery. Maybe you've decided to start a practice of self-reflection.

That's great!

But be warned: No matter which strategy you select, the journey won't always lead to a sense of peace and acceptance immediately. It's not all rainbows, butterflies, and puppies. Connecting to yourself can stir up a lot of unresolved stuff. I like to think of this as the layers of sand and algae that cover sunken treasure. We dig in order to access deeper truths.

As all this crap starts to rise and muck up the waters that once seemed clear, your first reaction might be to pull back. Stirring up old memories and touching unhealed wounds can trigger shame, blame, and feelings of guilt or anger or regret.

You know how this feels. You have a flashback to an experience of disgrace that makes you cringe. It can knock the wind right out of you. In an instant you are engulfed in humiliation. You might frantically look for an explanation or an excuse.

A trip down shame-memory lane can kick up a cloud of similar instances and experiences. When you are looking back like this, remember that regrets in the mirror are closer than they appear. No matter how far in the past the events are that caused them, your feelings are in the moment. And that's what matters. That's what you can address. Now is the perfect opportunity for another level of healing and release.

This takes a lot of love.

Appreciating and embracing yourself can seem easy when you're feeling on top of the world. Maybe you are proud of something in your life. Maybe you are in love with someone. Perhaps you just accomplished a great feat. Self-love in those moments can seem like a piece of cake.

Where self-love gets harder and even more essential is when you come face-to-face with truths about yourself that hurt. When you lied. When you abandoned your commitments. When you cheated on something or someone.

It may not be easy, but in a state of self-compassion, it can become possible to sit with everything that comes up and see all of it as separate from the core of who you are. Self-compassion opens up your heart to self-love.

Your self-love story will be filled with points of celebration, moments of acceptance, and countless opportunities for forgiveness and repair. Approaching life with self-compassion strengthens and encourages your inner hero through the unfolding journey of self-discovery, healing, and wholeness to which each of us is invited.

You may have heard the saying "You can't love another if you don't love yourself" or its companion "No one else is going to love you if you don't love yourself." You may have even read something like that in this book. And these old well-intentioned encouragements hold some truth about self-acceptance, but they also carry a warning: Even when we are not in a state of self-love, we still *attempt* to love others. We can still want good things for them and even work to help them flourish. Service providers do this all the time. It's what leads so many of us to burnout.

When we resist loving ourselves deeply, our capacity for love is not fully accessible to us. It doesn't disappear, but it's diminished. Without self-compassion, we simply cannot feel its depth and intensity. Without specific strategies for self-care, we cannot fully express our love.

The goal of self-compassion and self-love is not aimed first at enhancing our capacity to give to others. Self-compassion is something you offer to yourself because you love yourself. It is not a means to an end. It's not a box to check to satisfy the demands of a wellness program. Self-compassion is a heartfelt, soul-driven expression of accepting and embracing and embodying the fullness of your being—with all its beauty and scars.

Treat yourself with kindness.

Hold yourself gently.

Champion your own heart.

Embrace your spirit.

Wrap your arms around all your quirks.

Stand in awe of your brilliance.

Rock yourself to sleep.

Greet yourself with a smile each morning.

Try being in love with you.

Fill your story with you. You are the lead character. Reclaim the aspects of the tale that you have allowed to be taken over by the needs of others. Stand in the center of that chapter long enough to feel your personal power return. Then you can begin to reintroduce other key players.

The pilgrimage of self-connection is filled with wonder as well as repulsion. There are monsters on this road as well as miracles. Everything you could ever find in the world can also be discovered inside your own heart. The path of your personal pilgrimage will guide you toward the desires of your soul. Follow it with courage and curiosity toward a life that moves beyond ideas about selfishness and selflessness and embraces self-connection.

When are you conditional with your self-love?

Are there certain standards you must meet before you are okay with *you*?

CHAPTER 5

Communicate with Love

An Invitation to Enlightenment

For years I imagined that enlightenment was something I needed to *do*. I thought that there positively had to be some external activity I could engage in to achieve this sought-after state of being. I needed to acquire more techniques, more practices, more books, more meditation.

A passage in *A Year of Miracles* by Marianne Williamson turned the lightbulb on for me. She suggests that enlightenment is not about adding anything to our lives. It's not about doing more or achieving more. Enlightenment is about letting go. Finding enlightenment requires releasing everything that stands in the way of it.

Enlightenment has more to do with *being* than it has with *doing*. It has more to do with the patient process of simplification and clarification than with adding anything extra.

This insight about releasing things instead of adding them highlights a key difference between *effective* communication and what I call *enlightened* communication. Many of us have been schooled in what it means to communicate effectively. Most tools for effective communication are employed intellectually, and they're best used by those who can think quickly and speak eloquently (or sometimes just loudly). And because *effective* suggests a goal, interaction with others can quickly become focused on outcomes.

When a specific result is the measure of success, communication can easily be misused as persuasion or even manipulation. Any time communication is understood primarily as an attempt to get somebody to do something, it takes on the qualities of a game—with winners and losers.

And, of course, we know how much we like to win.

Rather than assembling a communications toolkit or amassing strategies for increased effectiveness, enlightened communication involves removing obstacles that block connection and understanding. It's about letting dust settle. It's about patiently attending to messages and meanings that travel along all kinds of routes.

Enlightened communication attends to our relationships with others and the world around us. It starts with self-awareness and results in a deeper and clearer connection to the divine nature we share with everything.

Thinking about communication this way might not be completely new to you. Setting intentions, active listening, noticing context, taking account of history, and paying attention to body language, tone, and nonverbal cues are wonderful communication skills that are well used by many service providers and can be developed in all of us.

The difference between effective and enlightened communication has to do with how we hold and use these tools, and what we hope will happen as we do. Effective communication focuses on exchanging information and influencing behavior. Enlightened communication understands that all communication is about establishing, maintaining, and deepening relationships of mutual recognition, trust, and growth. If effective communication is about results, enlightened communication is about love.

And the letting-go nature of love takes guts. Peeling away the attitudes and assumptions and impulses that stand between us and others requires a brave kind of vulnerability. The invitation to enlightenment is also an invitation to courage.

To communicate well with another person is to see them as clearly as possible and to love them anyway. We learn how to do this by starting with ourselves. As we explore the invitation to clarity and courage, we'll focus less on techniques and more on key principles that honor the relational heart of all communication, including intentionality, integrity, respect, truth, and trustworthiness.

We'll also explore some of the impulses inside us that resist this relational core, cloud our efforts to connect with others, and tempt us to use the awesome power of human communication to protect ourselves at the expense of the people we love and serve.

■   ■   ■

Ego and Other Obstacles

So, what interferes with enlightened communication?

To put it bluntly, you do.

Please don't be offended. I mean you and me. *We* are the forces that get in the way of the awake and aware communication this chapter explores. And by *we* I don't mean the fullness of our humanity. I mean the small but powerful part of each of us called *ego*.

In Latin, *ego* literally means I. Ego is the *me* in every human being, the one whose sole purpose is keeping us physically and psychologically safe.

Our egos normally express themselves through some variation of fear. Their job is to use anxiety to protect us from even scarier and more unpleasant experiences like shame, loss, and abandonment. This is not a bad thing. A little discomfort can help motivate us to improve our situations, to grow and change in healthy ways. There is a "right amount" of fear that befits situations where our physical and emotional safety might be threatened. There are good reasons for the ego to exist.

However, often—especially when we feel overwhelmed or under attack, or when we feel that we don't have what we need—we overreact to the ego's alarm bells and urgent impulses. We act out in ways that do not reflect our best intentions and our deepest values. This usually has a negative impact on ourselves as well as on the people with whom we spend our time.

One of the ego's greatest fears involves exposure and judgment. It's worried about being found out, or blamed for bad news, or discovered as weak or unworthy or vulnerable.

To protect us from this peril, the industrious ego helps us hide in all kinds of ways. Sometimes it hides us behind roles and credentials. It buries us in bureaucracies. It makes use of power imbalances. It makes excuses for insensitivity. It blinds us with assumptions about privilege or victimhood. In some circumstances it can puff us up with intimidating bravado. In other cases, it keeps us quiet and compliant.

In addition to employing these safety strategies, the ego often hides behind words. It uses the sophisticated power of language like the ink that frightened squids and octopuses squirt out to cloud the water while they slip away from danger.

Sometimes these words come out as lies, sometimes as omissions. Sometimes they come out loudly and aggressively, and sometimes they arrive bathed in tears and sobs. Sometimes they show up as jokes. Sometimes they come out vague and mysterious. Often, they spill out with such volume that they take up all the oxygen in the room and exhaust everybody.

The complexity of human language means our speech is prone to confusion, misunderstanding, and misinterpretation. Because of our highly developed brain capacity, human communication is susceptible to uncountable complications. Our egos know that we often have a hard time keeping it simple, and they make good use of this aspect of language.

Imagine a time when you were in conflict with someone. Did you notice that the harder you tried to fix the problem with words, the deeper you sank into disagreement?

Sometimes less is more.

Tempering our response to our ego's defensive alarms and developing a bigger imagination about what safety can mean in relationships of mutuality is a huge part of conscious service. It's also one of the keys to enlightened communication. This involves accepting the ego's alarm messages, getting clear about what's really happening in and around us, and choosing our responses with courage and intentionality. It involves thanking our ego for its service even as we step out from behind the shield it puts up.

How does your ego help you?

Are there ways its efforts might be harming you or holding you back?

Intentions, Good and Otherwise

Your intention sets your course. Sometimes our intentions are clear to us. This makes them easier to declare to ourselves and share with others. At other moments, they can be mixed or murky, or even unconsciously embedded in parts of us that we don't visit or acknowledge very often. Unexamined intentions often show up as impulses.

Our intentions are always present and active, whether we are aware of them or not. One goal of enlightened communication is to get better at being aware of them—to become more conscious of what we want to have happen in any given interaction. As we've discussed in previous chapters, awareness allows us the power to make choices.

When you are aware of your intention in any given interaction, you go into it with access to your inner resources and clarity about your goals. Even as we seek to move beyond understanding our interactions as win-or-lose scenarios, each of us has something that we're hoping to attain or accomplish or embody when we communicate with others.

When I speak of intention, I'm referring to whatever is my most genuine desire in any given situation. That doesn't mean it is the most noble, of course, or the best thing for me or for anybody else.

You'll recall the old saying about the road to hell being paved with what always seemed, at one point or another, like good intentions. I'd say the road to all kinds of hell is usually paved with *unexamined* intentions.

Spending a few quiet moments to clarify your intention prior to any communication with others can make an enormous difference to both the process of the interaction and its outcomes. This involves a little bit of self-connection, self-reflection, and channel-scanning.

Suppose you need to check in with a coworker on the status of a shared project. Prior to the conversation, spend a few minutes thinking about the questions you would like to have answered and the information you want to share. This sets the intention for the concrete tasks you hope to achieve.

Sounds great, right? Almost like it came out of a textbook on effective communication.

Now, let's also admit that you happen to be frustrated with this person or with the process the two of you are trying to work through. Maybe things have not been moving along as quickly as you would like, and you have a hunch that your partner hasn't been forthcoming with all the information—especially the parts that might be heard as bad news. Maybe you experience your coworker as abrasive or dismissive or defensive. Maybe they express self-doubt or fear in a way that annoys you or triggers your own anxieties.

Our intentions are rarely limited to the concrete concerns at hand. We enter a conversation like we enter any relationship: with emotional intentions as well as ideas and expectations from the physical and cognitive parts of ourselves. Taking a moment to tune in to your feeling channel and calibrate your emotional intention before going into your meeting will help ensure that you approach the matter with some awareness of the feelings at work between you and the other person, and how they might be present in your interaction.

Our intentions set the stage for all of our interactions. When we are aware of our intentions, we are more fully present, and we become capable of more enlightened communication, better relationships, and success in the broadest sense.

I'm Sorry You're Hurt

Think of a time when you said something that hurt someone. Maybe your relationship with this person was in turmoil. In a moment of frustration, you delivered a message that left a sting.

If you're at all like me, you first feel found out; your friend now knows that you're pissed and have been pretending otherwise. Then comes remorse and a stab of guilt.

If I'm honest, I knew I was angry before the moment in question, but I thought I could stifle that for the sake of getting through the conversation. As a matter of fact, I had been pissed off with this person for some time. Until that point, I was managing through avoidance and a bit of self-indulgent bashing behind their back with one of my buddies.

And I was called out on it.

Most of us twist into a self-justifying mode at this moment. "It wasn't my intention to hurt you." "I'm sorry you're hurt."

Are we, though?

This might not be entirely true. At some point in every relationship we do the math. We decide whether it's worth it to share our true feelings, or if we can get by with more superficial interactions that don't require as much from us. Dealing with drama is tiring and scary, so we often just let our anger or frustration simmer. If the conflict bubbles into view, we might be sorry that it's now visible, but our contrition usually feels more like impatience.

Regardless of what we pretend our intentions were or are, anger has been pushing its way to the front. It has been reminding us, quietly, then loudly, of an opportunity for self-reflection and honesty that we've been resisting all along.

There's nothing wrong with anger, by the way. Anger offers an alarm when something feels wrong or dangerous or scary. Anger is one of our ego's reactions to fear. Feeling anger, and asking what it's calling our attention to, helps us assess risk and choose our response in any given situation. As uncomfortable as it makes us, anger serves as a source of protection when what lies beneath (betrayal, heartbreak, insecurity) has the potential to hurt even more. It also supplies motivating energy that can help us act and focus even when we're afraid.

Unattended anger, however, can have very harmful consequences. When denied attention and left to brew—to keep sounding its urgent alarm—anger will start to influence not only our intentional action but also the elements of our behavior that float below the level of attention. This is true for all emotional energy.

As in the interaction I'm remembering, fear of accepting the reality of our anger often shows up as denial. *I didn't mean to hurt you.* It's not easy to admit that, on some level, maybe we *did* mean this.

Each of us can, in fact, want to harm someone else. Few of us enjoy seeing ourselves in that light, but when we do acknowledge the presence of unpleasant intentions in us, we become more able to explore where they came from and what's going on beneath them. We do this not to make excuses for these feelings, but to receive their wisdom.

When we don't take the time to identify and explore the emotional intentions we carry into our interactions with others, whatever has accrued the most power in the heart will show up in force. Our intentions, good and otherwise, will always become evident.

Remember that your ego wants you safe. Any desire to hurt someone is your ego's cry for protection and its declaration to go into battle on your behalf. When you acknowledge the ego's efforts, it is easier to understand what's going on, and it becomes possible to enlist its energy in finding more helpful and healing paths to peace and safety.

Competing Intentions and Hidden Agendas

Carol was the new CEO of a midsize mental health organization. Carol was a go-getter powerhouse when it came to pursuing her career. She had worked her way through the ranks, starting in team leadership and progressing to middle management and eventually senior directorship within the agency. She had tons of great ideas and good relationships with the service providers in her organization.

Stepping into her new role was a fairly smooth process. Carol felt connected to the people in the organization, and most felt comfortable that they knew what to expect from her.

Taking on the CEO role had been a part of Carol's long-term career plan. She worked hard to get here. But this position was only one part of a larger picture. Carol had plans that would take her beyond the leadership of this agency. Though she hadn't shared the specifics with anyone, Carol expected to spend about five years in this role and then leave to set up her own business. She envisioned offering coaching and training to health-care and human services agencies in ways that could capitalize on her years of expertise in the field as well as her newly budding interests in spiritual growth.

As CEO, Carol had strongly held values related to her role as a leader. She took pride in her ability to build community and foster transparent and honest dialogue with her teams. When she started, Carol had a vision for what the organization could achieve, and she was ready to get that ball rolling.

A few months into the job, Carol identified a professional development opportunity that attracted her, and she negotiated to have the expense of the training covered by the agency. She dove headfirst into learning the new practice and sought out ways to incorporate it within the systems of the organization.

At first, these efforts were well received.

But, eventually, Carol became frustrated at the amount of time it was taking to see the shift she had been expecting. She noted that not everyone held the same commitment to the practice as she did. She knew the merits of this new approach, and she was impatient that others couldn't or wouldn't embrace it as she had. After all, she also had her personal five-year plan.

Carol's frustration started to appear in her interactions with others. People began to notice her disapproving looks and impatient tone. They felt rushed when the conversation was not progressing as Carol wanted.

Carol lost the trust of those around her—trust that had taken years to develop and nurture. What had gone wrong?

It turns out that Carol had chosen not to consult anybody about her idea before selling it to the board of directors. She did not seek feedback from those who would be asked to embrace the approach in their work. There was no conversation with the teams about their professional development interests.

Carol knew how valuable successfully using this new approach could be when it came to furthering her own career plans. Soon it became clear to others that her intention had more to do with preparing for her future than with serving her current organization. This came through in Carol's communication—her disregard for input from her colleagues, her frustration with anything that seemed like pushback, her impatience with questions she felt were unnecessary. This not only hurt the training project but also left a number of damaged relationships in its wake.

Carol started off talking the talk of integrity and community and ended up unable or unwilling to walk the walk that supported these ideals. What she thought were her key communication skills eventually revealed gaps and holes that undermined years of her hard work.

There's nothing wrong with considering your own interests alongside others' when it comes to intention. It is often possible to bake (and have and eat) a cake that's your favorite flavor and your colleagues' too. In fact, when your intentional energy involves what's best for you and also serves the needs of others, you have hit on a recipe that will both satisfy and nourish your interactions.

Trouble arrives when we deny, downplay, or hide our personal agendas or cloak them in the sweet-sounding idea that our intentions are purely for the benefit of others. As we see with Carol, the effects of this behavior can be magnified when our roles include responsibility for leading large groups or organizations. When we can be honest about the full range of our intentions within any dynamic, we have the opportunity to consider how to express those intentions through our interactions and choices.

This kind of clarity and honesty isn't automatic. It involves the sustained self-connection and reflection we explored in the last chapter. And sometimes we really don't know what we want. If you begin an endeavor unsure of your intentions, any discrepancies between your heart, mind, and action will show up as the situation unfolds. As Carol found, this can be messy and include damaged relationships, bruised credibility, and lost progress. Difficult as it is, this process may be exactly what we need to clarify our intentions and align them with action.

Carol's reluctance to be seen as personally benefiting from the training she ordered for her organization led her to deny this part of her intention. When she experienced resistance or questions, her hidden motivations bubbled to the surface as defensiveness and impatience.

How have you felt when you sense that someone else has a hidden agenda?

What could you be more up-front about in your interactions with others?

It's Okay to Want Things, by the Way

The problems that can accompany mixed intentions and hidden agendas notwithstanding, it's okay to want things for yourself. It's even okay to want and need things from other people. It's actually good and healthy. The myth of the selfless and self-sacrificial service worker has invited many of us to deny our most important desires as well as our basic needs. Our egos have even joined this effort, employing their worry-power against our own hearts. We fear disappointing others, and we also don't want to let ourselves down.

It can be hard to admit our truest, most heartfelt desires. Most of us are afraid to set ourselves up for disappointment. Our dreams can seem so big that it can be scary to even hope for them to be realized. Even here, the safety-seeking ego will try to protect us by keeping that hope at arm's length. Awareness of this impulse gives us the chance to redirect it.

When avoiding disappointment looms large among our intentions, it can have devastating effects on motivation, courage, and our ability to believe in ourselves. Denying ourselves the joy of thinking big, following our passions, and expanding our lives really doesn't protect us from the possibility of disappointment. In fact, disappointment is exactly what awaits us if we deny our heart's desires over the course of our lives.

What gets in the way of authentic awareness of your deepest intentions?

If you're aware of what you want, what gets in the way of going for it?

Integrity

Integrity goes beyond the basics of honesty and truth. Integrity is alignment of mind, spirit, and action. Our thoughts, emotions, beliefs, and behavior are undivided when we speak and act with integrity. When we say yes and no, we mean it. "I don't know" and "Maybe" are also valid responses as long as they reflect the truth of our inner state.

Aligned in this way, we can become aware of how our behavior reflects our belief systems and recognize when limiting beliefs are calling the shots. A commitment to integrity shows us where we can alter those belief systems so our actions fall in line with our deepest intentions.

Coming into integrity with our intentions not only leads to clarity; it also makes it easier to accept outcomes and feel peaceful with our actions. When we don't get what we want, we may feel sadness or loss. That's different from the energy of frustration and disappointment that goes with inaccurate self-representation.

Do your best to find clarity with your intentions. When you are cloudy and experience the disappointment of unmet expectations, you have an opportunity to get to the bottom of what you really want. Sometimes, we don't know our pure intention until we're chewing on an unsatisfying outcome. These experiences can offer insights that help us try again. Like every aspect of conscious service, getting in touch with our intentions is a process of ongoing learning, and we'll be doing it for life.

Living with integrity does not put us above others. It simply allows us to express our truth clearly and enter into relationships authentically. When we know where we stand, we connect more meaningfully with others, and our integrity invites them to feel more comfortable sharing where they're coming from and what they want.

Clear intention and commitment to maintaining personal integrity will help you remain true to yourself and your values in ways that do not diminish other people. As you practice integrity, you will more quickly recognize the feelings of discomfort associated with misalignment, and you will become more aware of when you're out of step.

Underground against Carol

At the same time Carol was mired in the consequences of denied intentions and lack of integrity, two of her program managers, Sam and Elaine, were struggling with their own demons.

Sam and Elaine had been colleagues for many years, working in different organizations together. They shared similar belief systems and values when it came to service, and both were committed to making a difference where they could.

This thing with Carol was bothering them. Each had felt the brunt of Carol's frustration lately, and they suspected her personal agenda was fixed in ways that didn't welcome feedback. Assuming that any alternative strategies they might offer would be rebuffed, they had gone underground with their dissatisfaction.

The two would get together outside of the office on a regular basis. Sometimes they met at a local pub near the end of the day. They'd get their business out of the way, manage their schedules, and then have a beer or two and kibitz about life in general. Inevitably, the conversation would come back to their irritation with Carol and what was happening at work.

Sometimes they considered speaking candidly with Carol. They thought about sharing their observations in a loving way with a view toward reaching a resolution. They had liked Carol, and in some ways they wanted to support her. More often than not, however, the conversation would drift back to critique and move beyond professional concerns to focus on personal shortcomings they saw in Carol.

At first this was strangely fun. It felt good to get it all off their chests, to see the humor in it, and to point out the wrongness of it all. Sam and Elaine got used to their gossip sessions without paying attention to how this energy was impacting their ability to communicate well with Carol. They also became really good at ignoring the fact that they would not have found it acceptable if they themselves were ever the subject of similar gossip and behind-the-back complaint.

The more they bashed Carol behind her back, the harder it became to listen to anything she had to say. They took everything with a grain of salt, and they found that they felt little respect for her anymore.

One evening over a bottle of wine, as they laughed their way through another familiar rendition of "What's Wrong with Carol," they revisited the idea of approaching her with their concerns. Elaine immediately expressed her fear about Carol's response. She expected that they would be met with anger and that they would feel the afterburn for months to come.

Was it even worth it?

Neither felt ready to go down that path.

Over the next several weeks, they continued their backstage banter, but now an element of helplessness was in the mix. Elaine and Sam had tricked themselves into believing that they were powerless in the situation with Carol. They started to buy in to their own excuses. They began to blame Carol for the fact that they didn't feel safe to address their concerns.

As we saw earlier, it was true that Carol had some problems. Misaligned and unhappy about it, she was attempting to assert control. But Carol's choices had stopped being the issue. Elaine and Sam had relinquished their power to respond with integrity.

And they knew it.

It was actually their job to know it. Elaine's and Sam's official roles in the organization included enhancing community and communication—practices that included speaking up and embracing personal responsibility. It became clearer and clearer to them that their own behavior regarding Carol was completely out of whack with what they were trying to promote professionally. Like Carol herself, they had stepped out of integrity.

Even if nobody else could identify what was going on behind closed doors, you can be sure that they felt it. Sam and Elaine felt it too. In the office, they kept talking as they always had about the importance of open communication, but at some point they could no longer deny or avoid the discomfort they felt with their own actions.

Had another colleague approached them bothered by challenges with a colleague, both women would have immediately encouraged face-to-face, direct, respectful communication. And they would have offered support in the process.

So, what was blocking Sam and Elaine? What was making it so difficult for them to apply what they would guide anyone else to do in a similar situation? What was keeping them from addressing Carol directly?

You may suspect by now that the primary human experience that blocks enlightened communication is fear. You're right.

Sam and Elaine were afraid. They were afraid of the discomfort that would inevitably be part of speaking their truth with Carol. They feared that things might get worse. They dreaded the thought that the energy in the office would get thick with defensiveness and anger. What if Carol started to plot ways to get rid of them? Their fears interfered with their capacity to be true to the principles that they were so diligently trying to guide other people to follow.

A tinge of guilt now colored Sam and Elaine's fear. They hated the idea that they might be exposed as leaders who failed in their duty to address the problem. Neither could ignore the fact that they had spent countless hours behind closed doors engaging in conversations that had added nothing to resolving their problems with Carol. They knew, in fact, that their actions actually put an energetic cloud over the whole office, even if they never discussed them within those walls. They had given up their integrity and, along the way, they forfeited their personal power as well as their responsibilities as professionals.

How has fear of discomfort interfered with your expression of integrity?

Have you ever chosen to stay in the suffering you know to avoid the suffering you fear?

Power and Truth

When it comes to relationships and the energy of the social channel of our human system, our personal power depends on the quality of our integrity. When we step out of integrity, whether we're aware of it or not, our sense of personal power begins to diminish. If we don't stand for the truth of our heart, we begin to feel helpless, and this shows up in our behavior with others.

Personal power is not tied to our role or our credentials or the authority of our position. It is not about having control over anyone or anything. Personal power comes from within and is accessible to all. It is the opposite of fear-motivated ego. Power is not about exerting energy or applying force as much as it is about simply embodying integrity in all our relationships and interactions.

A truly powerful person has a strong sense of who they are and is comfortable stepping into their being. Powerful people do not overextend themselves by taking on false responsibility for others' lives, nor do they hold back by editing and censoring themselves. Truly powerful people are not threatened in the presence of another's expression of personal power. They understand that power comes from an internal experience and does not involve control or manipulation of people or events. Truly powerful people know where they end and others begin. This allows them to develop deep and respectful connections. Truly powerful people are able to create a space where others can realize the fullness of their own personal power.

Not everyone has equal access to personal power. Some people are more attuned to this energy than others. Some have learned how and been encouraged to access it more consistently. Life circumstances and unhealed wounds can create barriers to naming and claiming innate power. And for many, even when we are able to access and embody our power, our expressions of it are too often disrespected, devalued, and rejected by systems and structures shaped by sexism or racism or exclusion.

Societal and structural realities affect each of us differently. Some of us live with much more privilege than others. This undeniably affects our access to and embodiment of all kinds of power in our lives and in the world.

It is also true that each human being is created with the capacity to fully embody their personal power. Personal growth and human flourishing require us to claim and access this source of stability and energy. Without it, we wither.

Elaine and Sam knew they had stepped out of personal power when it came to their interactions with Carol. Instead of acting with integrity, they ultimately let fear motivate them, shrinking themselves in an attempt to avoid discomfort. In the end they realized that this had only added to and prolonged their suffering.

The fear-based notion that they needed protection from Carol is exactly what kept them separated from their personal power.

In relationships, power is about perception and belief. If I believe you have power over me, my behavior will show my sense of inferiority. If I believe I have power over you, I might communicate with aggression or condescension. If I'm unaware of my power in any given situation, I will likely express myself in ways that are confusing and out of integrity.

When we believe we have lost control of ourselves and our destiny, we can be tempted into mind games. Afraid of powerlessness, we may begin to anticipate others' needs and desires before we commit to our own truth. We may manipulate our messages to control the responses we want. We may start thinking two steps ahead so we can get to the finish line first. This behavior flies in the face of what we know is right for us. Our impulse to control keeps us attached to certain outcomes, and this self-defeating cycle eventually limits the options we're able to imagine.

As we embody the truth of our personal power, we let go of outcomes and open ourselves to possibility. We understand that one person's loss belongs to all. Personally powerful people are able to hold a vision of the highest possible good, even when they don't know the details of how that will be achieved. They are unafraid of ambiguity, because they recognize what we all have in common, and they know how to recognize the power that each human being holds.

Fear of the unknown and discomfort with the universe's lack of guarantees may block our personal power. When we don't know what lies beyond the familiar and the comfortable, we may hedge our bets and accept less-than-ideal conditions. When we sense we're losing control in a situation and feel threatened by what that means, we comply with the undesirable. Ironically, this almost always leaves us feeling controlled by life and others.

And then we wonder why we feel so depleted.

Personally powerful people have a sense of freedom. And, as we've seen, freedom comes hand in hand with responsibility. As we claim and embody our power, we also respond with care in our relationships. We value other people and affirm their right to personal power alongside our own.

Embodying your personal power offers very practical energetic gifts. Here are just a few:

- Courage to share your out-of-the-box thinking, even when it might be met with resistance

- Grace when you find yourself experiencing intense emotions in the midst of your interactions

- Loving-kindness as you challenge the status quo

- Acceptance of the diversity of perspectives and beliefs

- Excitement as you let go of personal agendas in favor of the possibilities you cannot currently see

- Faith in the process when resolving conflict and navigating disagreement

- Trust in yourself as you create trust with other people

Standing in a state of personal power is not a stationary experience or a onetime achievement. As with integrity and self-awareness, it requires commitment. We move in and out of touch with our personal power.

With practice, we can identify the specific ways our urges to control situations and outcomes create barriers to relationship. This awareness can help us stay attuned to the source of our power and keep embodying it in our connection with others.

When you consider your own personal power, what does it look like?

What is the source of your personal power?

Respect and Conflict

Our capacity to hold the vision of a person's full humanity, beyond outward appearances and actions, forms the basis for respecting them. Respect is the simple recognition of every person's inherent and equal worth and dignity for no reason other than the fact that they exist. The capacity to see this and act in ways that align with its truth is part of our personal power.

We often treat respect as a commodity. In many interactions, respect seems rare and precious—it must be earned or proven, then guarded, because it can be threatened or stolen or lost, especially when we disagree with each other. Mutual respect is frequently assumed to be conditional—kind of an "I will if you will" sort of thing.

In enlightened communication, respect arises from the unconditional energy of love. Respect has nothing to do with approval or agreement, so it never needs to be earned. Respect for others is a commitment and a behavior that arises from the integrity of self-respect. We offer respect to others, but in order for it to be real we must first be able to receive it from ourselves.

Respect is demonstrated through what humanist psychologist Carl Rogers calls "unconditional positive regard." Imagine this as a type of window through which I commit to seeing you. No matter what you believe, what you think, what you say, or how you act, I recognize you as a fellow human being. I may not like your behavior or beliefs or the words you speak or shout, and I may tell you that; I may disagree. I may walk away from a situation that is hurtful to me or threatens my safety, but I will do so without denying your humanity. Your inherent worthiness frames whatever response I choose.

I can be angry and still respectful. I can feel hurt or happy or amused or anxious about what's happening, but self-respect prevents me from collapsing my own emotional experience into yours. My integrity keeps me from matching or mirroring whatever energy you're expressing.

In conflict, maintaining respectful connection can feel challenging. Our sensitivities are heightened, rattling our egos into action and making patience and perspective difficult to embody. When we feel defensive, it can be hard to choose respectful responses. Learning to calm our ego in these moments and act out of self-respect takes practice and commitment.

When it is aligned with respect for you, my self-respect lets me act from a place of power and personal responsibility. When we behave in this way, we feel better and we'll likely have fewer regrets. No matter what another person is doing or how they're doing it, we claim our power to demonstrate the innate human value we have in common.

How do you maintain respectful communication in the midst of conflict?

What might cause you to make an exception to a rule about respecting yourself or another person?

That Thing with Carol Isn't about Carol

Elaine and Sam came to understand the link between respect for others and self-respect as they grappled with their personal and professional responses to Carol. At first, their one-on-one discussions provided grounding relief and gave them a safe place to air frustration and troubleshoot. Over time, however, these conversations became a type of entertainment that linked them in self-perpetuating behavior.

Each time they indulged in this weird guilty pleasure and then sat in a team meeting intended to facilitate conscious conversations, they felt misaligned. Laughing and complaining behind someone's back while encouraging a more enlightened form of communication among colleagues was an act of self-disrespect. Their behavior left them feeling out of alignment, guilty, and ashamed. Knowing their own communication was far from enlightened, they began to find it difficult to encourage others to reach for that ideal.

With every gossip session, Sam and Elaine each were ignoring their deeper commitments, honoring instead the allure of one another's approval. Have you ever found yourself going along with certain activities because you wanted to be liked or accepted by a certain person or group? Have you, like Sam and Elaine, compromised your own commitments to yourself because you put another's opinion before what matters to you?

I have done this too many times, in too many ways, for the sake of too many relationships. And each time I thought I couldn't live without these connections. Each compromise was an act of self-disrespect by which I ended up hurting myself more than anyone else ever could.

These compromises can take many forms. We chase after people for approval or acceptance, grovel at their metaphorical feet, accept harmful behavior, or lie down so they can walk on us. Each time, we are sacrificing our self-respect for the sake of an unattainable goal.

Self-disrespect always seems like it's going to hurt less than facing our fear. Denying ourselves seems like it takes less energy than stopping to listen to what's driving our pursuit of misery, what keeps us engaged in this awful form of entertainment.

Whatever acceptance we're seeking from others will always feel insufficient until we are able to accept and respect ourselves, honor our values, and embrace our integrity.

Acceptance recognizes and respects autonomy: the simple freedom we all have to be who we are, where we are.

Acceptance adds openness to our relationships—a space where people are valued for their whole humanness. Having been seen in this way, people can start to feel safe. They can become less reactive and more open to exploring options for behavior and belief, more willing to see possibilities beyond the present moment. Whenever you are able to create a safe and accepting environment for yourself, your capacity to help hold it open with and for others expands.

How has self-disrespect shown up in your life?

What are you still learning to accept about yourself?

Language Is Power, Listening Is Love, and Precision Honors People

In a textbook on effective communication, we would have started with the tips and tools way back at the beginning of the chapter. This is not that textbook. Instead, through the loving practice of clear and courageous connection with ourselves and others, we've built the muscles we'll use for enlightened communication. Now we can visit the toolbox; we're ready to use the tools with care and strength.

In our daily acts of communication, we have the opportunity to integrate all of the qualities discussed in this chapter. We can set clear intentions, maintain our integrity, embody our power, and respond with the generous openness of unconditional respect—all in service to the simple human tasks of speaking and listening. When we do, we find clarity, connection, and understanding.

Speaking

Much of the time, we agree on the meaning behind the words we use. But our words, voices, and sentences are energetic. They carry with them a certain frequency. Interpretation is always subjective, and meaning frequently moves beyond dictionary definitions. Language can be freighted with emotional weight; it matters to people in ways particular to their histories and personalities. Communication—especially with people we don't know well—always carries some measure of risk. We are building a kind of bridge, which we hope will support the weight of whatever we bring to the conversation. The complexity of human language allows us to connect with people in profound ways. And it can lead to misunderstandings and hurt feelings.

We can't always anticipate what people hear when we speak, but we can recognize and respect the power of language. Whenever we use words, we must consider the context of our communication as well as the elements of delivery we choose, such as tone, pitch, volume, and pace.

Our language represents what we believe to be true. The words we select express our values, attitudes, and perspectives as well as whatever other information we intend to convey. It is imperative that we choose our words wisely and find ways to express them in alignment with what we feel and believe.

Listening

Like any form of active love, listening can sometimes feel like a challenge. Internal and external conditions can make full attention more difficult. Noisy or busy environments require a great deal more energy to remain focused. When we interact is also a key consideration. Are you more alert later in the day or first thing in the morning? What happens to your capacity to listen when you are fearful or overwhelmed, sad or anxious? Which fears will your ego bring to the party? If your body calls for attention, how will you address its need as you also honor the person you're with?

When we truly listen to another, we are present, we seek to understand what they are telling us, and we remember what has been shared. In doing these things, we create a sacred space that honors both the speaker and the hearer.

Challenge yourself to move beyond the skills of active listening. In addition to demonstrating that you have heard by reflecting what people have said and asking for clarification when you need it, listen to the silences. Note how people hold their bodies when they speak, where their eyes go, how their breathing reflects the emotions beneath their words.

Practice bringing your whole self into your interactions. What happens to your ability to pick up on subtleties and silence when you engage with all your channels? The more attuned we are to another person, the easier it becomes to understand what they're communicating and why. Pay attention to where you need clarity or more detail in order to fully understand. In this state of attentiveness, it is much easier to receive the emotional quality of the conversation as well as its content, and to remember both.

Remembering the details of what people choose to share with us, as well as the energy that accompanies those messages, is an expression of love. Remembering well is evidence of listening with full awareness.

People First

Health-care and social service settings are full of acronyms and short forms that effectively dehumanize people and exclude them from conversations. This usually impacts those whose voices deserve to be central. Trying to be concise in our communications, we can inadvertently perpetuate jargon, stigma, and generalizations. These linguistic barriers tend to separate us from the people we hope to connect with—people who are best served through connection, humanity, and respect.

When we refer to people as *cases, suicides,* or *overdoses,* we're using language as a way to help us feel safe. This is the work of ego again. These words keep some definitional distance between ourselves and the human reality of the painful situations we are witnessing. These labels shore up the comforting belief that similar tragedies won't come to pass in our own lives or touch the ones we love.

Whenever we use the power of language to reduce the reality of any human being to their experience or condition, whether it's to soothe our fears or to save a few minutes, we move away from the core power of respect. Whenever possible, use a person's name.

If using names would impact a person's confidentiality or privacy, or if you don't know what they like to be called, embrace person-centered or person-first language. Refrain from referring to "the homeless woman" or "the autistic boy," for example. Instead of pointing out "the former addict" or "the HIV-positive man," you might refer to the gentleman who lives with HIV as a result of using IV drugs in the past. Acknowledging humanity first is more important than any efficiency that dehumanizing shorthand might give us.

Service-based language is in a constant state of flux. We come up with new terminology that might sound better in the moment, but eventually just becomes another way to label. Person-first language recognizes that any given condition or category can describe only part of an individual's reality. Labels cannot define any person's identity, nor what they mean for the world you share.

When you are in a position to describe someone, slow down, connect with your own humanity, and choose words that honor the fullness of their being. Think of how you want someone to feel when they hear you speaking about them. Consider how you would like to be described by someone in your place. Choose words that create the energetic experience of being respected and cared for.

Better yet, ask them who they are and how they express their identity in words. Welcome them to speak on their own behalf.

Be Gentle with Yourself

While we aim for honor and strive for impeccability in what we say and do, we accept and embrace our full humanity. We trust that we will make mistakes, that the ego's alarms will distract us from hearing right or speaking plain. We will put our feet in our mouths through ignorance or ineptitude. Our biases will emerge, sometimes unexpectedly.

Don't be discouraged by this.

Self-acceptance allows us room to grow; self-respect motivates us to work for this growth. Pursuing the clarifying path of enlightened communication with courage will help us expand our ability to navigate all our interactions with others with more care and precision. It will also expand our capacity to communicate with and represent ourselves in ways that respect our humanity and honor our needs.

And on those occasions when we do stumble, we will have tools to help us clear the air, re-center ourselves in the limitless power of love, and strengthen the integrity of our conversations.

CHAPTER 6

Focus on Transformation

An Invitation to Vision

Way back in chapter three, we explored our responsibility, as service providers, for holding on to hope, even when present circumstances do not appear to support such an outlook. We identified this as one aspect of the spiritual work of service—a matter of believing beyond immediate evidence and acting from faith that a different and better future is possible for anyone and everyone—including ourselves.

This chapter invites you to explore more deeply how that active faith works in real life, and how our human relationships serve as containers where hope can happen. We'll examine what limits and constricts our vision (judgment, prejudice, assumptions, overwhelm) as well as what conditions (relationships of empathy, honesty, integrity, respect, humility, and humanity) help expand our vision and create space for healing, perspective, and awareness, as well as action toward those possibilities.

Accepting an invitation to focus your vision for any relationship relies on the power to make choices and the ability to direct the energy of your attention where it's most needed. Enlightened communication is about our capacity to remove obstacles to connection and see clearly, and *focus* is about putting this clarified perception to work in and through our personal and professional relationships. It's about our ability to accept what is and what has been while also making space for and moving toward a future that doesn't have to be defined by the past.

As with every other aspect of conscious service we've explored so far, our capacity to see beyond the present moment's unexamined certainties and scary-seeming uncertainties must begin with ourselves. Without a broad and generous vision of our own possibilities for transformation, healing, and hope, our efforts to open this space for others will be limited, inauthentic, and unsustainable, even if our intentions are pure.

■　■　■

Invitation, Intimacy, and Trust

The urge to fix people and manage situations is a powerful one. When paired with what feels like the best intentions and put to work with a toolbox full of techniques, this urge can be nearly irresistible. When we feel equipped and empowered by our training and calling, and authorized by our roles, it can seem like our job is to steamroll in with answers and take over as caretaker and cruise director of another person's life—all in the spirit of being helpful.

If we have not been invited into that space, it is more likely that forcing our way in will shut down all communication. It's like crashing a party.

And invitations to relationships of service don't always arrive gold-embossed in your mailbox. We are not given automatic access to the recesses of another's heart, even if they've taken a step toward seeking service.

Just because someone has appeared at your door or in your chair or on your massage table, it does not necessarily mean that you have received an intimate invitation. As relationships deepen, there will be moments when we are invited to more personal connection with others. Trust is an essential element of this process. Continual openness and a genuine desire to understand are required ingredients. In a safe space, we are all more inclined to reveal our true essence.

As you stay self-connected and present, you're less likely to miss invitations when they arrive. Be patient as you anticipate these moments. Be careful not to overstep your welcome or presume to have a permanent seat at the table. Stay in tune with all the channels of your human system to sense when it's best to wait and when to move closer.

It is possible that you may be asked directly to help in specific ways. People invite us into relationship when they say "I need you," or "I'm lost," or "I don't know what to do." We are extended an invitation when someone discloses a secret. Or words may come later. Often, the more vulnerable another person feels, the more language might fail them.

Many people indicate their needs through an exchange of emotional energy or in ways that feel safer than speech. Maybe it's something in their eyes or the tone of their voice. Perhaps it is a look on their face or what you sense them saying between the words. Either way, our presence, engagement, curiosity, and patience are necessary if we are to be prepared to receive and accept the invitation.

We know we are welcome when we feel it. It is an energetic exchange that says, "You can be here with me."

When the invitation comes, we might feel ready to get down to the nitty-gritty, but that doesn't imply universal readiness. There is a big difference between open questions and interrogation. Some people live their lives like open books, and others don't answer the door until you've knocked three times. Sometimes, the entrance is completely blocked.

It is our role in service to others to keep coming back, to continue to show up in our humanity, and to be ready to enter the sacred space of relationship whenever the door opens.

We can't make the door open. Responsible and respectful service will never include acts of manipulation or abuse, shaming, blaming, or impatience. Relationships that support transformation are characterized by acceptance, understanding, resourcefulness, and a reverence for the wholeness and strength of the human spirit.

When the time is right, people will teach you about who they are at their core, what matters to them, how they have been shaped by their life experiences. People will show you how they came to develop their rough edges and their soft spots. They will guide you toward the ways in which you might be of service. Through your human relationship with those you wish to serve, you will be offered a vision of what life is like for them.

Tuning in to your own human desire to be heard and seen will expand your ability to be patient. Acknowledge that, at times, what matters to you makes no difference to anyone else. But honor your very real need to sometimes think out loud in order to make sense of what's happening in your world.

Whenever you allow yourself to soften to the impact of another human being, you become open to being touched and transformed by their story. You might see yourself in what they share and suddenly understand something you've never been able to wrap your head around. You may meet kindred spirits or wise teachers or careful messengers in the most unlikely places.

As a service provider, you are responsible for creating spaces safe enough for people to reveal their hurt, claim their healing, and embody their personal power. In the strong and powerful container of a trustworthy relationship, the concepts at the heart of conscious service become real.

What are some strategies you use to create safe space with others?

Rapport and Reciprocity

Developing a trustworthy service relationship is about helping someone realize their capacity for growth. Rapport functions in a relationship the same way resonance works with energy. Good rapport exists between two people when they share a high level of trust, respect, and a kind of mutual understanding. In service relationships, the rapport that we establish with others is meant to be purposeful and meaningful.

People who access social and health-care services are usually seeking to meet a need they have identified. We service providers have a specific role to fill. This role includes an agreement that the focus of the relationship is the needs of the person seeking service. Sometimes this agreement is formal, sometimes informal.

Most of our personal relationships don't include such an agreement. They're more reciprocal. Even if the balance is not always equal, we assume each party's needs and desires matter. We give and take. This is part of what makes personal relationships satisfying and energizing.

And reciprocity is an important aspect of all relationships—including our service relationships. Transformative relationships—the relationships that conscious service asks of us—are partnerships. Both people have a role and are aware of this role. The partners share a vision of what is to be achieved and how communication will be handled. This is especially important when conflict or disagreements are possible. This requires a process of continually checking in to ensure that things are on track and refocusing when perspective has been lost.

The best partnerships are based on an understanding about equality. Transformative service relationships include balance. At no time does either partner have dominion over the other. The atmosphere is one of safety and shared power in which each person feels a sense of being fully connected to the process and each person has a voice.

At times, the other partner in a service relationship may not be willing or able to embrace a transformative connection. But you have the capacity to be a dynamic and valued partner in any relationship, whether others acknowledge it or not. What matters is that you recognize your worth, and that your vision is grounded in possibility and power as well as self-awareness and the humility of your actual humanity. What matters is that you trust the value in your contribution even when it appears to go unnoticed.

Obviously, service providers bear the primary responsibility for outlining the structure of the service relationship. Creating partnerships that include reciprocity while honoring roles requires us to be resourceful and have a variety of skills and tools to offer to the process. But even when we have strong skills and experience in our area of service, ours cannot be the only voice that matters. Shared responsibility for the relational space encourages both partners in the service relationship to bring the truth of their being to each interaction.

Reimagine Where the Lines Get Drawn

Service providers have been encouraged to maintain "boundaries" intended to protect us from the dangers of burnout, enmeshment, and overidentification with the people we're supposed to be serving. Such safeguards are also designed to protect others from us. These concerns are real, of course. We all know about situations and can imagine scenarios in which people are and have been harmed by the people authorized to help them. We do need structures that promote safety and prevent abuse in service relationships.

There's nothing wrong with the idea of a boundary. But we need to reconsider where boundaries need to be built.

Helpful and connected service relationships require presence, patience, commitment, partnership, and vision. Their purpose is to act as an incubator for the sensitive processes of self-discovery and transformation. When people seeking service perceive a safe and supported space, they are more likely to utter and honor their hopes and fears, explore possibilities, and emerge in new forms.

Our role as service providers isn't to erect a wall of separation between ourselves and the people on the other side of the service equation, but to build and maintain a powerful boundary that focuses the purpose and protects the safe nature of the relationship.

Instead of drawing a line that divides us, we can mark out a circle that includes and honors provider and recipient both. Our job is to hold open this space where the magic can happen, where hope can take root, where what once seemed impossible or out of reach can be tried on and tested out. A safe relationship is the container where the potential for positive transformation exists.

The problems that anti-burnout boundary prescriptions seek to avoid will not be solved by further separating the real humanity of service providers from the real humanity of the people we serve. In a transformative relationship, the boundary belongs around us instead of between us.

Of course we need sensible practices and supports and skills and self-awareness to keep us grounded and safe and healthy as service providers, to keep our personal concerns from becoming entangled in the lives of those we serve, and to prevent us from abusing or mishandling the power our roles entail. Responsible and self-reflective service providers will choose carefully what we bring with us into this sacred space and what is best left outside it. When it comes to boundaries, we need them to guard the integrity of the service relationship and protect the processes of positive transformation—not to lock our humanity away from those we serve.

When have you built a boundary between you and another person?

When have you drawn a circular boundary around a relationship?

What emotions do you associate with each experience?

Enmeshment, Estrangement, and Engagement

Most of us are familiar with the experience of finding ourselves at three o'clock in the afternoon not really aware of where we have been or what we've been doing since we rolled out of bed that morning. Perhaps you have ignored your body's signals or you have been ruminating in the back of your mind all day as you checked items off your list of things to do. Maybe you find yourself in traffic but really not aware you're behind the wheel.

How do we stay engaged in the moment? Well, it's not something that falls into place easily because we meditated for fifteen minutes when we woke up. Engagement, by nature, requires a continual process of coming into the present moment, in real time. This is especially powerful when we're able to do it in difficult moments and with people in crisis.

Engagement can be described as the physical, mental, and emotional condition that makes responsive presence possible. As you become more familiar with how it feels to be engaged in this way, you will notice more quickly when you are not.

Engagement isn't activated by a switch or a shortcut, however. It's one experience along a spectrum of emotional and attentive states that characterize relationships. We move in and out of these states all the time, depending on all sorts of inputs and conditions, both internal and external. Imagine engagement as the sweet spot on this spectrum. It's a place of balanced attention and grounded focus.

The sensory experience of engagement is your most powerful indicator that you have found this sweet spot. Some people describe these feelings as when things "click" or when we're "on the same wavelength" with another person. I experience engagement as a distraction-free, open, and receptive energy that emanates from my heart. When I feel fully engaged, my jaw isn't clenched, my breathing is even, and I'm often smiling.

If engagement is the balance point of the spectrum, the poles that sit on either end are enmeshment and estrangement. These states of being are often connected to relationships with others, but we can experience them by ourselves as well. I can become enmeshed with or estranged from my own thoughts and inner turmoil, even if the people or situations involved are far in the past or haven't yet happened.

Enmeshment occurs whenever we become overly entangled with something or someone beyond ourselves. In relationships, enmeshment can include the experience of codependence. When we have become enmeshed, we've usually lost sight of the limits of our role in a situation and think it's all up to us. This often means we're overstepping our responsibilities in relationships and inserting ourselves where we don't belong. When we're enmeshed, we believe there is something only we can do to save someone or something from an undesirable outcome. This experience often comes along with feelings of anxiety or panic and a kind of jittery exhaustion.

Enmeshment takes us out of the present moment through the power of fear. When we're enmeshed, we believe we need to protect other people from themselves, and we're convinced that we have the power to do so.

When we become enmeshed with other people, external situations, or problems that we have no business trying to solve, we're unable to act from a place of balance and perspective. At best, we end up missing any real opportunities we might have for service. At worst, we cause harm, both to ourselves and to the people we're attempting to serve.

On the other end of the continuum, far from the sticky tentacles of enmeshment, lies the lonely experience of estrangement. When we're estranged from people or situations, we're often feeling some kind of anger. This could be bitterness at being pushed away from something or somebody, or a judgy righteousness by which we've separated ourselves from everyone and everything involved. When we cannot understand other people's choices or thought processes, when we feel attacked or dismissed, or when we get tired of trying to connect, we often check out. This means moving away from a relationship where engagement is possible to one marked and limited by estrangement.

Estrangement also includes an element of fear. Moving toward this end of the relational spectrum is often a form of self-protection. It can become so difficult to watch others' behaviors, or witness patterns unfolding that make us afraid, that we feel a need to protect ourselves from the situation. Rather than enduring or exploring this fear, estrangement offers us the option to harden ourselves and add distance between us and the person or situation. In this state it can become easy to blame the other, whose choices scare or infuriate us.

As service providers, many of us move along this spectrum of experiences and feelings all day long. We might relinquish our personal responsibility for engagement when we become afraid or frustrated and swing to either end of the spectrum. The further we get from the sweet spot of full engagement, the more limited our access to insight, intuition, and inspiration will be. Learning to sense how our internal resources slow, shift, and recharge will help us know when we need to rebalance and re-center in order to stay present.

Engagement allows us the chance to be present, even when the present moment is fraught with feeling or compromised by chaos. Operating from a place of engagement allows us to recognize and respect the shifting nature of our personal resources of peace and serenity, and respond to our own needs as they arise. Your ability to remain engaged not only will honor and benefit those you serve; it will allow you to do this while avoiding the lure of fear-based self-protection.

When we learn to engage with the full range of our human system, we become more naturally responsive and present. I'm not saying this will solve every dilemma or heal the wounds in our world, but it will expand our capacity for innovation and compassion. And these things do make a difference.

When you slip out of balance, are you prone to enmeshment or estrangement?

When have you experienced trouble maintaining the balance between yourself and another person? What helped you cope?

Empowerment and Power

What does it mean to be empowered? Is it really possible to empower other people? I believe we can learn to empower ourselves, and I believe others can play a pivotal role in that process. In the end, however, empowerment doesn't happen for anyone until they choose to step into it.

This is often tricky in service relationships. We often find ourselves engaged with people who have lost touch with a sense of self that includes power, or who never had their power named or noticed by the important people in their early years. This doesn't mean that it will remain forever elusive. And it doesn't mean that someone took it away. Just as I doubt any human being's ability to empower another, I'm skeptical about the possibility of anyone stealing another person's power without their consent.

Some define personal power as the ability to control events or other people. This is not the kind of power I have in mind here. At times, we do try to control or influence the conditions of our lives. That's about willpower. But what I'm talking about is retaining a sense of resilience and possibility in the face of circumstances that no amount of effort can seem to alter.

Holding personal power in such an unyielding situation is a struggle. But it's precisely in these times of felt powerlessness that we have the chance to assert ourselves where we can make a difference. Even when we have no control of events and circumstances, we can control our perspective. We can change how we choose to understand what's happening and how we choose to respond.

There is a delicate balance here, because we tend to seek evidence of our power in the external conditions of our lives. And over time, as we step more fully into a sense of personal power, we do see subtle shifts in our physical realities (and sometimes huge ones too). But that is not necessarily the goal.

Many people in the world appear to have significant power. They can influence others and get what they want. And often these same people never feel a sense of personal power, because they know that if their money or prestige were taken away, they would be left with very little.

Claiming the power to alter and expand our outlook is where our capacity for resilience begins. When we learn to tap into this personally powerful place, we start sensing the depth of our core resources and become grounded in a self-trust so deep that we are reunited with a hope that once seemed impossible.

From here, it becomes much easier to see a path forward, even in the midst of confusion. Hope combined with clarity tells us that there is a way. Resilience combined with courage allows us to persevere until we get to the other side.

Most of us know someone in our lives who seems to exude this kind of power. Often they are service providers, though their roles are not always formal. These are people who make an impression but aren't intimidating. Personally powerful people exude safety. You know that you can be yourself with these people. Instead of being anxious about your vulnerabilities, you find that being with them offers you courage. Seeing through their eyes shows you that what you assumed to be insurmountable obstacles are actually challenges you can meet with resourcefulness and hope. You start to understand that there are ways over, under, or around, and you begin to trust that you will find one such way that works.

Personally powerful service providers recognize the inherent capacity of others to claim their power, and they are able to share that vision with the people they serve. They recognize and address the obstacles that keep people from recognizing, accessing, and articulating their personal power. Rather than assuming a position of controlling power over others, they focus on fostering the unique expression of power within each person.

In service with others, you will quickly come to realize that not everyone you meet is in touch with their sense of personal power. Quite often this becomes the most profound aspect of your role with others.

Some aspects of your role may clearly give you authority over the lives of others. This authority can impact others' reality in profound ways. These are positions of great responsibility, and if you are honored with one, never confuse the objective powers of your role with the personal power that will keep you grounded and guide your vision.

You may have protocols that must be followed. How you interpret and apply these policies is fully within your personal power. Rules and regulations on paper have no power. They are made effective only by those who enact them. When you are the human being in that equation, your sense of personal power is the feather in the scale.

Never hide behind your code of ethics or your agency's mission statement. That just feels slimy. Codes, missions, guidelines, and policies are best-guess constructs meant to be adapted to human realities. Use them as they are intended—as resources to assist decision-making and safeguards to honor and protect everyone involved.

When you know your own journey of claiming and embodying your personal power, you will be a responsible lantern-bearer for others on that path. Empowerment cannot be forced. It must emerge from within each person. Your usefulness and effectiveness in this process has little to do with what you do and so much more with how you show up and how you bear and share your own power.

Suspend Judgment Long Enough to See Past It

We often define people by their actions as they interact with us or near us. It's easy to assume that what people do is a clear window into who they are. While there is truth in this claim, especially as it asks us to examine and assess patterns of repeated behavior in relationships, we too often use our immediate experiences to form snap judgments. We let individual moments of isolated behavior define people. In the process, we're liable to reduce someone's complex humanity to a narrow category—often expressed as a label.

Dull, drunk, spoiled, stuck-up, asshole, bitch, weak, damaged, irritating, needy, problem, trouble—these are a few of my ego's go-to labels. I'm not proud of them. I'll bet you have your own list.

Those of us with access to other frameworks and more clinical words might even go about diagnosing people based on a first impression or brief interaction: *narcissist, bipolar, codependent, psychotic.*

First, let's admit that this happens constantly, both in our personal lives and in our callings. Then let's get to work understanding what's happening when we do this and how we might expand our vision.

It would be a mistake to ignore or deny our natural tendency toward immediate evaluation and easy characterization. Snap judgments rise and fall within us every moment of every day. They are part of the complex and lightning-fast mental system of perception and action that allows us to navigate a million decisions each day of our lives. When it comes to sizing up other people, a snap judgment is a risk-assessment function of that self-protective ego whose alarms we examined in the last chapter.

If the ego gets its way, we will begin to behave in unkind and demeaning ways whenever we perceive that somebody doesn't look, think, choose, or act the way we want them to. These responses stem directly from the ego's basic belief in our own inherent superiority or supremacy. This is actually a self-protective response intended to shield us from a deeper fear about our inherent inferiority, unworthiness, and unacceptability.

Noticing our ego-fueled impulses to quickly assess and categorize potential threats is a fundamental step toward receiving information about people as input instead of conclusion. The key is to be aware that these impulses are trying to tell us something, and then to question that message. Connection to our core values and intentions helps us meet the ego's fear with alternative information. Self-awareness allows us to suspend judgment long enough to see what might be standing beyond it.

People tell us about their *current and unique experience* through their behavior. Any person's actions in any given moment provide a single window into what they are going through at *that moment*. Whatever we're seeing, feeling, hearing, and noticing is only a brief glimpse into a much bigger picture.

Holding this larger vision of another person can be difficult even in ideal circumstances. When emotions are high or conflict is involved, the ego's alarms within us get louder and strain our ability to keep the big picture in focus. Our urge to label and limit can become hard to resist.

This is where our enduring commitment to self-connected self-reflection is critically important. Let's explore the sensations, ideas, emotions, and actions that can be connected to the experience of judgment.

What does judgment feel like for you? What are the physical sensations that alert you to displeasure or disgust in response to yourself or someone else? I get a queasy, heavy feeling in my belly. I might also notice a quickening of my breath or an increase in my heart rate. Exploring judgment on the sensory level is a valuable initial step in the process.

Consider the thoughts that go through your mind when you notice yourself judging. Are you working out who's right or wrong? Are you preparing arguments or explanations defending your verdicts? There's no need to judge the voice of judgment. We seek to recognize it so that we can be aware of when it's speaking and decide how to respond.

Invest in your desire to understand what drives behavior in other people—especially the behavior that irritates or scares you. This has benefits beyond your capacity to help anyone. The simple desire to understand can interrupt your impulse to categorize or condemn. You cannot judge and understand at the same time. Invest in understanding.

Tune in to the emotional energy that arises for you when judgment narrows your vision. You might sense anger or sadness. It might feel like helplessness or hopelessness, frustration or rage. Opening to the messages of these emotions and responding with self-kindness allows us to dial down their energy and choose our behavior more freely.

And it's freedom we're seeking. The relational space beyond judgment is a place of mutual freedom in relationships.

As we access the wealth of information provided through our senses, thoughts, and emotions, we are more equipped to act in ways that align with our integrity. This is what transforms the limiting energy of judgment to the expansive energy of possibility. Without this ongoing transformation we risk treating ourselves and others with disrespect, disregard, and disapproval. These energies erode and undercut relationships and sabotage our service.

Become aware of your specific triggers and points of ignorance. Your list of snap judgment labels can be a good place to start. And start with yourself. Try treating your own limitations with respect and kindness. Love is always a safer place within which to evolve. Continue to cultivate your awareness and reflect on whatever comes up as a biased belief or unfair filter that is ready to be abandoned or altered.

As you do this, you'll be better prepared to notice and navigate moments of snap judgment and limited perspective. Be patient with yourself in the process. Count to ten when you need to. The space beyond judgment is a place where empathy can thrive.

What does judgment feel like for you?

Where does this feeling show up in your body?

Empathy and Imagination

Do you see yourself as an empath? Recently popularized, *empath* describes a person with heightened sensitivity to energy and emotions or someone who believes that they have the ability to absorb other people's feelings and states of being. Though it's defined vaguely and variously, the word gets a lot of buzz these days. It's a descriptive concept that many spiritual care providers, energy workers, and healers of all kinds identify with or even hang on their shingle.

Don't get hung up on the title. A capacity for empathy simply means that you are both attuned and sensitive to the energies around you. This might include people and environments and even animals.

Your sensitivity is a gift. Not everybody finds this gift helpful, though. Google the word and you'll find reams of information describing the downsides of being an empath, common characteristics of people who "feel too much," frequently asked questions about overload, and even guidance on how not to be such an emotional sponge.

As a service provider, you likely know a bit about empathy, and maybe you even see it as one of the tools of your trade. Empathy allows us to connect with and relate to people on an emotional level. Strike a bell and place it next to another bell, and they both begin to resonate with the same frequency. Empathy works in much the same way. An empathetic response to another's emotions provokes a similar note of vibration in our own emotional energy.

Contrary to popular belief, empathy is not the ability to feel another person's feelings. We can only feel our own feelings. It's possible you're very sensitive and have a heightened capacity to pick up on the vibes around you—remember, this sensitivity is a superpower—but it's impossible to make someone else's experience our own.

Whenever we feel an emotional response to someone else's emotional experience—regardless of what they're expressing—we are engaging in near-instant interpretation. We are effectively telling ourselves a story about the person's experience and responding with our own emotions. Empathy and imagination go hand in hand.

You may feel unrest or unease in certain situations or surroundings or after spending time with certain people. You are not, however, feeling other people's feelings. You are feeling your own feelings in response to your awareness of emotional energy. This may seem like a subtle difference, but it's important.

Empathy is a type of perception. It tunes us to another person's emotional reality. Empathy is part of our ability to connect meaningfully with others. Conscious service depends on our capacity for this unique aspect of emotional intelligence, and on the drive to care that often accompanies it.

Empathy is a powerful tool for service providers. It can bridge gaps between us and the people we serve, offering context that language isn't always able to convey. Empathy allows for an energetically informed glimpse into another person's experience. In an empathetic moment, we sense the nature of their emotional energy. We then interpret that sensation through our own personal lens.

Sometimes these moments become triggers for our own emotional response.

When that happens, we can lose touch with ourselves. This often starts with a feeling of surprise that quickly becomes resistance as we try to limit or control our own discomfort. Our resistance response not only temporarily shuts down our emotional expression; it also diminishes our ability to stay connected to what is happening in our interactions. Knowing how to be present and connected to what arises for you in these moments helps you stay engaged with the person across from you.

To remain present, we rely on the self-connected foundation for conscious service we established in the earlier chapters of this book. As your internal awareness and alignment skills deepen and mature, you become increasingly able to recognize your own resistance and soften it with acceptance. As you do, you become able to more quickly acknowledge and integrate your personal experience while remaining centered in your service role.

Scary as it may seem, the triggering moment can be your best friend.

All your emotions want is to be acknowledged. When you can gently say "I feel you," they will stop clamoring for attention. Space will open, allowing you to return to the present and remain engaged. When there is more for you to work through, you can return later to that emotional state and spend more time with the feeling.

Since emotions can feel so big, it's easy to mistakenly assume that dealing with them requires hours, days, months, and even years of heavy work. This mistake is rooted in our fear of discomfort. The longer we resist what we feel and the harder we try to ignore our emotional responses, the longer and more arduous the emotional journey.

As we practice attending to our own emotions with kindness, we can learn to connect with others without becoming confounded by the emotions they carry into the relational spaces we've built together. We will know more clearly when we're feeling personal emotional responses and when we are resonating with what another person has shared or expressed.

This is not always easy, of course.

Whether you're a hairdresser, a flight attendant, or a board-certified psychiatrist, people may share stories with you that are very difficult to hear. Sometimes we simply cannot imagine what their situation might feel like. Sometimes all we know is that we don't know, and all we feel is a kind of bone-chilling fear.

Fear is often a first response when someone shares a story of personal trauma. This is also empathetic. You are likely picking up a bit of the fear that this person is feeling as a result of trauma. However, even more so, you are likely to feel your own fear that something like that could ever happen to you.

In these moments, you might find that you resist the vision empathy offers. You don't want to go there. You don't want to even imagine what it feels like for that person. And it's okay. You can respond to your fear in the moment and come back to give it full voice later on.

At times like these, the most responsible move might be to share the truth. You honestly can't conceive of what they are going through, but you would like to be with them as they need and desire your presence. You are there. You are open and willing to sit with what might be very, very uncomfortable. Commit to drawing closer instead of stepping away. Commit to learning from the other person what will help them. This is exercise for your empathy muscles and the enduring challenge of self-connected service.

Is Empathy a Gift or a Curse?

Some see empathy as something we need to protect ourselves from. They point to emotional exhaustion, compassion fatigue, secondary trauma, and high rates of burnout among those of us in helping professions. They blame our capacity to feel for these real instances of suffering.

As well as being an insidious way of blaming victims for their own suffering, this perspective also offers solutions that ignore the relational reality of service and depend on disconnection rather than conscious connection and self-awareness.

In fact, as we care for people on their worst days, it's usually when we resist our natural talents and the places they guide us that we experience the most pain. When we buffer ourselves from the harsh realities we witness, we may arrive at disconnection, overload, or self-abandonment. Our frightened egos are screaming for the safety of distance while our empathetic hearts are urging us to remain close. This tension can create a great deal of disharmony inside us. Learning how to recognize and cope with it in healthy and positive ways will involve developing the capacity to be aware of the ego's alarms without allowing them to disrupt our focused presence with and for others.

Empathy is hard. People with empathy gifts often benefit from practices and strategies that help them navigate their highly tuned sensitive natures. Knowing when to open wider and when to conserve and cocoon can mean the difference between powerful connection and unbearable overwhelm. There is a time to express and a time to reflect. There is a time to absorb and a time to release. When we value the power of empathy instead of fearing it, we can create systems and structures that take these needs seriously and offer supports and training that encourage empathy instead of working against it.

How do you express your humanity within service-based relationships?

How are the gifts of empathy viewed in your workplace?

Each of Us a Mosaic

Broken. In bad shape. In need of repair. Used up. Empty.

These are words that we often use to describe the human condition. I feel this way more than I like to admit. Many of us who are witnesses to the worst of what people can do to each other have developed a bleak view of human nature and a skeptical stance toward possibilities. It's not just service providers, either. Whether it's through daily news reports or word-of-mouth stories of suffering or by their own direct experience, people can have a hard time feeling hopeful.

Our hopelessness is not limited to the way we see the outside world. When our gaze turns inward, it's often filtered with the same lens. We're disappointed by our mistakes, regretful about our choices, still stinging from old hurts. We look in the mirror and are exhausted by what we see. Too often we view ourselves as fixer-uppers—works in progress on our way to a set of goals that might make us more tolerable to ourselves and more attractive to others. Even our hope in these imagined outcomes is clouded by our doubts about our abilities to reach them.

Seeing yourself as broken and in need of fixing will eventually erode your ability to recognize your own light, and without that you become unable to detect wholeness in anyone else. No matter how strongly you try to resist it, you will end up seeing everyone as broken.

In service to others, we are already tilted toward this dim view. We have come to anticipate problems. We expect people to be in need of healing when they come to us. If everything were okay, we would wonder what they were doing here. Our experience has wired us to look for the points of pain, the scar tissue, the signs of shame.

Then we take it a step further and convince ourselves that we somehow have the power to fix what's broken in the people who come to us for help. We buy into this even while we're mentally mired in what we suspect is an irreparable state of personal brokenness—a state that we spend little energy trying to embrace or understand and use every available trick to hide.

How do we honestly admit all the brokenness that is so immediately apparent in the present moment while also holding the vision of our enduring wholeness? It can seem like either an impossible balancing act or an exercise in self-delusion.

It's neither. It's a matter of vision.

Instead of a sad pile of broken bits that need to be denied or hidden, what if each person is a beautiful mosaic that records the story of a life? What if nothing is broken after all? Rather, as the whole beings we are, what if all of our experiences—every lesson, every gift, every sorrow, *everything*—is ongoing evidence of our existence and our impact?

There is no one on this planet without importance and influence. This includes you. We may not be able to see all the ways in which our existence affects anything or anybody, but we can trust that it does.

Any healing journey requires this kind of trust. Transformation requires us to accept the truth of our worthiness and hold a deep inner assuredness that we are being led out of our woundedness and more deeply into integration. Healing demands surrender. And surrender occurs in the trust-filled moment.

As service providers, we must remember that this core worthiness is true for us and also for all who cross our paths. The man who spends his days on the street with a cardboard sign and a shopping cart has impact and purpose that surpasses his last known address.

The young woman with a developmental disability who struggles with her mom may be working through a lifetime lesson that will deepen her capacity for independence and offer an immense learning opportunity for her mother.

Your colleague secretly goes home every day to a bottle of wine and sinks into the depression and anxiety she has held at bay all day. She thinks she hides it, but everybody can sense she is struggling. She, too, is worthy—not only later, when she enters recovery, but today.

Yet, too often, we stand in the shadows passing judgment and soothing ourselves through comparisons of brokenness. *At least I've got a place to live,* or *What does she have to complain about?* or *I've got it worse.*

Are other people more or less broken than we are? Does having an addiction make you broken? Are people with developmental disabilities in need of fixing? Does staying in a shelter mean you are damaged goods?

When we have a vision of wholeness, we know that the answers to these questions are no, and no, and no and no. If we don't have a vision of wholeness, we need to pursue it, both for our awareness and acceptance of ourselves and for our capacity for compassion and connection with others. It will inform how we are led to respond in any situation, especially those in which our first impulse is to fix or flee or freeze.

Holding the vision of another's wholeness does not mean that we minimize their experience or their pain. Holding this vision invites our compassionate presence—a presence that's big enough to contain explanations, plans, strategies, and goals but will never be reduced to the task of fixing.

In a recent session with my spiritual advisor, she suggested that perhaps I was actually healed enough for the next part of my journey. Could it be possible that all my traumas and sorrows were not destined to forever be obstacles I could not live beyond?

What would happen if, as service providers, we took this same stance with the people we serve?

Embracing and embodying this generous vision means that we can see a path beyond the trauma and we'll keep our eyes on it for them while they make their way through the brush. We become truly equipped for that role when we ourselves have begun the journey.

Embrace the entirety of your being. Honor the wholeness of who you are, even as you are aware of every flaw and wrong step. Treat yourself gently. Not everything can be fixed and not everything needs to be. Let's instead celebrate the beautiful perfection of human imperfection. Everything leads us home eventually.

Which of your long-standing personal "flaws" can you embrace with kindness today?

We Are All Experts

In your role as a service provider, people will come to you seeking your guidance and input. At times they may even ask you to tell them exactly what to do next.

You may be tempted to oblige. It's an honor to be invited into someone's life.

And, as we've mentioned before, we also like to fix things we think are broken.

Desperation, self-doubt, and lack of experience can lead people to believe that they are not capable of determining their next best step. People can desire to be free of their current circumstances so deeply that they will follow any suggestion, even if it goes against their gut. Many people have struggled for so long that they can't even feel what their gut is telling them.

We have to get away from the idea that there is a single right or best answer to the problems and challenges that we human beings face. There isn't. There are as many paths as there are people, countless choices along each route. And each of us has the potential, whether it has been developed or not, to determine what direction is best suited to our moment and our need.

Someone may tell you a story that resonates so strongly, it propels you back to a similar experience of your own—how it felt and what it meant. In those moments, you will be strongly tempted to tell them the exact steps you took to move through the challenge. Try to breathe through this urge when you feel it. Give yourself a chance to contain your personal feelings and reactions, and return your presence and attention to the person across from you.

Insights gained through personal struggle are not one-size-fits-all. The pathways that led us out of despair or into health may not even show up on another person's radar. The tools that worked for us or the solutions we finally found may not fit their needs or match their goals. Just because something worked for you or didn't work for you doesn't mean anybody else will have the same outcome.

Our urge to supply solutions is not limited to practical problem-solving. It also affects our emotional care for people.

In an attempt to demonstrate your empathy and prove your ability to relate to someone's story or statement, you may have the urge to tell people, "I know how you feel." Don't. Resist that impulse. We don't know how another person feels. We know how *we* feel. When we suggest that we know what someone is going through, we minimize their experience. Even if we intend our remark as a way to make connection or establish rapport, this kind of us-centered interruption undercuts that desire. It may even shut down the possibility of further communication.

Why should I continue sharing my story if you already know how it ends? Why express myself if you can read me like a book?

Even when two experiences overlap so much as to appear identical, each one of us has our own interpretation of what has happened and our own complex response to it. We have our own journey through the event and its aftermath as well as any healing or integration that followed.

Taking a moment to remember and respect the difference and distance between you and the person you are with allows you to offer ideas and observations from a place of detachment. Detachment doesn't mean that you don't care; it means that you are able to stay open to outcomes that don't depend on you. Detachment means releasing any hold we have on whether the person we're serving accepts or rejects our offering. It helps us step away from our impulse to meet our need for significance by writing the next chapter in somebody else's story.

Detachment respects that we are all experts. Nobody knows me like me, and nobody knows you like you. Our self-perceptions may be skewed or undeveloped or limited, of course. We may need assistance and intervention and advice from people we invite into our lives, but each of us is uniquely equipped and intimately connected to our own stories.

Michael Ignatieff writes, "There are few presumptions in human relations more dangerous than the idea that one knows what another human being needs better than they do themselves." Taking this seriously means admitting that even if someone appears to be out of touch with their own good, we do not necessarily know better. To paraphrase St. Francis, we must wear our self-certainty like a loose garment. Our role is to walk with others as guides in a walk of mutual exploration and discovery. We may know the terrain, but we do not know the path. We don't take over. We don't impose. We don't get in the way.

When paired with trust and connection in respectful relationships, this kind of detachment sends the message that you see the other person as capable and whole regardless of their struggles and no matter what choices they may make. It allows you to stand in support of their discoveries and encourage the steps they take toward their own breakthroughs.

Bearing Witness

We service providers are less like carpenters and more like midwives. Our work is not so much about building from scratch as it is working with what is already taking place. Our efforts may facilitate growth and change and healing, but we don't make these things happen any more than a midwife creates a newborn child or a farmer causes the corn to grow or a parent makes a baby crawl.

Transformation is not something we do; it is something we witness. It's a process and a force that we participate in. Depending on our roles and our investments of energy and care, we can participate with skill or indifference, with love and vision or out of fear and ignorance. Conscious service asks us to take up this work in every area of our lives with skill and commitment powered by love.

Transformation simply *is*. It's how our lives work and how the ever-moving universe continues to exist. The changes we experience may be positive or negative—those are subjective judgments we make, and we've seen and endured both. We may be ready for it or completely surprised when it appears, but transformation happens.

People who are able to pay attention along multiple channels of awareness and communicate from a place of internal authenticity are better equipped to notice where and when transformation is happening and hold space for it to occur in the best possible way.

The vision of transformative relationships at the core of conscious service is about unity and partnership. It involves recognizing that we and the people we serve are together supporting the living thing that's coming to birth. Each person in the relationship has a role to play, energy to add, limitations and sources of power and hope to share.

If the carpenter stays asleep, the house won't happen. It's not the same with the midwife or the mother when the baby is on the way.

There's a limit to this metaphor, of course. What I hope it communicates is the truth that transformation happens in each of our lives whether we're attending to it or not. Change may be slow or subtle sometimes, but it is constant as corn growing and unstoppable as children learning to move under their own power. The crises that cause people to seek service and support from people like us are moments when some kind of change has suddenly sped up in their lives, or slowed to an unbearable crawl, or veered away from the direction of growth and expansion into scary territory or along an unknown or unwelcome trajectory.

Our roles and our gifts are intended to help us meet people in these places of crisis and build safe relational containers in which the worst effects of negative transformation can be softened and the most promising possibilities can be seen and grasped and lived toward.

No matter how much technical skill you bring to this relationship, it is not your expertise or sage guidance that will make the most difference to the people you hope to serve. It is your humanity. What makes it possible for connection to happen? Your capacity to show up in the fullness of your being while also recognizing and respecting a vision of the other person that both acknowledges and transcends the present moment. Embodying these qualities with integrity communicates your openness to the intimacy required in relationships of service.

When we embrace and deepen our capacity to create transformative relationships, the focus shifts from fixing broken things to engaging with other humans in a journey of mutual evolution. We move from seeing everything as a problem in need of solving to a vision of opportunity and possibility. This allows us to work for and witness positive transformation for others as well as ourselves.

CHAPTER 7

Create Community Together

An Invitation to Leadership

To create community together, there must be a *together*. For most of us, *together* means that we're in proximity to others as well as being closely associated with others. Our work as service providers requires us to be with people, for people, and about people. Our closeness and connection in these relationships is physical, mental, emotional, and spiritual. We've explored the intimacy and complexity of these connections and our responsibility for them in previous chapters.

It's worth noting that we are also closely associated with one another in our professional communities. Many of us serve alongside other people who share the same calling. This happens within our organizations and professional work structures as well as in the guilds, affiliations, and other formal or informal organizing structures that unite and support our vocations of service. To be able to make what we do together possible and productive, we must be organized and collected. Our communities—their systems, cultures, values, and people—must work.

In the last chapter, we explored relationships as places of power—places where the possibility for transformation begins. Our focus was on individual relationships, including the ways our personal relationships of trust and respect and honor can become containers for hope and growth. This includes family and friendship connections with the people closest to us, as well as the relationships of service into which we are invited as professionals and practitioners. In this chapter, we'll reimagine the broader organizational relationships of community and organizational life with similar ends in mind.

So often, we service providers experience our greatest stress in the context of community life. When we strive to meet deadlines, budgets, mandates, and missions that are seemingly imposed from beyond and directed by needs we can't understand, we can come away with a sense of powerlessness. We feel unable to effect change or experience growth. We feel isolated. We feel like whatever power or agency we possess is unwelcome or suspect. And as we immerse ourselves in the unrelenting demands of helping others, too many of us feel as though we've abandoned ourselves to a job that doesn't value us as people and a culture that doesn't practice what it preaches.

And we feel helpless to change any of it.

Health-care and human services organizations are often the least healthy places of employment. There is a paradoxical disconnect between what we know to be beneficial within helping relationships and what we ignore or overlook in our work environments. Stressful conditions between colleagues, misunderstandings with managers, and opaque or impersonal directives from on high too often make these cultures and communities draining instead of energizing, even if the stated mission is about wellness or health.

Within these organizations, at all levels of responsibility and role, we are at risk of disillusionment, disengagement, and burnout. Our organizations and communities have become fragmented, and they will eventually break down. We already see this in too many ways, including employee sickness, high turnover, and reduced quality of service. Our community dis-ease costs money and endangers people.

We know that this is the crux of many of our problems as we serve others. We need to rethink our systems, cultures, values, and structures. We need to heal our communities so that they can be a source of healing for the people we are driven to serve. To do that, we have to first see where we need to reconstruct our approach to working with each other—then we have to know how to change the ways we do our work. Only then can we become together the community we wish to be.

This requires leadership.

It is time for the innate strengths and natural talents of the individuals who make up the system to be freed to lead it. We need to use each person's deep capacity for engaged and creative leadership to help our organizations and communities become healthier and function better. When the structures that guide and support our work genuinely invite input and value personal expression, they can become communities of unbridled creativity, passion, and shared energy.

As we develop our shared workplaces along these lines, we will create opportunities for transformation in our multimember relationships as well as in our one-on-one interactions. We will begin to function less as a collection of individuals grinding away at unending tasks within inhuman organizations and more as a gathered group of leaders whose strength and focus combine to make our shared communities of care greater than the sum of their parts.

The system does not exist without the people. We are joined in creative communion, always.

■   ■   ■

Geese

I once heard a story about leadership from an Indigenous worldview.

A young man noticed one day how the geese fly in a V formation. He wondered why they did this, so he met with the geese and questioned them.

"Who is your leader?" he asked. "How do you know who's in charge?"

The geese replied that they were all leaders in their own way.

The young man had a better idea. He suggested they choose just one leader and fly in a straight line following the chosen goose.

The geese agreed to give this a try. The next day, they formed up and took off, flying across the sky in a straight line, with one special goose in the lead.

This went on for days, and day after day, the last goose in line became dinner for the eagle's family.

Acknowledging our own leadership qualities strengthens our ability to follow our own sense of guidance. Understanding that leadership is a shared responsibility allows us to be open to other points of view and find value in the challenges of collaboration and conflict, even as we stay grounded in our own integrity. And as we find this balance, we will be more likely to notice when one member of the community is in danger; that includes ourselves.

Like the geese in their formation, we all have responsibility to lead from our places along the V. Each of us has the potential to offer our unique gifts and talents in service to something beyond our own goals. We can fly for ourselves, even as we add our strength to the direction and movement of our community.

What characteristics of leadership do you already embody?

Which ones would you like to develop?

Power Is Power, Regardless of Role

In a hierarchy, just like in a single line of flying geese, it stands to reason that those at the top have the most power and decision-making authority. Some would say these positions entail the most responsibility as well. In the story about the straight-line geese, these also happen to be the birds least likely to get grabbed by a hungry predator.

Responsibility is subjective, however. The responsibilities of high-level leadership frequently come with a great amount of flexibility as well as freedom to delegate or make decisions that ease what could otherwise feel like a burden. These aspects of executive roles are luxuries that those lower on the ladder often lack.

Traditional views of supervision, management, and leadership are premised on the hierarchical structure we are used to in organizational systems. Power and authority go with specific roles, and these things flow upward on the org chart.

For too long, leadership has been equated with the duties of management. Managers oversee the work of others, direct projects and initiatives, determine what constitutes success, and reward or reprimand other employees. In many organizations, leadership only means being *the boss*, the person with the power to hire and fire.

What if we considered the possibility that our role in an organization—our job title—does not determine our power in it?

As we've explored the shape and use of personal power in previous chapters, we've seen that it isn't a commodity that can be banked and traded or bestowed or lost; it's an energy that is available to everybody, even as we access and express it in ways that are unique to each of us. The power we connect to in our personal and service relationships is the same power we bring to our communities and workplaces. How we use and share this energy within our organizations can make all the difference in the world when it comes to co-creating community.

Regardless of our role, each of us has the power to contribute to the overall health of the organizations we serve within, as well as the specifics of their shape and structure. It's helpful to think of this type of power as authority.

Authority, in this case, means what you bring to the table—what you authentically contribute. Seen in this manner, authority isn't what gives you power over other people or situations. Instead, it's a demonstration of the personal power that grounds and focuses your gifts and makes who you are and what you do matter to the people around you.

You can probably picture the people you've worked with who have had an authoritative presence and shared it in ways that went beyond their assigned role in the organizational hierarchy. Their contributions likely emerged in a manner that deepened the bonds you had as colleagues and made the organization's mission come alive in ways that made you proud to work there.

These personal aspects of authority and power don't always translate into an official position of leadership within organizations. As we actively cultivate the capacity for co-creating community in our workplaces, we will provide opportunities for all members to embrace the responsibility for leadership at various times.

Leadership does not happen *to* us. We are active participants in offering our authority and exercising our power for the well-being of the community. You may lead various committees or work groups involved in specific projects or share your burning passion for something that would benefit the workplace. Opportunities to lead will present themselves. As you step into them with integrity, others will resonate with your authority and follow your lead. Whether your contributions are recognized formally with an enhanced position or increased salary won't matter as much, because you will feel fulfilled and energized by what you are doing and how it enhances the community.

And, quite often, more opportunities for leadership, as well as the change in roles and recognition that can accompany good leadership, will begin to emerge.

Culture and Change

The role of workplace and community culture has become a major focus in discussions about organizational development and effectiveness. What do we mean when we use the word *culture* to describe an organization or an industry?

From an anthropological perspective, culture consists of norms, values, rituals, traditions, beliefs, and symbols that any group of human beings agree have a shared meaning and enough significance to guide our common life and work. Culture establishes the rules we generally operate by within these human systems. Of course, not everybody in any group follows these rules to the letter, but even rule breakers and outlaws have a sense of what it is they're breaking and what the law that they're trying to elude looks like.

Culture provides a road map of sorts, or a basic blueprint that frames and informs the actions, decisions, approaches, and practices of any group. One of the beautiful aspects of human culture is that its details are constantly changing and evolving to fit the needs of the time and place.

The culture of a workplace or an organization shares the qualities of any human group. Among a great many other things it does, culture describes what's acceptable and expected in the organization, who has formal power, who has informal power, how we do things around here, and what language we use to describe our work and communicate with each other. Culture defines which contributions matter and what they're worth in terms of reward. It outlines how conflict will be handled and what resolution looks like. It even covers aspects of behavior as basic as dress and tone of voice and what kind of coffee ends up in the break room (as well as who makes it).

Across the countless individual workplace cultures, there is also a basic understanding about healing and helping professions and vocations that serve human needs. Sometimes we call this the *culture of service*. This understanding has been influenced by religious ideas, political and economic structures, educational agendas, and the changing demands of our humanity.

Many of the assumptions that underlie the idea of a culture of service deserve a review and reboot. As I've mentioned earlier in this book, we often equate service with sacrifice. Being "selfless" has been touted as an indicator of pure intention and noble character. Guided by this basic image of altruism and other-focused self-sacrificial generosity, our society has drawn a simplified image of what happens in a vocation of service: a person who *has* something gives it to someone who lacks it—an act that declares and demonstrates a greater interest in others than in oneself.

Even if we disagree with such ideas about service, we can't blame anybody else for the creation of these cultural assumptions. We are each involved in creating and perpetuating culture, even if we feel mired in it without a choice. Culture is created through the active, albeit often subconscious, participation of everybody it encompasses.

Must we stay stuck in this old paradigm of sacrifice, lack, and dysfunction? Must we unreasonably and unsustainably elevate those who provide service and unfairly and inhumanely denigrate those who receive it? Are we able to shift into a new paradigm that holds the promise of creativity, fulfillment, and quality? The service culture I want to promote and enjoy—as provider *and* as recipient—is characterized by transformation, connection, contribution, reciprocity, growth, and joy.

When we talk about organizational culture, it can be easy to think in terms of what seems impossible to affect or influence. Culture feels so big and enduring that it seems like individual actors have no power to make change. We are, of course, influenced and shaped by the cultures that we are involved in. But we are also influencers in these human systems. To think of culture as an entity that exists beyond us is to deny our inherent role in creating it, keeping it going, and changing it when it has outlived its usefulness.

Just look at how we rallied to respond to the immediate needs that emanated at the onset of the coronavirus pandemic. If we have learned anything in this season of challenge and change, it's that we have the capacity to respond and shift culturally when it's a matter of life and death.

I'd like to think we can do it with much less pressure.

Ideally, we are nurturing organizational and community cultures that allow us to not only survive threats like pandemics, but also meet all kinds of challenges and thrive while we do it.

The fear of trying new things is often met with the old adage "We tried that before and it didn't work." Cultural change-makers will, instead, say, "That was then and this is now. Things have shifted, and what was not feasible then might now be the perfect solution."

Don't get stuck in thinking that culture is just the way it is. It's not. It is mutable and malleable, and we have the collective power to mold it.

How would you describe the culture of service?

What are the characteristics of the current cultural environment within which you serve?

Supportive Community and Service Provider Well-Being

What happens to our health when our happiness is seen as optional in our organizations, or when we're stressed by competing demands? What happens to our presence in and commitment to our work in these times?

The view from joy is vastly different from the view from despair. When I feel good, I have greater understanding and compassion. When I'm feeling bad, I become more cynical. Feeling bad makes it more likely that I will see myself as bad. Remnants of shame often become more evident when we are distanced from the energy of love. This can create an opening for self-abandonment to creep in. Maladaptive and addictive behaviors are directly related to the state of our health and happiness. When we exist in a state of balance and harmony, there is little desire to seek outside of self to feel better. It's not even a question.

When we are in the business of service to humanity, these concerns must affect our organizational commitments. We are entitled to receive the benefits that we offer the people who depend on our care. Our health, happiness, and well-being must be part of the equation. Our organizations' mandates call them to respond to our needs just as we respond together to those we serve. We cannot have one without the other.

When we service providers become overwhelmed and feel overlooked—when we begin to slide into spaces of self-abandonment and despair—it is crucial that we can experience our work communities as safe havens. Just as individual service relationships can be secure containers for crisis and incubators for healing, our organizations can hold these things when we need them ourselves. We need built-in support to explore what ails us, and we need active partners in the restoration of our physical, emotional, and behavioral health.

So, how do we do this?

A community's responsibility to people on the brink of self-abandonment begins long before that crucial moment of crisis. We have to build relationships of trust—relationships with the strength to contain the types of transformation we explored in the last chapter. The more we invest in relationships of mutual respect, patience, and intuitive intimacy, the earlier we'll be able to recognize when those around us might be challenged by things they aren't talking about.

Transformative relationships are most easily cultivated when everyone is feeling good, open, receptive, and healthy. In times of conflict or collective stress, it can be easy to shy away from friends and colleagues when we're struggling personally. Taking the time to cultivate transformative relationships in the easier seasons builds a bridge that you can cross when someone has slipped into self-isolation.

With this groundwork laid, you will have the courage required to open up sensitive conversations and ask difficult questions. To do this is to demonstrate loving-kindness. This gesture may be the key to another's restoration.

Many service providers pride ourselves on our ability to show up for other people in ways that many would see as being superhuman in nature. In the process, we can get used to bypassing our own needs and, before we know it, we slip into a hole of self-abandonment so deep that our only chance of survival is to reach out for someone's hand.

As a service provider, you will experience times when you are that hand for others and times when you will need another's hand to cling to. Be willing to flow in that reciprocal space. Reach out when you need to, and extend when you can.

Suspend judgment and see beyond it. We don't need to concern ourselves with how someone has found themselves in their circumstances or why they didn't seek support sooner or how easy it appears, from where we sit, to make the necessary changes or fix the situation. When we extend our hand to someone who is struggling, our only concern is to be real and present with the intention of being kind.

Culture is what we do. The integrity of our cultures of care depends on how what we do relates to who we say we are together. The culture we create demonstrates how we support our community as well as how we define it. Any organizational policy or set of guiding values that articulates or suggests an approach of openness, acceptance, kindness, and compassion for those served by the agency must extend the same to those who serve *within* the agency.

There Is No Such Thing as Neutral

In our discussions about personal responsibility, we explored and embraced the freedom that comes with the ability to respond to situations instead of reacting to how we feel about them. We get to choose how we respond.

I don't always feel like I'm fully standing in the power of this freedom. Sometimes, I feel myself reacting as though it's beyond my control. These days, this reaction is usually internal, and I am grateful for the opportunity for space and time my modicum of self-awareness provides before what's going on inside me becomes apparent to everyone around me.

At our best, we take moments of self-connected pause to reclaim our power to choose, and then respond in ways that align with our values. This level of responsibility does not make us immune to the natural gut reactions and emotional triggers that arise within; it just gives us the freedom to decide how we will move through the next steps as they unfold.

But one thing is for sure: we are always choosing something. Always. Yelling your head off in frustration is a choice. Sitting quietly while you fume on the inside is a choice. Being mindfully present in a place of peaceful detachment is a choice. And our choices matter. Each action or nonaction is a contribution to some relationship. In community context, our choices affect the greater whole.

I used to believe that if I kept my mouth shut during a discussion that was leading to a decision I didn't agree with, I was remaining neutral and could not be seen as a contributor to the outcome. I was wrong. Everyone is contributing—either to maintaining a situation or to changing it. There is no such thing as neutral. We almost always have a preference, even when we might feel detached from the outcome.

Withholding my concerns or refusing to suggest alternatives was actually silent agreement. Each time I sat on my hands, I was accepting the freedom to choose, but I was rejecting my responsibility to align my actions with my values. Each time I stayed silent instead of speaking up—whether out of fear, frustration, or just plain fatigue—I stepped out of integrity. And every time I did that, I felt more and more discomfort.

Even in my silence, I was sharing. Even in choosing to hold back my comments, I was contributing an energy of *againstness* that I didn't have the guts to own and offer. I secretly hoped someone else would speak up and share my views. Maybe then I would second the motion.

Who wants to be the one that always goes against the grain?

If you see yourself here, this is a time for immense grace and gentle care. It's only fear that stands in our way when we hold our tongues. At some point, the fear will pale in comparison to the discomfort of misalignment you feel. Sooner or later, this pain will fuel your courage to voice your truth.

Just remember that you don't have to wait for the pain. Choose integrity every time.

Detachment is not the same as neutrality. And compromise always has a place at the table when we are co-creating community. But we must follow through on the commitments we make to ourselves, even when we worry we won't be heard.

When have you kept silent in order to appear neutral?

What scares you most about disagreeing in public?

Anita's Gift

Anita invited me to develop and facilitate training activities for a team of early childhood educators in a local child care center. She was the director of the center and was excited to learn more about the relationship between personal and professional development. She spent a great deal of time nurturing her personal curiosity, reading and learning as much as she could about emerging philosophies.

Anita found ways to incorporate these new ideas into her approach to leadership. She wanted me to help her bring these ideas to the rest of the team and to work together to find ways to apply them to their workplace. She saw this training as a way to help her team members celebrate their strengths, build their capacity for self-connection, and more creatively address the challenges they encountered. She wanted to make space for leadership to develop in every area of the organization.

Anita and I worked together to gather resources and plan out the workshops. At times we invited other members of the team to share input and suggest direction. We planned ways to invite participants to contemplate questions and set intentions even before the workshops began.

When we did gather the team in session, the content was relevant to their context. Instead of using outside case studies or scenarios to illustrate the concepts, we drew from the experience of the organization and the expertise of the team's members to create opportunities for meaningful discussion focused on real circumstances.

We talked about the qualities that the group admired in each member and also discussed the challenges and tensions that might be present within some working relationships. Because Anita had established clear guidelines for this work, we were able to use these real situations to apply novel approaches to communication and reflection. Learning and application happened in real time and had immediate effect.

It was hard work for those involved—emotional, thought provoking, and in-depth. Because it was both relevant and respectful, it was meaningful and useful. Anita's initial effort set the stage for authentic transformation to occur within the workplace. Her collaborative approach created safety, promoted personal responsibility, and honored individual needs.

This particular leader treated her group well. Because they were included in the design and prepared for the process, they were ready and willing to engage in this deep-level interpersonal and intrapersonal work. They could grasp the work's importance to their personal well-being as well as its impact on the quality of their service as child care providers.

Most of us know what it's like to attend a workshop or seminar and leave at the end of the day feeling inspired and renewed in our perspective. We also likely share the experience of arriving back to "reality" and feeling these things fade into memory. It's really challenging to step outside of our comfort zones when we are back in the midst of daily busyness. Applying new ideas and practices to our routines takes a huge amount of cognitive and emotional energy—sometimes so much that we're tempted to stop even before we start. This is where an enlightened leader can make so much difference.

Anita was this leader. She integrated the ideas shared in the workshop into daily, weekly, and monthly practices. She incorporated the insights of the team into policies and procedures as well as encouraged their application in both face-to-face and written communication. She made sure that the philosophies were applied and supported. Plainly put, Anita demonstrated integrity. This is the single most powerful thing that any leader, teacher, or service provider can ever do.

Anita also recognized the leadership skills and potential possessed by the people she worked with. She became committed to nurturing the expression of each member's personal genius. The team members who were ready to step into leadership positions were poised for breakthrough opportunities and growth. As she went about consciously building a culture and community based on the values of mutual honor and shared curiosity, Anita also developed a brilliant way to begin succession planning. The community they built together formed a pipeline of committed, connected, and deeply co-creative leaders.

Leaders like Anita have vision not only for the overall direction of an organization, but also for the culture of the workplace. This vision allows them to see the best in all community members. Leaders with vision are able to believe in possibility, approach change and growth from a place of creativity, model and promote the spirit of inclusion, and celebrate the journey from beginning to end with all its ups and downs. If this reminds you of the qualities of the transformative service relationships we explored in the last chapter, it should. They grow on the same tree. Truly transformational leaders make it their business to encourage all community members and to set the stage for enlightened communication, connected relationships, and creative communion.

Who has been your best boss?

What made this person's leadership valuable and memorable for you?

"Labor vs. Management" Is Unhelpful

Most of us have experienced some kind of us-against-them mentality in our work. Sometimes this shows up as service providers seek to self-protect from the emotional demands of the people we serve, but more often than not it applies to tension with our colleagues. Sometimes it can seem as if people who share an organization and a values-guided mission aren't on the same team.

Many of us have experienced difficulties with or disconnection from those tasked with managing or leading our organization. This includes doubt about their plans or goals, confusion about policy decisions, and professional disagreements about where the boots-on-the-ground work needs to be done and how it's assessed or valued.

Remember, all of this is information, even if it comes freighted with emotional energy. Disagreement indicates a need for discussion. If things were perfect, we wouldn't be having these conversations.

Many organizational cultures have attributed high levels of power, superiority, and value to management and leadership roles. This has contributed to inequality, competition, and control in the workplace.

But it doesn't have to be this way.

Leaders and supervisors are human beings. Despite what you may feel at times, they have not been granted power over you. Unfortunately, some leaders believe that they have. This often leads them to abuse the authority of their position. Even if it doesn't cross the line toward abuse, it always feels awful.

In truth, no manager or leader can inhibit your progress along your career path. I know that might be a tough pill to swallow. You might be shaking your head in disagreement. You'll argue that your current supervisor could easily get in the way of your progress at work if you didn't abide by their wishes. You can't wrap your mind around the idea that they really have no power over you and your success. And it certainly might feel like a power imbalance. I'm telling you this is a matter of perception.

I can still feel your disagreement. And I know that it can be very challenging to work through a situation with your supervisor where you feel you have no control over what happens.

The first step begins with shifting your view of the situation.

Suppose your supervisor continually overlooks your contributions, rewarding a colleague for similar actions while refusing you a raise and promotion year after year. You could let this make you feel thwarted, nervous, angry, and without options. On the other hand, if you take away the superhuman qualities that you have assigned this person, you might connect with your sense of personal power and responsibility for your own intentions, and then you would have greater potential and energy for finding common ground.

No matter what anyone else is doing, you still have the ability to declare what and how you wish to contribute. You can still embrace and employ your innate talents. You can give voice to the directions you would like to move in and take responsibility for your own learning curve. You are ultimately responsible for how you show up. You do not need to allow narrow-minded thinkers and outdated models of leadership to stand in your way.

Even when it might feel like there is nothing you can do, there is always a choice to be made. You never have to remain in a position where you feel controlled or stagnant. You have the power to create a different experience for yourself. Reclaim that power.

If we stay connected to ourselves and our power, if we stay engaged in clear and courageous communication, and if we trust the strength of safe relationships to support transformation, we decrease the chances that we will find ourselves in interactions that feel nerve-racking and personally threatening. Issues that need to be addressed will come to the table and be sorted as they arise. You won't have to wait for a periodic review or be blindsided by unexpected feedback.

Even when our supervisory relationships are imbued with a sense of partnership and reciprocity, too many of us continue to suspect that we might "get in trouble" for something we have done or neglected to complete. We worry that we cannot trust our own intuition or that some-one else knows more about our work experience than we do ourselves.

Don't get stuck in old thought patterns that leave you feeling less than powerful. Don't surrender self-connection for self-doubt. Know yourself. Be confident in what you bring to your role, and allow yourself to be filled with enthusiasm and energy for the work of your calling. Be proud to identify your areas of highest contribution as well as those areas you wish to cultivate. Be open to others' input and actively seek out feed-back and alternative perspectives.

Do you look forward to connecting with your supervisor? Why or why not?

If you supervise others, how do you interpret your role?

Transparency and Authenticity Go Hand in Hand

Building communities and cultures that respect and value all their members requires transparency between the organization's leadership and each person within it. Not everything can be fully see-through, of course. Rules about personal privacy and confidentiality exist for good reasons. Privacy respects autonomy and prevents abuse—central concerns in any organization with integrity.

The type of transparency required of us as we create community together is about honesty and inclusion. As we build these types of partnerships, transparency essentially means we know all we need to know about the things that involve or affect us and the people and processes we are responsible to and for.

Transparency doesn't mean every little detail about every little thing. It's about relevance. Most of us don't actually want to know every detail about everything. We want and deserve the pertinent information about matters that impact or include us.

As it relates to the co-creation of community and the functioning of our organizations, transparency is similar to the clarity at the core of enlightened interpersonal communication. It means relevant information is delivered in honest and open ways to whoever needs it. The aim is for everyone to be well equipped to manage whatever situation is at hand and to be prepared to operate in the highest capacity.

Many organizations operate with an open-door policy. In these communities, people with offices rarely close their doors. When they do it is for privacy and confidentiality. Apart from those times when interactions with others require the confidentiality of a private space, lots of closed doors in any office often indicates that something might be brewing beneath the surface.

Emira recalls such a time in her organization. Several coworkers, including the CEO, had endured a year filled with losses, including divorces, and personal struggles. Walking through the hallways sometimes felt like entering a morgue. Some colleagues lacked energy and seemed unable to focus, while others were irritable or downright angry. People were ineffective at their work, communication was stunted and rigid, and the overall feeling was stagnant.

At times, Emira could literally feel certain people walk through the door. She could sense their scowl before she laid eyes on them.

It was not an easy time.

In addition to the dampened day-to-day community spirit, morale was eroding at a deeper level. Emira began doubting her safety and stability in her work. She started to second-guess herself, and she didn't feel nearly as comfortable voicing her concerns or opinions as she had in previous years.

A clandestine fog overshadowed the daily operations, coupled with a tight-lipped and impatient tone at team meetings. Everybody noticed, but nobody spoke of it. People seemed to just adapt and cling to the hope that this would pass.

But, when the agency was faced with an unexpected dilemma that threatened to cost them significant funding, the state of the community could no longer be ignored.

The senior management team decided to meet on their own to figure out what needed to be done. They decided to come up with a plan and then just tell everyone how it would be. They wanted to be true to their values and ensure the clear and transparent communication process that they used to enjoy, but they doubted it was possible in the current climate. They all knew morale was low, but even among themselves they didn't want to talk about it. There just wasn't time to get into the feelings involved. They had to make some decisions, and they felt they had to make them fast.

LaDonna, one of the program directors, convinced the team to at least seek some feedback from others. The team invited a few key people to a brief meeting to get their reactions to the solutions that they were considering.

Emira was one of those few who had the opportunity to offer her ideas and feedback. She did her best to be honest and forthright, but she held back. Even though the team presented the meeting as an open discussion where all ideas were welcome, it didn't feel that way to Emira. She had the sense that there really was only one acceptable answer, and she had a feeling the decision had already been made.

And she was right.

When Emira reflects on this event, she can see that her trust in the process was damaged because the leadership team handled this challenge without regard to the enduring problem of morale. She sees this event as a direct catalyst to the movement to unionize that got underway about six months later.

Describing a process as open and transparent and actually *being* transparent are two very different things. At times, of course, full disclosure and consultation are not possible. But if this particular incident had been one of those times, then there would have been no need to ask for input from workers like Emira.

Had the leadership team instead made the decision and shared their solutions while honoring the reality that there had been little time for consultation, people might have been angry, but they wouldn't have felt duped. This challenge also could have been an opportunity for the leaders to acknowledge the low state of morale and invite people to work together toward improving the agency culture and returning to the shared values at the heart of their purpose.

Respecting other people means sharing your truth with them—especially when people might already sense that you're not coming clean. Nothing damages a relationship or frays a sense of community more than trying to convince people to go against their own intuition.

When we own our opinions and observations as well as our intentions, we reduce the potential for developing mistrust. We might be wrong, and we can be responsible for that too, but at least we are telling the truth about where we stand. This is transparency. And, as in Emira's situation, these decisions can impact an entire group of people.

Transparency and authenticity go hand in hand. This means that, as leaders, we reflect the truth of who we are, what we think, and how we feel in clear and direct ways. You are not required to share what you are not ready to share. Choose your transparent moments with courage and clarity. Reflect upon any fears that might be holding you back, and be patient with others as they work through their own.

Where is your comfort level with transparency in your personal and professional relationships?

What can you do to create a greater sense of security within?

When We Need the Support of Our Community

Service providers who struggle with substance use disorders or other addictive patterns commonly go into hiding. Many of us don't feel safe enough to disclose these conditions and the problems they create in our lives and seek the support we need. As a result, our struggles stay isolated from any possible help. They go underground and frequently become more and more destructive. When I realized that I was at my lowest point, I considered making up a story about it all—anything to keep from having to reveal what I felt at the time was a personal weakness. I tried to justify this avoidance by telling myself that my employer wouldn't understand and I would somehow tarnish my reputation or destroy my career.

Intuitively, I knew that trying to keep hiding would have caused the real damage. If I wanted freedom, I wouldn't find it by covering up the truth.

So, I told it.

And my employer met me with respect. I had a conversation with the executive director on a Sunday at her home. I acquired a doctor's note, sought out a referral, and before I knew it, I was scheduled to enter treatment.

I found myself in a constant state of "What the fuck?" Was this really happening?

It was the best thing I ever did for myself. I developed skills and strategies. I received compassionate service. I engaged. I connected. I met people. I found myself.

If you've struggled with substance use or any addictive pattern in your life, you can likely relate when I say that this experience, now thirty years in the rearview mirror, was not the end of my story of healing and recovery. My twenty-eight-day program wasn't a fix-all that prevented me from ever dancing with that particular devil again. Our shadows are lifelong companions.

But I have come to recognize that I have learned enough and healed enough to be ready to face what is in front of me now.

The messiness of life is not the exception; it's the rule. Life, with all its conflicts, setbacks, and suffering, is an ongoing opportunity to learn and grow, even when we are in the thick of it.

And when we who have benefited from the kindness and respect of those who received us with compassion can become strands of the safety net for others, we have the chance to pass along that grace and love.

That is what authentic community is about. We don't say, "You are a part of us as long as you meet these specific criteria." Rather, we gather around each other. We shelter in times of heavy rains. We don't hide the umbrella.

When we don't meet each other with care, we run the risk of losing each other.

I was lucky. My employer supported me, no questions asked. They worked with me to prepare for my absence and to ensure that continuity of service was held. Our collaborative, proactive approach prepared me and the organization to move through the process with a sense of security. In a time of great personal uncertainty, this was one less thing I had to worry about.

My employer did not pressure me for details. They did not compel me to share. I was not required to provide updates about my treatment. Disclosure was my call. My choices were respected. I shared what was relevant to the community as it impacted them and held close what was private to me.

I had decided early on that responsible transparency would be my ultimate protection. Authenticity did not need to mean full disclosure with everyone around me. I could trust myself to share my experience where and when I felt safe to do so, and as it was relevant to the situation or relationship. Truth was safer than fiction. It was a relief for me to not have to put up a front. I hope that I led by example and encouraged others to do what I did.

Sometimes, our darkest hour can illuminate the path we need like nothing else. You can tap into personal courage and power to create the safe conditions in which you can speak up about private struggles. Each of us has an opportunity to shift the expectations we hold of ourselves and each other as service providers. We have the opportunity to reconnect to our humanity, which enhances our ability to connect with others. We are not immune to the challenges that face those we serve, and faking it only weakens our ability to help.

If you find yourself struggling with personal challenges, resist the urge to hide. Even if others don't fully understand you, you are demonstrating your desire to understand yourself as you claim the truth of your circumstance.

There is power here, and it ripples. Even if some others offer judgment and harsh assessments, you will not notice it as much as you would if your own internal space were one of criticism and condemnation. Be the first one to step up for yourself. Even here, embrace your leadership. Show others how to treat you in your time of need. Expect to be met where you are.

I can say without doubt that I was met with love.

When it's a matter of our life and death—literally or figuratively—we are in the vicinity of our deepest stores of resilience. When you think you can't continue, you actually stand at the gateway of expanded capacity.

Just walk through.

Navigating Conflict with Safe Sounding Boards

How do you feel when you think about being in conflict with someone? Most of us dread this part of community life. If you're like me, the prospect of open conflict makes you clench up. Our throats close and our insides become knotted. Fear leads us to imagine that facing the conflict will have disastrous outcomes. Our self-protective egos tell us we are better off avoiding the disagreement and anyone connected to it. Call in sick. Fake a cramp. Run and hide.

If left untended, however, conflict only gets worse and our discontent brews and amplifies, leading to an ongoing sense of irritation. That irritation will play out in our interactions with the other person—our tone of voice, our quick dismissal of anything they say—and it will inevitably affect us in truly negative ways. Long-standing low-grade annoyance rooted in unresolved conflicts with others is a slow and invisible killer of your spirit and your capacity for compassion.

It also hurts, slows, and complicates whatever you're trying to do together.

When conflict arises in a community and you have a responsibility for addressing it, a great way to start is by processing your options with a person you think of as a safe sounding board. Safe sounding boards are people you trust who can offer you sacred space for reflection, support, and redirection.

Together with a safe sounding board, you can experiment with ideas and test possible responses before you go into a conflict-heavy situation. You can float ideas and concerns in exchange for impressions or opinions. This feedback is crucial when you need clarity or simply another perspective on the matter.

In practical terms, safe sounding boards embody unconditional acceptance and respect. The ability to listen with openness and support is the primary qualification. The best sounding boards are able to provide an engaged and focused presence—even if you're angry or upset or emotionally activated.

Your safe sounding board sees *you,* beyond whatever you're experiencing at the moment. They know you to be capable and are highly skilled at transcending their own judgment. You've selected this person because you know that you will not lose their respect, no matter what you divulge.

It may be tempting to try to recruit your safe sounding board to your side of the conflict. This is natural. We all want and need allies. But this person is not here to fight. They are on your side without taking sides. They will not add fuel to the fire. They will not provide you with reasons to stay angry, hurt, powerless, and frightened. Their task in this role is to help you shift away from the heat and emotion of your struggle and to encourage you to see more deeply into the learning opportunity it offers.

Safe sounding boards are like champions who help you keep your eyes on the prize. They don't try to protect you from experiences that are designed for your growth, because they know you've got what it takes to master the challenge.

Choose your sounding boards carefully. Identify these people before you're mired in conflict, while you're self-connected and thinking clearly about what you'll need, a state that might be harder to reach after an upsetting conflict arises. You may want to seek out someone who has a different worldview than you. A contrasting perspective can be helpful.

Your sounding board must also be able to listen without defensiveness. If your respect for a person under consideration as a sounding board is at all tentative, do not ask them to fill this role. You are not likely to clearly hear their input, let alone consider what they offer as an option for your growth.

As you speak with your sounding board, work to remain open and receptive. Center yourself before you begin. Ensure that your heart feels safe and protected enough to receive whatever may arise. This fosters self-trust and a sense of control. Know that you can stop the conversation at any moment and come back when you feel ready.

In this state of open receptivity, it will be easier to let go of your defenses and suspend your own judgment as you receive feedback. You will be more able to remain in a state of curiosity as you consider any questions your safe sounding board might pose. In the safety of this space, you can begin to detach from the outcomes that you thought you wanted and open to alternatives and possibilities.

In the midst of our struggles, it can be extremely difficult to resist the urge to defend ourselves. If we feel we have been wronged, it's hard to consider what part we have played in the whole mess. Safe sounding boards encourage us to do that in loving and nonconfrontational ways, always with the intent to grow.

Life is one big learning journey. There are opportunities to grow and expand every day. Sometimes these opportunities arrive wrapped in delight and ease, and sometimes they come salted with conflict. There is always something new to discover. Safe sounding boards can provide powerful support for this process.

Whom do you go to for the kind of feedback a safe sounding board can provide?

What steps can you take to become a sounding board for someone else?

No Room for Ego

Close your eyes. Imagine a time when you were in the flow. Everything was moving along with ease. It almost felt like floating. Other people were involved, each acting and responding with complete precision. Effortless. Alignment. Ease.

Remember our discussion of synergy? The word literally means "together energy." It's a term that describes how community functions and feels when it's at its best.

Does this sound like a fantasy? Is it beyond imagining that you could function this way with the people who share your life?

It takes a little work and a lot of patience, but creating an energetic symphony of momentum and collaborative creation is a real possibility. And once you've got the momentum, it's hard to stop it.

I recall an experience I had with group synergy that has since become a benchmark for me in terms of ideal teamwork situations.

Our organization pulled together a committee tasked with the job of reviewing our ethical practices and policies. We had faced a couple of situations that we hadn't seen coming, and as a community we were questioning our capacity to meet the changing needs of the people we served over the long term of their care.

People came from different parts of the organization to form this committee. Some of us were aligned in belief and approach, and others seemed to be coming from left field. Luckily, our team had already invested time and energy in developing our capacity for enlightened communication within the organization. We had become more comfortable facing our conflicts and more patient and willing to understand our differences. So, even if handling those conflicts wasn't particularly fun, it was more comfortable than it might have been.

In our shared work, all of our efforts to improve communication were put to the test. We grappled with challenging scenarios that stirred up varied responses. After all, ethical considerations frequently reside in gray areas, even as we often have very black-and-white views of what seems right and wrong. We all had to look inward and bring our authentic selves to the work we did together.

Reviewing current policies, modifying language that we had outgrown as an agency, aligning practices with our newfound values, and creating fresh and innovative approaches to serious situations proved very challenging.

We started out by creating some ground rules to guide us through the process. This included how often we would meet and for how long, as well as how we wished to communicate throughout the meetings. We identified the tasks we needed to complete and created timelines within which to reach our goals or evaluate our progress. We agreed to delegate research between meetings and be prepared for each gathering with the information required to take the next steps.

It was clear that each person sitting at that table was committed and interested. It was easy to invest energy in a group process aimed at a common goals that we all held close to our hearts: our own well-being, the safety of those we served, and the quality of our service.

Committee members wanted to be on the cutting edge of a more progressive approach to ethical management. We felt like pioneers, and we carried that sense of adventure into each meeting over a period of several months.

When we completed the project, every member of that committee felt more connected as colleagues. We had all known each other as part of the agency, but we left this experience feeling a much stronger sense of camaraderie and personal and professional connection.

The varied perspectives around the table could have easily gotten in the way of a smooth and productive process. Instead, we became able to appreciate the differences. In fact, we celebrated them, because we trusted each other and valued input, even when it challenged our own personal viewpoints. We knew that we needed a variety of perspectives in order to see what we might otherwise miss. We embraced the positive energy of conflict. We sought reciprocal interactions, calling on each other to serve as sounding boards and to give feedback. We each spread our wings and felt our power as we flew in the same direction, each taking the lead at different times—each watching for each other to be sure no one was left behind.

In the end, not only did we innovate a whole new process for ethical management that aligned with our declared values and mission; we also strengthened our relationships. The policies produced by this co-creative community made a difference when the agency was faced with changing and challenging situations. The renewed relationships reverberated through the community in powerful ways. Their ripple effect impacted morale and bolstered enthusiasm. It's an experience I will never forget—one that deepened my belief and trust in the power of conscious collaborating and co-creation.

The key to success in any group endeavor lies in our willingness to show up with courage, authenticity, and vulnerability and to responsibly detach from any particular outcome. As members of this committee, we had to silence our egos over and over again in order to keep coming back into a space where both transformation and co-creation were possible. We had to surrender to the synergy of the group process.

We also had some secret weapons in our pursuit: an unwavering commitment to a set of values to guide our work and a steadfast dedication to our cause. We built our community and our culture on these values. We took our task seriously. We trusted in our capacity to be successful and maintain integrity, and we were loyal to those who would be most impacted by our decisions and recommendations. These commitments kept us motivated and in touch with the goal of the project.

We worked together to redefine our culture and our community. We became leaders, together, all flying in the same direction.

Your Joy Matters

I believe that we are all connected. Just as the suffering or dehumanization of any human being affects all of us, the joy, fulfillment, and contentment of each individual impact the optimal health and functioning of our families, our organizations, and the human community we share. The overall energetic imprint that each person contributes to the greater whole will have an impact upon the energetic state of that greater whole.

This includes you.

Your transformation transforms us all.

When you identify a pain point, bottleneck, or dysfunction in your community, claim your leadership. Step fully into your responsibility to change the situation. Do not wait for others to do it. If you have identified even a partial solution before anyone else has, why waste precious time hoping someone else will initiate some action? When you notice something worth celebrating, look at it with delight and call together a crowd. If you have found a source of wonder, why let it pass unnoticed and unshared? This practice alone will create huge shifts for you personally, and it will make a rippling impact in your community that will reach people you may never meet.

Your leadership matters.

So does your joy. Take charge of your own behavior. Be accountable to yourself for the ways you engage with others. When you can look back and know that you maintained your integrity without compromising compassion and openness, regardless of another's actions, you will feel light. You will feel strong. You will be free. You will have become a co-creator of community within your organization.

CHAPTER 8

Seek and Share Support Continuously

An Invitation to Compassion

In various roles, I have been a service provider for about forty years. Throughout these decades, I've also cared for members of my family and other loved ones as they faced illness, accidents, and deaths both slow and expected and tragically too fast. And I've received the care and amazing assistance of countless other service providers along the way. This has included practitioners and professionals in traditional and alternative healing roles as well as wise counselors and dear friends and family members who met me in my lowest moments with compassion and kindness. Some were paid for their service, and others gave it without cost.

Each of my experiences of service, as provider, recipient, or observer, has offered me a window into the nature of the energetic exchange at the heart of our vocations, a deeper appreciation for the humanity of service providers, and an opportunity to enlarge and refine my vision of service as well as my personal approach.

I've also noticed how fluid these roles can be. What we offer today, we may need tomorrow. Most of us professional service providers will at some point seek services for ourselves or our loved ones. The line between provider and recipient is worthy of respect and attention, but we never want to lose sight of the truth that the common ground we share runs under whatever fences we build to sort us into categories.

And this is a beautiful thing. When we're acting in our role as service providers, our personal experiences don't take center stage as we attend to others' needs, but they can soften us to our shared humanity. This is where our empathy and compassion are both urgently needed and deeply right. It's also where we will find the best opportunities for expressing compassion in tangible and practical ways.

The invitation to compassion is also an invitation to recognize how deeply we're connected. We're all in this together.

■ ■ ■

The Energy of Compassion

Many of us might describe compassion as the driving force behind our desire to serve and to make a difference in the world. Compassion and its role in relationships of service have often been misunderstood and misapplied, however. We sometimes confuse the internal experience of compassion with the related feelings of sympathy or empathy. Some people also explain away emotional experiences of fear by identifying tears or other expressions of anger or sadness as evidence of compassion.

We took up the topic of empathy in a previous chapter. *Empathy* refers to our capacity to relate to another person's feelings. It's a type of understanding. It involves our ability not only to sense others' emotions, but also to imagine what it might be like to be in someone else's situation and to connect another's situation to our own emotional experience. Empathy is what it means to try to walk a mile in someone else's shoes. At its best, the resonance of empathy can create a special energetic bond that allows us to stay focused on and present with others even as they experience and express deeply difficult emotions.

Whenever empathy stalls at imagining how others feel and comparing it to how we might feel in a similar place, it's expressed as sympathy or feelings of pity. When we say, "I feel sorry for you," we're expressing our discomfort with their experience.

Compassion is a form of love. In relationships, it is an acknowledgment of connection. In action, it is an expression of profound kindness. It's a shared and paradoxical understanding that allows us to be present with someone who is suffering. Compassion admits that we are fundamentally separate from the emotional realities of another person. It also embraces and embodies the message that we are deeply attuned to and present with what they are going through. Holding these two truths in tension, we can accompany another's experience without succumbing to an urge to fix them or an ego-driven desire to make the situation better in order to make ourselves feel better.

It's easy to confuse a compassionate desire to assist someone with a fear-driven response that leads to the same desire—or even the same actions.

Well, if the outcome is the same, you might wonder, what's the difference? And if there is a difference, does it matter? People are still being helped.

The energy of our actions reveals whether they originate in compassion or in fear. The recipient of an action that is intended to help feels this energy, as does the giver. Fear-motivated behavior feeds on the energy of self-protection. Like all our efforts to shield ourselves from what the ego identifies as dangerous, it is draining. True compassion is energized by the endlessly renewable resource of love.

When our actions are motivated by fear, those on the receiving end often sense apprehension and distance. The action says, "I'm helping you but what I really want is to get the hell away from you as fast as I can." The energetic imprint is one of separation.

On the other hand, when we reach out to someone with the energy of compassion, people feel seen. This action says, "I see that you are struggling. I also see that you are more than this moment." The energetic message is a sense of hope and respect.

Speaker and spiritual teacher Iyanla Vanzant says that compassion has often been misunderstood to mean that we do for others whatever we feel they may need us to do for them. This can cause us to either hold ourselves back from the service relationship or extend ourselves into the center of it. Both extremes are ineffective means of truly supporting another person. Both extremes often conjure up in us a variety of ego-fueled emotional responses, including frustration, anger, helplessness, and guilt.

These are common responses for any of us called to serve. We see that someone is hurting or suffering. We want to reach out and be supportive and loving. But another part of us feels afraid, wants to avoid this person and run away from their suffering. We want to be compassionate, but we also don't want to feel anything like what this person is feeling. We don't want that experience. In an attempt to separate and protect ourselves from what is happening, we too often disconnect from the interaction and turn away from the person.

You cannot hurt for another. You can be with them in their sorrow. You cannot heal for another. You can accompany them on their journey. You cannot grow for another. You can open to the human capacity for change. You cannot do the work for someone else, but you can be present in the process.

Where does compassion fit for you as an internal source of motivation?

How do your actions express the unique energy of compassion?

No One Is Immune

If we've learned anything since the spring of 2020, it's that the unpredictable reality of this world impacts all of us. Viruses have zero respect for borders and don't discriminate between people. Many of us who never imagined we'd ever have to rely on government assistance to get by faced the uncertainties that came with layoffs, reduced income, and no guarantees for the future.

This pandemic leveled the playing field in many ways. But even as its danger underscored our common humanity, we shouldn't minimize the fact that it hit different people differently, around the globe as well as within our respective countries and communities. Individual health status aside, people living with oppression and marginalization were impacted in more catastrophic ways than those of us with access to savings, backup plans, resources, friends, and family.

One place the pandemic hit hard was among the community of service providers.

If we didn't have a sense of our emotional and physical risk factors before COVID-19, we are likely more attuned to them now. For the first time in the history of professional human services—in my lifetime, anyway—there was a collective recognition of service workers as essential, and a dawning realization about the impact this emergency was having on frontline and face-to-face service providers.

Those of us with any experience in these roles had concerns about our risks long before a global pandemic arrived to highlight them. The virus underscored what we already knew: service providers are human like everybody else, and we are at risk by the very nature of our work.

Beyond the possibility of infection because of our proximity to the people we serve, service providers in the early days of the pandemic were also exposed to a more insidious danger: a combination of self-imposed standards and unrealistic community expectations.

As we explored earlier in this book, most service providers come to our vocations with a sense of being called, a natural inclination toward giving, and a heart attuned to others' needs. As a group, we arrive at work primed for overextension. If that weren't enough, our academic preparation may note the risks of burnout in helping professions, but it rarely offers practical strategies for meaningful self-care. Add to this the informal but effective message, often sent by leaders and peers in fast-paced and high-stress work environments, that service providers must have their proverbial shit together if they really want to last in this job. If we can't hack it, we're told, we should never have signed up in the first place.

Alongside the too-common culture of service that says, "Toughen up if you want to make it," society's pandemic-provoked celebration of service providers as heroes put us in a precarious position. How could we admit we were struggling when everybody was banging pots and pans for us at shift changes? What could we complain about now that we were finally being recognized as essential?

Anyone placed on a pedestal will eventually disappoint. Elevating service providers to superhuman sainthood does nothing but deny their humanity. It also offers an easy excuse to attack us when we fall apart, fail to help ourselves, or prove unable or unwilling to live up to the standard of self-sacrifice.

Mental health challenges, addictive behaviors, and substance use disorders among service providers are lamentably common; this was true for decades prior to the pandemic. Whether it shows up as a nurse helping themself to narcotics, a physician on the brink of suicide, a community support worker gambling themself into bankruptcy, or a family caregiver crawling into a bottle every night, the results of silenced pain, overlooked trauma, vocational stagnation, grief, and loss can be devastating. When we've become disconnected in these ways, it can be nearly impossible to help ourselves. In workplaces and other cultural climates that assume you can't do your job if you are facing your own struggles, it's scary to reach out for help.

We're not only struggling with the physical and emotional toll of our work; we're also laboring beneath the assumption that we had better be strong enough to simply shake off these challenges and their effects. It's no wonder people abandon themselves to coping mechanisms that seem to offer even temporary relief.

No one is immune to suffering. Your role as a service provider may equip you with certain information and skills, but it doesn't automatically protect you from pain. Tragedies can befall anyone, and we all have our limits. Life does not differentiate when it comes to hardship or challenge. Depending on the day, it may seem like others are either worse or better off than we are. But comparisons like this don't help. No matter how we imagine our difficulties compared to others', each of us has to face our own battles and climb our own mountains. There's little relief to be found in the idea that your neighbor's struggles might be more difficult than your own, nor is there much motivation in longing for what appears to be an easier life that somebody else is enjoying while you struggle.

Your role as a service provider was never meant to add to your pain.

We can help ourselves, but we must do it together. Movements and organizations that claim missions of healing and human well-being are uniquely positioned to understand the needs of service providers philosophically and to address them tangibly. We have the resources and the heart to recognize and respond to human need with compassion, even when the need is our own.

Resilience Is Hard-Won

Tough things make us stronger, right?

Shortly after my first divorce, I took up a walking practice. I would head out each morning before the crack of dawn and walk for miles. At the end of my workday, I'd do it again.

I walked a lot.

As I paced out the miles, I would imagine that all the worries, concerns, or challenges in my life were somehow being resolved. I would visualize these things falling out the back of my head and being absorbed in the sidewalk behind me. Many days I would be aware of leaving my house and arriving back home, but I'd remember very little detail in between. Walking cleared me out.

We had two young children at the time of the divorce, eight and six years old. In the years since, they have come to realize how much better it was for everyone to end the distress and conflict we were in at the time. But this childhood trauma hit them hard and left a lasting impact. As adults, they've had to work through their attitudes and assumptions about relationships with themselves and with partners.

I can recall, just prior to our separation, firmly resisting the idea of divorce. There was no way I wanted to be a divorcée. I just couldn't fathom that I would experience a failed marriage. I suppose there was some element of shame and guilt. I had contributed to the problems our marriage faced in all kinds of ways. But mostly I was bothered by the idea of failure and by how a divorce would make me appear to others.

Nobody is at their best during the dissolution of a relationship.

It is challenging to be present for loved ones—including children—when we are in the thick of the trauma. When a marriage falls apart, all the roles seem up for grabs. Thanks to the assistance and support of my parents and sister, my kids had a safe place to land while we worked on picking up our broken pieces.

I walked. And walked and walked. I worked a lot out on those walks. I pondered my role as the kids' mother and my ex's role as their father.

I recognized my desire to control the relationship between the kids and their dad. Finally, I settled on what felt, at the time, like some deep truths.

All I could do was be my kids' mom to the very best of my ability. This was a significant realization, because for months preceding that particular walk I had been less emotionally available to them than I needed to be.

I also realized my limits. I could not control the relationships they had with anyone—including their dad. In the end, I wanted them to have strong, loving relationships with both of us and with anyone else who became part of their family.

I decided that this experience would help my kids become resilient. I wanted them to be able to weather the difficulties in life. Through this hard time, they would develop strength and courage and learn to trust themselves. I clung to this desire for years, all the while grateful for the time I still had with them at home.

It's true that resilience is hard-won. We don't learn it through easy times. The very nature of resilience demands that we face uncertainties and challenges that force us to access the depths of our being.

But let's be careful.

While resilience is a positive trait, we shouldn't seek out suffering in order to earn it. And the idea of encouraging or excusing or inflicting harm on another person in the name of building their character or somehow making them more able to handle hardship is plain wrong.

I had to step back from my easy embrace of resilience. I had to admit that one reason I hoped my kids could develop this capacity was because I knew I shared responsibility for what was harming them, even as I tried also to be a source of safety in it.

Only many years later did I have this epiphany. My kids had moved away and lived across the country. As they faced struggles in their personal lives and relationships, as they managed these without my physical presence, I found myself rethinking my previous position about resilience.

What if they had had enough difficult experiences already? Instead of wishing for their resilience, I decided to hold an ongoing vision of their joy.

When we too quickly tell others in pain some version of "You're going to be okay" or "This is going to make you stronger" or "Others have suffered worse and turned out fine," we run the risk of denying the weight of their present experience, even while we believe we're offering comfort or encouragement. If you are tempted to offer these encouragements to another, examine whether your intention is to soothe your own worry about their eventual well-being or to join with them to create a future where hard-won resilience is accompanied by the free gift of joy.

My family's story now includes a great deal of joy. The dynamic my ex-husband Greg and I have worked to create during the decades since our divorce is a source of personal pride and gratitude for me. Our family has grown and changed over time. We aren't perfect, but we show up for each other in ways that we weren't able to before. The transformation of our relationships has been one of the greatest learning opportunities of my life and an experience I wouldn't trade for the world.

Most service providers I know have had the blessed opportunity, through their personal life experiences, to understand more deeply what is needed in their professional lives. This has certainly been part of my journey. Resilience is not automatic and does not automatically erase the painful experiences that may build it. Only when we can stop denying or minimizing times of grief, loss, struggle, or change in our lives and in the lives of those we love and serve can we start exploring and embracing the lifelong gifts these experiences can offer.

Stevie

"Please don't let her be here for me. Please."

I was pleading from every part of my being as I saw the face of my colleague peering through the window in the door of the classroom.

I was in the middle of teaching a class. It was nearly two o'clock, and we were ready for a break. The topic was drug and alcohol addiction. I had been feeling uneasy for the past few days. Something didn't seem right.

The knock at the door was for me. It was about Stevie.

My nephew Steven was twenty-six years old when we lost him to suicide. I had been blessed with a renewed closeness to him during the months prior to his death and found comfort in that gift, even as our family was devastated. Many family members did not want to acknowledge that Steven had killed himself. There is so much taboo surrounding suicide.

As I prepared to return to my teaching duties a week after Steven's death, I knew there would be no way I could walk into a classroom full of adult students, some of whom knew my nephew, and not acknowledge what had happened. I brought a picture of Stevie and shared my family's story. I acknowledged that I would be there for the remainder of the semester and would do my very best to be as present for them as I possibly could. It was a relief for me, but I believe it also was a relief for them.

Sharing in this way made it okay for them to talk about it and to approach me. The material we covered in class paralleled my personal experience in many ways. Many of the students had experienced similar losses or had personally lived with depression. I firmly believe that it is important to attend to the holistic needs of learners, just as we aim to do in health care and human services. When institutions of higher learning don't acknowledge the social and emotional realities that face adult learners today, we're missing an important opportunity.

Making it through those first few weeks and going to work was tough. I was still numbed by shock, though, and with the heightened adrenaline pumping through me, focusing on the duties of my job was not as hard as it would become later. When I returned for the new semester following the holiday break, I was ill prepared. It became apparent to me that it was only a matter of time before everyone knew I wasn't holding it together at all.

In my role as a service provider, I had many experiences with people who struggled with addiction, depression, anxiety, and suicidal ideation. In my teaching, I engaged learners in reading and reflection about these challenges. We examined and dissected them from a clinical perspective as well as through the lens of trauma care and emotional resilience. Meanwhile, someone I loved had been experiencing these struggles right in front of my eyes.

Family members of someone contemplating suicide are often both highly tuned in to the reality of their loved one's despair and in deep denial about how bad things actually are. We obsess about what we can do to change things, to make whatever hell they're in stop. And at the same time, we block away the very real possibility that the person we love so deeply and need so badly may end their life. The reality of the danger they're in gets obscured by our sheer inability to fathom it and our intense hope that things will get better.

My sister and I had talked about Steven's state, both with each other and with him. We had called the crisis line just a few weeks earlier when he was particularly distressed. Steven had the opportunity to go into detox that night and begin a process of recovery, but as soon as the crisis responders left, he changed his mind. Steven saw his doctor and obtained a referral to the local mental health association. On the day he died, he had received a letter asking him to confirm his appointment.

My sister had brought Steven to the local hospital a couple weeks prior to his death when he shared with her that he was having visions of killing himself. They sat for hours. My nephew was interviewed in an open space while waiting for the doctor to see him. When that time came, he was asked if he was currently homicidal or suicidal, to which Steven replied, "Not right now." He was sent home.

In the months after Steven's death, as we worked to care for my sister's grief and despair, one hospital social worker had the audacity to suggest that family members should step out of the way when it comes to mental health and suicidal ideation or attempt—that we should "leave it to the professionals."

It was very difficult not to be angry at the system and the people in it. I couldn't understand how this beautiful young man could have fallen through the cracks in such a profound way.

It is high time that we, as service providers, recognize the unique and important role family members play in the care of their loved ones and suspend our impulses to judge long enough to see beyond our biases. It is not up to us to analyze family histories, take sides, or assign blame, no matter how fucked-up we think a family's dynamics are.

Compassion accepts the reality that we're all fucked-up to some extent. We are in this together, so let's act that way.

Family members deserve respect. They are to be honored. Loving and caring for someone who is not well is no easy journey, and different people will walk this path as well as they can. Ask yourself how easy it would be for you to step aside and "leave it to the professionals" when a loved one was facing demons or despair.

No matter how many skills and techniques we bring to our work, or how much patient presence we are able to offer as service providers, we cannot replace the love or replicate the bond of family. Someone who has known me forever has unique access to my core, regardless of how dysfunctional our relationship might appear in the current moment of crisis. Rather than get in the way of these natural supports, or judge them as insufficient, let's honor the power every family has and work to support and strengthen it.

Family members have rich lived experience as well as traditions, stories, ways of speaking, and patterns of relationship that we can learn from and use to shape how we show up in service to others. They are not the enemy. Rather than seeing family members as a nuisance or obstacle, we can treat them as a living, breathing resource, and as an opportunity to serve with even more awareness. Organizational policies and guidelines around confidentiality and consent may govern the content of our conversations with family members, but these relationships, grounded in mutual respect and infused with trust, can become powerful partnerships.

Learning through our own lived experience allows us to become teachers who know in our bones what we're talking about with our mouths. Learning from the people who show up requesting our service allows us to ground our service in compassion. This is the most valuable tool we can access as service providers.

Remain curious. Family members in crisis may not have the language to express their needs. They may assume you already know what has happened, how they feel, and what will solve their problem. Be willing to read between the lines when others are unable to speak clearly. Get ready to make offers and suggestions based on what your intuition is telling you. Prepare to switch gears when you miss the mark and to forge ahead when you are invited deeper.

Before we are service providers or recipients, we are human beings. It's okay if we don't have all the answers. It's all right if we are still learning. Stay open—especially in what feels like the darkest moments. It is there that your role will be organically illuminated.

When someone shares their life journey with you and you are moved in some way, you have received a gift. How you learn from what you have been offered, and how you incorporate this gift into the specifics of your service, demonstrates your ability to receive as well as give.

Family Caregivers

We are here to serve each other. Sometimes this is basic and mundane, as daily as washing dishes or making dinner. Though the intensity and details shift over time, we experience the push and pull, give and take, and shared responsibility of friendships, family, and romance throughout our lives. Balanced relationships are reciprocal.

And sometimes they change.

Sometimes we are handed a set of extraordinary circumstances that upset the balance, put us in positions we didn't ask for or expect, and call us to roles that require a greater intensity of service than we ever thought we'd be asked to provide.

Millions of people are responsible for the care of loved ones who face exceptional challenges. These can be related to physical conditions or mental and emotional struggles. Often, they include a combination of these factors. Family caregivers are thrust into a complex set of circumstances requiring a balancing act between the nature of the relationship as it existed before and the demands of the present reality and the possible futures it presents.

I have had the opportunity to work with several people whose lives and loves were altered when their partners became ill or frail. Their stories and situations were unique, of course, but they shared a broad pattern. Slowly but surely, the landscape of the relationship changed. Romance faded. Dreams dissolved. The sense of shared experience and companionship that had once defined the relationship became elusive and complicated. Loneliness and isolation became unwelcome parts of life, even as caregiver and partner were still together.

As a new kind of relationship formed, it often didn't feel good for anybody. Frequently, failing health exacerbates personal idiosyncrasies. Negative relationship dynamics and habits that once could be managed can become heightened by increased stress, lack of support, and reliance on unhealthy coping strategies. Caring for someone we love in ways we didn't see coming can become a living hell.

It can also create the space for an intimacy profound enough to expand hearts—in ways that no candlelight dinner could ever accomplish.

I recall a conversation with a former girlfriend of my nephew's. Following his death, she was feeling bad about their past conflicts. This seems to be a common response to loss—heightened where self-harm or suicide are involved. We like to think that our loving relationships should be free of conflict, or at least that we'll have an opportunity to someday make them so.

That couldn't be further from the truth. Quite often our relationships don't become meaningful until we have experienced and worked through some form of conflict or disagreement. Conflict doesn't automatically create healthy intimacy, but it is an indicator of connection. Few of us will try to resolve a conflict with someone unless we are already emotionally engaged with them.

Conflict and disagreement give us opportunities for greater intimacy. When we engage these opportunities with courage, we allow ourselves to be seen, and we create the space for forgiveness, healing, and unconditional love. Realizing this truth somehow made me less apprehensive about the conflicts in my own life.

This truth can be very powerful for family caregivers, who enter their roles as service providers from atop a mountain of shared history, including unresolved conflict or unhealed hurts. When the relationship roles change, this resource of shared story and experience has great potential and power. Being of service to someone you love is a complex process. It requires developing the ability to navigate dual roles, shift perspectives, and embrace possibilities that are informed and energized by a shared history, even as you construct a new future together.

This is hard work. When we serve family caregivers, we're positioned to help them access their own resources of compassion, forgiveness, and hope as they find their way through some of life's most difficult challenges and reinvent their identities.

In addition to offering caregivers practical solutions and access to resources, we can also begin to build partnerships with them. These partnerships can reflect the transformative relationships we intend to create with those we serve. No matter what form they take, they require a continuous balancing act. Knowing when to lead and when to follow, when to speak and when to remain silent, when to act and when to wait are intuitive steps in the dance.

People often need to talk their way through what life is throwing them in order to access their inner resources. Quality service relies on our ability, as service providers, to understand this and intuitively respond to the unspoken fears and anxieties that lurk beneath the surface for caregivers. Your ability to acknowledge these forces at work in yourself as you witness and support the process can make all the difference.

Strangers in the House

When my dad was dying, my mom held the role of his main caregiver. She had some paid supports, but most fell short of her expectations.

Family caregivers face many challenges. Their worlds have been upended. Not only are they dealing with declining health or other struggles in the lives of those they love; they also suddenly find a whole new group of people traipsing through their homes and lives—people they rarely get to choose and usually don't know.

Even though I have worked with family caregivers and been one myself, I'm still challenged to imagine what it would feel like to expect a parade of people to whom I'm not related entering my home every day. A certain feeling of exposure comes along with that process.

As my mom tried to care for my dad, I think some of her challenges, including her discomfort with the outside service providers who became part of her life during that period, stemmed from the simple fact that she did not want what was happening to be happening.

She knew her husband was nearing the end of his life, and she was resisting this reality with every ounce of might she could muster. When we are in resistance, we might feel angry. And when we are angry, it's easy to lash out at whoever's available. The personal support workers (and sometimes us kids) were perfect targets.

I share this with the deepest sense of compassion for my mom—a compassion that I wasn't in touch with at the time. When we were going through it, I was in my own personal denial. I didn't really know how intense it was for either of my parents. I just showed up when I wanted to without any real responsibility or change to my role as their daughter.

When one member of the family is in distress, the whole system is impacted. While many family caregivers rise easily to the occasion, others struggle to find their capacity. Others fall apart. My mom needed to vent. She needed to talk about what was not working and about the challenges my dad was facing. She needed to blow off steam. She needed to grieve.

Family members who care for a loved one are human beings with a full range of emotions. Some form of guilt often tops the list. No effort is ever enough. The hours suck. The desire for freedom is palpable. So is the ongoing presence of love. It is a delicate balance. Service providers can either enter into the dynamic as partners or stand on the sidelines watching. We can be strangers in the house with a job to do, or allies in the sacred spaces of life transition.

To be an ally is not a self-proclaimed position, however. It is an intention. Make yourself available for partnership. Know your role and its limits. Resist the urge to overextend or control. Offer support without condition.

It's important for professional service providers to consider the courage it can take for families to allow strangers into their private worlds. Most of us will experience, at some point, the need to rely on the expertise and kindness of someone we don't know. When, as service providers, we are able to listen without the need to fix, offer ideas at the right moments, and allow for the full expression of feelings and frustrations, people are more likely to feel safe and heard.

A Word to Family Members (from a Family Member)

As family members of people receiving services, we cannot expect the professionals to do all the heavy lifting. If we are to be honored and useful parts of the team, we have just as much responsibility—and often even more motivation—to contribute to the development of genuine partnerships. Remember the advantage you have in the relationship with your loved one. Strained as it may be, or buried as it seems beneath dementia or confusion, you still sit atop that mountain of shared history. You know and are known in ways that transcend the connections even a skilled service provider can establish in the weeks or months they might be with you. Claim your role as an illuminator of what will be most helpful to you and your family. Don't expect others to read your mind.

The fear of being judged often clouds our relationships with service providers. We fear that these people don't or won't understand our motivations, or that they will question the amount or quality of our love or commitment. It can be tempting to embark on perpetual missions to prove them wrong.

Yet if we don't trust each other, we won't be able to create relationships with enough strength to endure the challenges ahead. Even if conflict arises or if someone feels betrayed at some future point, trusting in the people and the process can bridge the gap toward reunification.

If that type of trust seems like too big an ask, perhaps we can trust each other to do our best. Whether you are a family member, a service recipient, or a service provider (or all of the above), you have a personal responsibility to establish your commitment to partnership within yourself before you can see it happen with others.

Embrace the idea that we all have something to offer, whatever our situation, and stay true to your contribution. Speak with clarity and compassion whenever there is a derailment. Let kindness be the vessel to hold even the most difficult messages.

When we learn to honor each other in this shared journey toward living, learning, and loving, we create the conditions for partnership.

Intimacy and Codependency

Service relationships are intimate. When we try to fight against that truth, we lose something. Denying this quality of connection diminishes our capacity for presence and engagement. Intimacy is revealed not only in what we share with another, but also in how we receive what is shared, both verbally and energetically. Service providers have been encouraged toward professionalization at the expense of intimacy and love. But if we are to show up with our whole selves—if we are to send the message of unconditional positive regard—then we must be able to love.

How do we possibly differentiate between love as an expression of service, an act of intimacy, the core pulse of a personal relationship, or a demonstration of kindness? I'm not sure that it's so much about searching for examples we can wrap our minds around. Rather, it's about identifying the feelings we can sink our hearts into.

Too often, we are enticed into *thinking* our way through love. "Don't lose your head," we say. "Don't wear your heart on your sleeve." We are encouraged and conditioned to hide our feelings of love and our desire for intimacy with others. It's almost as though having love on the table means fear is inevitable.

And I suppose that is true to some extent. But maybe it doesn't have to be an either/or situation, but instead can be a both/and situation. Perhaps we simply need to be willing to dance with a certain amount of uncertainty.

Intimacy invites us to reveal ourselves when we most feel like hiding. In the exposure of our hearts and souls, we lose and find ourselves all at once. In the risk we take to connect with another, we access a place of safety that cannot be taken away.

Codependency deserves some attention here. Codependency is common not only in romantic relationships; we can also experience it with family members, with friends, and with those we offer our service. Most relationships characterized as codependent have elements of other-focused love and care combined with a whole lot of personal insecurity.

Codependency shares roots with concern or worry. It's easy to worry about the people who matter to us. We worry about the effects of their decisions and choices. We are kept up at night gripped by the fear of what might happen to them. When concern for someone we love morphs into a desire to protect them from the consequences of their actions and behavior—even at the cost of our own pain—our love has become unbalanced. When our personal equilibrium is toppled by the actions of another person or when our self-worth seems to depend on what other people say or do, we are experiencing some level of codependence.

If you're recognizing yourself here, even a little bit, breathe.

Remember that we often learn through contrast as much as we do in congruence. My own history of codependent behaviors has helped me learn more about love. This includes how I'm able to love others, but also—and perhaps more importantly—how I have learned to love and care for myself.

The only way beyond codependency in our relationships is to connect with and respect ourselves. It won't suffice to *talk* about self-esteem and acceptance. When we're on the precipice of self-abandonment, we must *choose* in our own favor with concrete actions on our own behalf. We must love ourselves.

For self-love to matter, we must embody it consistently. But it starts with a feeling. Get in touch with what you personally experience when you are aware of self-loving energy. Notice the clarity you are granted. Recognize the peaceful joy that washes over you. Take note of the grace and ease with which you move through your day. Sense the depths of freedom granted you in that loving space. Intimacy with others begins with your ability to intimately see and know your own heart.

The depths of intimacy lie right beside the pit of self-abandonment. When we open ourselves to be seen without safety or security, we will feel exposed. Intimacy requires that we create internal safety. Truly intimate connections give rise to a wellspring of courage that allows us to feel strong in our vulnerability. As service providers, we facilitate spaces that help others find this courage and grow to create and maintain a personal sense of self-security.

When we confuse intimate connections with codependent relationships, we are liable to open ourselves without these internal safeguards, and we run the risk of losing our capacity to honor our own needs and respect our own integrity. That's when the spiral begins. Obsessions set in. Caution gets thrown to the wind. We find ourselves behaving in ways that pull us out of alignment. Where a capacity for intimacy keeps us grounded in positive self-regard, codependency moves us toward self-destruction for the sake of somebody else.

Codependent relationships are gateways to other forms of self-abandonment, including substance use. Through the relationship, we escape the pain of facing ourselves. Then we need to escape the dysfunction of the relationship, so we turn to coping mechanisms like alcohol or drug use or other addictions. This makes it harder to face ourselves with love. It's a vicious cycle.

The compassionate clarity of intimacy interrupts this cycle. Rather than providing escape, it offers us repeated opportunities for forgiveness, relational repair, and the self-respecting connection of love. Perhaps that is the only way out of self-destructive patterns. Hopefully, we'll make progress as we learn and grow, but I'm not sure we will ever be able to move beyond the need for forgiveness and love.

I hope not.

In our service relationships, intimacy means that we feel secure enough within ourselves to fully witness the lives of others. Instead of worrying that we will be triggered or traumatized by what we experience as we accompany others, we come to realize that we have what it takes to love ourselves through any emotional experience that arises in us. We begin to trust in our ability to show up entirely engaged in service to others, knowing that we are both seen and safe. And so are they. In all our relationships, intimacy is a gentle force that, like water over stones, has the power to soften us.

Creating intimate relationships will scare you. It scares me to this day. But this is only fear. And on the other side of fear is love. If we have trouble allowing ourselves to be seen because of shame or fear of rejection, we'll have difficulty seeing others at their depths as well. The truth that lies in that space is a beautiful mess well worth the risk it takes to discover.

What does intimacy mean to you?

How do you express intimacy in your personal and professional relationships?

The Problem with Compassion Fatigue

Compassion fatigue describes a challenge often experienced by those in helping professions. I have experienced its symptoms myself and know many others with similar stories. It has become accepted as inevitable that at some point in your career as a service provider, you can expect to be overcome with fatigue related to compassion. There are books, workshops, strategies, and practices to help professionals cope with the impact of this phenomenon within their work.

I'm ready to call BS on compassion fatigue.

As a service provider, you will be exposed to a number of challenging situations involving the pain and suffering of other human beings. You may hear horrifying stories of abuse, loss, and illness on various levels. You may also feel a strong sense of responsibility to the people who cross your path—a responsibility to help, to support, to provide resources, and to have answers. You may eventually become aware of the fact that many of the answers are impossible to come by, and over time you may find yourself disillusioned at best and in intense despair at worst. You might even feel an urgent need for self-protection. Compassion fatigue is based on the idea that this is inevitable.

You will likely witness many challenges and struggles in the lives of others. Problems are often the reason people seek our service. As a result of what you witness, you may experience a number of the symptoms of so-called compassion fatigue. These can include exhaustion, guilt, shame, sadness, depression, hopelessness, helplessness, lack of motivation, inability to focus, anger and resentment at the system, anger at the people you serve, and a desire to escape—just to name a few.

Those experiences are authentic. Many service providers from all walks of life experience these. The impact is palpable. The effects are not in your mind. The struggle is real.

But you are not in this mess because you are too compassionate toward others. You are here because you lack compassion for yourself.

That's it. Bottom line. Compassion does not make us tired, but lack of self-compassion is exhausting.

Compassion is an expression of love. Love is energizing, uplifting, and light. Love is a central characteristic of service; it is not about having weak boundaries, becoming too attached, or caring too much. Loving-kindness for our fellow human beings is a prerequisite to high-quality and sustainable service relationships. Compassion that springs from this source of loving-kindness will be expressed in clear, caring, and conscious actions.

When we talk about feeling tired or worn out because we are too compassionate or we care too much, we must ask ourselves, "Is this compassion that I am feeling, or am I operating from another emotion or motivation?" Perhaps we have crossed over into caretaking, worry, fear, or a desire to control an outcome or any number of things. We noted earlier how the ego often tries to disguise its fear in a cloak of compassion.

These emotions and motivations emerge when we step out of or away from love. That doesn't mean that we are acting in unkind ways; it just tells us that we have slipped into the denser and heavier energies of fear and are looking for our way back to loving-kindness.

Love benefits everyone involved—including you. If you are struggling with exhaustion or overwhelm, reconnect with yourself. Consult a safe sounding board. Take time to examine your personal lens. How are you interpreting things? What beliefs can you identify behind your interpretations? What would loving-kindness look like in this situation? Being truly compassionate will never leave us fatigued.

Compassion guides our response to others and their needs in ways that honor their unique personal processes and their capacity for resilience. Self-compassion affords us the same respect. As we are invited into relationships of service, we maintain connection to ourselves and our personal needs. The moment we find that we are giving when we don't want to give, we are no longer in a state of compassion. When we lose sight of our personal needs—when self-care becomes an optional one-hour activity every third Friday of the month—we have lost touch with compassion for ourselves. When we start to believe that we are better off ignoring our emotional needs and instead lose ourselves in others' feelings, we are setting ourselves up for suffering. When we break down sobbing after a heart-wrenching interaction with someone and don't treat the tears as an opportunity to explore what has touched us so very deeply, we are cheating ourselves.

We react and respond to the experiences of others in deeply emotional ways because a place within us relates and resonates. Self-compassion allows us to explore that place and to open to the healing that such exploration can offer. This kind of compassion is restorative. Self-love reconnects us with the sustainable energy of compassion and renews all our resources.

Good Grief

Health-care and social service organizations can play an important role in the safe grieving process of their service providers. Most employers provide a certain amount of time for people to navigate loss. In too many cases, this amounts to a few days of bereavement leave. That seems like wishful thinking to me. For most of us, the grief process is an extended one. It takes time to stop reeling from the impact of loss. The work of absorbing, let alone integrating, life-changing losses in healthy ways involves long-term labor. We can and must do better.

Some are doing it better. Several years ago, I had a refreshing conversation with a friend who was navigating heavy grief following the loss of both parents as well as her family pet. She told me about the encouragement she was receiving through her workplace community. She had worked for many years in human services and was committed to maintaining the high quality of contribution she was known for.

This woman's colleague had suggested that my friend consider all that she was learning as she went through this process of grieving such losses. She encouraged her to recognize how the experience might contribute to her professional growth as well as her personal healing. The process and the journey could ultimately enrich the depth and quality of her service as well as her sense of fulfillment in the work. Her painful losses could become a kind of good grief.

We need more of this in the communities we form around service.

Even though grief is a common human experience, it is a unique personal journey. And with every loss, we encounter new layers, new insights, new wisdom, new pain, and new possibilities for joy. Through my life transitions, as loved ones left my life or I left theirs, I had repeated opportunities to learn, to shrink, and to expand. I wasn't always a willing student, and I got stuck more than once.

I still do.

I don't tell you my stories of personal loss, grief, change, and healing simply to get them off my chest, but rather to illuminate the learning possibilities that our lives offer each of us at every moment of every day. Our experiences shape our personal lens and inform our practice as service providers; the more profound the experience, the more profound its gifts. Each of us is one human being having continuous experiences on many levels and through all our channels of attention. It all influences the ways we express ourselves in the world. Our vocations of service are an important form of this expression.

Everything counts.

If there is ever a time requiring compassionate patience with self and with each other, it's in the depths of despair. Grief is not reserved only for the loss of loved ones. It permeates our lives in the wake of lost dreams, dashed hopes, broken relationships, and everyday disappointments.

As a service provider, you will accompany others in their experience of grief and loss, even as you make your way through your own. Consider both the responsibility and the gift offered you in this capacity. Challenge your assumptions and strive to continually enter this space with renewed insight and courage.

Grief is an intimate journey. In our deepest sense of despair, we might find a profound presence if we can allow ourselves to open to it. When we are least aware of the net, we learn to trust that we are somehow held.

What role has grief played in your life?

What lessons has it offered?

How have these experiences shaped who you are in the service of others?

CHAPTER 9

Learn from Your Life

An Invitation to Openness

In the ancient imagination, alchemy was a mystical blend of magic and science that offered people a chance to control elements and transform one thing into another. The highest of the alchemical arts was the ability to turn lead into gold. These days, *alchemy* is most often used as a metaphor. We use the word to describe the way things can sometimes come together as if by magic. Alchemy is when basic or simple things suddenly combine or coalesce into something more complex and precious.

In this way, the human process of learning is a type of alchemy. Information, data, and random experiences somehow transmute into what we call knowledge and use as wisdom. Things that happen to us and around us are alchemized by our unique worldviews and patterns of experience and expectation into the thoughts and concepts and connections we rely on to understand and navigate the world. This happens within every human being and takes an incalculable number of forms. All it requires of us is a capacity for wonder and the ability and willingness to remain open.

If that's not magic, I don't know what is.

This chapter doesn't offer an exploration of learning styles or a how-to manual for getting the most out of educational opportunities. Instead, it respects that each of us learns in different ways and for different purposes, and it challenges us to make openness a defining characteristic of our approach to anything and everything.

The invitation to the openness that comes from learning is also an invitation to humility. Learning anything entails admitting that we don't know everything. Our ignorance only becomes a problem when we deny it.

As we explore a handful of specific life lessons in the pages that follow, you'll become aware of an ongoing theme that connects this invitation to everything else we've come to understand about conscious service. At the heart of any authentic act of learning is a fundamental openness to self-understanding and growth and a desire for transformation.

Not all we teach is knowledge, and not everything we learn is limited to the kind of information that can be spoken. We teach and learn through all the channels of our human system—including the frequencies of emotion, relationship, and spirit. Some of the greatest lessons in our lives have little to do with intellectual capacity and everything to do with the ability of our hearts to remain open. In the previous chapter, we explored how grief and loss have functioned as sources of profound wisdom in my own life. My experience is by no means unique or exceptional. While any of us would rather learn in less painful ways, we rarely get to choose or control what happens to us—only how we respond. And we can remain open to the possibility of learning through joy.

In life's wide and weird classroom, we can choose to keep our heads down, stick to what we know, and try to make it through without rocking boats or risking failure. Or we can show up open to change, curious about how the future might connect to the past, and ready to learn from everything we encounter. This second path is the way of conscious service. As we embrace the call to openness in our service and in our lives, we learn to alchemize our most joyful heights as well as the depths of our sorrow into self-knowledge and energy for service. We become better equipped to respond to ourselves as well as the people we serve and care for. We can choose hope over bitterness and love over loss.

And we don't have to wait to learn the hard way. We can use what we know to create new paths. The most repetitive life lesson can deliver a fresh insight—even if it's only a vision of how far you have come. Your expanded ability to embrace your unique learning process and to marvel at the universe's generous shower of lessons can become a source of ongoing excitement and enjoyment.

The impulse to simply push through, keeping on doing what we have always done, will continue to be strong. We can ignore the signs that come our way and refuse to accept the teachers life offers. Resist this urge. The safety it seems to offer is an illusion. Learn to see familiar paths with new eyes—and see people you thought you had figured out as the mysterious beings they are.

A life of learning is a life that will never feel fully settled. Growth and change are constants. Balance is realized in the moment. Remaining open to these forces means they will work their magic in us as well.

■　■　■

Stay Curious

Sometimes it's hard to imagine learning from people or situations we already seem to know inside and out. Familiar patterns and personalities seem unchanging and unchangeable. Many of us have friends or loved ones whose sentences we can finish and who can just as easily complete our own. The intimacy in these relationships offers a deep connection. It's tempting to assume they can't surprise us.

This can be a dangerous assumption, especially during times of conflict or personal change.

Knowing anybody very well is a double-edged sword. It grants us a foundation for real and meaningful intimacy, while at the same time interfering with our ability to see anything new about that person. We start to feel like they can't show us anything different. In the process, we diminish them, limit ourselves, and freeze the relationship we share.

A similar dynamic often complicates service relationships. Even if we don't know the people we serve as well as the people with whom we share bonds of friendship, we often have a great deal of knowledge about them. Our roles often offer access to people's information: files, records, histories, reports, and narratives. Sometimes it can seem like we have more information about a person's life than they do.

Those of us who serve in roles that address specific social conditions have an additional layer of knowledge-based assumptions. We know things about disability, or homelessness, or hunger, or domestic abuse, or chronic pain, for example. The insights offered by this wealth of professional data can cloud our ability to recognize the people we meet in our work.

As soon as we feel there is nothing left to learn, a part of us begins to wither and die just a little bit. We get bored. If this persists, we can start to lose connection with what we do, and the competence that was once evidence of our learning will start to fade.

It is easy to lose sight of the fact that the people to whom we provide service have a great deal to teach us. People who have been living life under the shadow of stigma and labels have some of the greatest lessons to offer the world. It can be tempting to think that someone struggling with day-to-day life is occupied solely with trying to survive. In such a circumstance, how could they possibly offer us anything in the way of wisdom or insight?

What a missed opportunity.

Not only can we learn about a specific person's particular challenges; we can also learn about their humanity. When we are open to learning from the people we serve—not just as a population, but as discrete and whole human beings—we might get a glimpse of what it's like to walk in their shoes. We might be invited to learn how another person perceives the world and their place in it.

From this perspective, if we are humble enough to earn it, we will be best poised to learn a specific person's needs and to begin to imagine practical responses that make a difference to them. People are the best sources of information about themselves. Compassionate curiosity can help us learn how to serve in each situation we encounter. It also offers us ongoing lessons about ourselves as people and as professionals.

Curiosity can sustain you elsewhere as well. When—perhaps in the midst of a staff meeting or professional development session—I find myself wishing I were anywhere but where I am, I try to shift my energy toward curiosity and openness. I make the effort to stay connected with the speaker, to interact through nodding or smiling as they share information, even if it's already familiar to me. I challenge myself to stay open for the nugget of novelty that will offer me a chance to see beyond my preconceived notions.

It is remarkable what happens to our energy when we make the decision to be present and engaged. Time begins to move more quickly, and we notice a certain lightness return to our bodies. Impatience and boredom are replaced with a sense of peace. This becomes the perfect space for breakthroughs, insights, and connection.

Respecting each person who crosses our path as a teacher in our lives makes each day an opportunity to learn. Wake up in the morning with the intention to be open to the wisdom of that particular day, and receive all the individuals who enter your life as infinitely interesting. Make learning an active choice. Notice themes. Connect dots. Commit to learning out loud by asking questions, sharing doubts, and letting your ideas be challenged and sharpened by others. Let learning expand your horizon and alter your perspectives. Whether we put it to work in the intimacy of a personal relationship, in a classroom, or in the context of our service, the energy of curiosity has the power to transform and dynamically shift our perspectives.

New people may show up in your life as your own energy and vibration shift. A new character may emerge in place of the old you. When you tune in to your learning and open yourself to it, you set intentions and send out the vibes that attract more opportunities for expansion.

What are you most curious about right now?

What can you learn from your interactions today?

Lead Like a Learner

Many leaders struggle with learning. I have had challenges with this myself. Most of us assume that leaders are supposed to have everything figured out. If I have questions, my leaders are supposed to have answers. I should be able to go to this person and they will tell me what I need to do. They'll fix the issue.

That's why they get paid the big bucks, isn't it?

Even if we don't accept such an extreme image of infallibility, those who find ourselves in leadership positions often feel the pressure to demonstrate competence. Leaders and would-be leaders absorb such expectations. Many find it hard to admit their need to learn, much less do so in public.

And among the rest of us—among those of us who look to leaders for answers and solutions—there is a corresponding assumption. Leaders get where they are because they know stuff. We trust that someone further up the chain from us is ultimately responsible, and we feel a collective fear if there is any indication that they don't know what they are doing.

When we together embrace the gift of learning out loud, we can relax a little. When it's safe to entertain the idea that any of us might be wrong—and that there are always alternatives to the ways we're able to see in the moment—we step beyond discomfort about our ignorance and into the place of growth, exploration, and possibility.

This takes some courage, of course. But the blessings are worth it. As leaders, we can put down the burden of pretending to be the smartest person in the room, having to always get things right, and being the sole source of immediate answers. Most of the time, we can—and are better off to—take our time.

Those of us who have yet to realize our potential to lead can step more bravely into our own capacity, trusting that an ability to learn is one of the attributes that best qualifies anyone for leadership. The ability to learn and adapt is increasingly recognized as one of the most important resources for any organization.

Peter Senge introduced the notion of "learning organizations" many years ago in his book *The Fifth Discipline*. Senge argues that decentralizing leadership in organizations is key to enhancing everyone's capacity to work toward common goals. He describes learning organizations as places in which "people continually expand their capacity to create the results they truly desire, where new and expansive patterns of thinking are nurtured, where collective aspiration is set free, and where people are continually learning how to learn together." Learning organizations are built and sustained by people who have personally embraced their ongoing need for shared learning and are able to celebrate and expand their ability to consider and integrate new information, new perspectives, and innovative approaches. These organizations see all people, regardless of title or role, as active participants in the creation of the organization's future.

If you're a leader, embrace the position of learner. If you're seeking leadership from somebody else, take a look in the mirror. Take back your power for expression. Figure out how you can create a renewed sense of security within yourself. Be brave enough to step outside of your comfort zone.

List three leadership attributes that come naturally to you.

What do you still need to learn as a leader?

Not Everybody Will Like You

This can be a tough pill to swallow.

Lots of us like to please people. Helping others, which sometimes involves supporting their happiness, is a core part of many vocations of service. It can be painful to accept that some people don't like us. Sometimes I wonder if it's as hard, or even harder, to admit that there are some people we simply don't like.

I am most bothered by these ideas when I am in a state of not liking myself so much. When I've become disconnected from myself—maybe knocked off the beam by an uncomfortable interaction or a long-term simmering conflict—I get prickly. In this state, I am more inclined to notice things that irritate me. I am also more likely to assume that someone else doesn't like me. Why should they? It becomes very difficult to resist the urge to find some sort of explanation and justification for the dark feelings that seem to want to take up so much head and heart space.

It doesn't have to be so complicated or intense. All relationships involve friction. You might be rubbing someone the wrong way without having any intention or inkling of what you are doing. Maybe you remind them of someone else. Perhaps they feel their worldview being threatened by your perspective. Who knows?

There doesn't need to be a reason, though we'll likely spend time searching for one.

And it is much the same when you find yourself bristling around certain people. Your mind might scramble to make sense of it so you can find a reason for your ill will or avoidance. We usually have more luck plumbing our own feelings and functions than others', but you still might not get to the bottom of it. The reason for your annoyance may be too subtle, or you may not be ready for it.

And that's okay.

Relational discomfort is a teacher. When we need to have that information, we will get it. Our work is to try to open ourselves enough to receive the message and its meaning. This takes patience, of course, and benefits from all the self-connected reflection you can muster. There's learning available to you, even within the weirdest interactions or random encounters.

These uncomfortable events can be mirror moments in which you recognize your own need for growth in what feels like offensive behavior from somebody else. They may come as divinely timed pokes at your internal bees' nest of unresolved experiences—a core shake-up that opens the door to healing and forward movement.

The power of love at the heart of our practices of enlightened communication entails an unplumbed resonance with and care for humanity and the world we live in. It is grounded in profound respect for the inherent worth of all living beings, and for life itself—beginning with ourselves. In this vision there is no hierarchy. There is no competition. There is no graded value. It is all valuable. We are all valuable.

To infuse your service in the world with the energy of universal love takes away the ego's need to judge anyone, including yourself. When judgment arises, you have momentarily stepped out of the flow of universal love.

Step back in. Start with yourself.

Notice how shitty you feel when you decide you don't like someone or you determine that they don't like you. Something must be wrong somewhere, you tell yourself. Something's wrong with you, and there definitely is something the matter with them. Your mind can keep you stuck in this investigative process for as long as you allow it.

When I decide that I don't like someone, I often begin to justify my feeling with evidence. Here's all the reasons why I don't like them. Look at all the examples I can point to that make them wrong, bad, or in some way undesirable. How can I separate myself from them (oh, let me count the ways)? How am I different from them (translate that to mean *better*)?

Let me sit just a bit taller on my high horse now.

Eventually the arrogance of this perspective hits me. Now I don't even like myself. Meanwhile, the other person is nowhere in the vicinity.

I have created my own private project of self-sabotage in response to somebody who I already decided is not of great importance in my life.

Doesn't make much sense.

When my contact with another person evokes such a strong response within me, I have a golden opportunity to look in the mirror that person provides. If I can embrace the truth that my reactions and responses live inside of me, I can use this mirror to learn. I can start to trust that my discomfort is a catalyst to another layer of personal awareness and growth that is ready to be discovered.

When we find ourselves feeling disliked, what might that tell us about our internal state of self-connection? Is there an aspect of me that I don't like or accept right now? Is my antagonist reflecting that back to me? What if I take this opportunity to like myself a little bit more? To act from a place of self-respect that naturally leads me to respectful communication with them? To be a person who doesn't require the approval of someone else in order to feel worthy and deserving?

It is common to believe that serving others automatically leads to liking them. This belief creates dissonance for many service providers. It leads to questioning ourselves and our power to do good. How can we serve somebody well if we don't like them?

Remember that these feelings are more about us. They provide an opportunity for reflection and self-understanding. These situations challenge us to reconnect to our values. Doing so can help us expand our capacity for unconditional positive regard.

Grappling with the feeling that someone you serve doesn't like you offers an equally valuable opportunity for self-connection and self-respect.

When I believe that someone doesn't like me, my impulse is usually to try harder. A part of me is determined to change their mind. I am convinced that I have the power to win them, to worm my way into their heart no matter what that requires or how it makes me feel. I find myself measuring every word and second-guessing every action from the perspective of how I'll be received. I lose touch with my heart and what feels right to me, and my sole purpose centers on trying to figure out what will make them happy with me.

It's exhausting. I'd like to tell you that I have completely outgrown this well-practiced song and dance. I haven't. At least now this impulse has my full attention and I can recognize when I'm doing it. I am becoming increasingly attuned to what triggers a launch into my "Please, like me" mode.

I'm also aware of how much I hate it.

My frustration with these tendencies in myself is highlighted when the dancing shoe is on the other foot. When someone else seems to suspect that I don't like them and begins trying to win me over, I can feel the same sad familiar energy that has sapped me for too long.

The "make them like me" project doesn't usually end well. Eventually it provokes a kind of arrogance. This usually arrives on the heels of anger and bitterness at being slighted or dismissed. When the ego wants protection, anger is an easy choice. "I don't care what they think of me!" "If they need a reason not to like me, I'll give them one." "After all I've done for them!" Acting from self-righteous indignation has rarely produced the results I sought, and it's never made me any friends.

Feeling disliked by anyone, whether we've got it right or not, offers us a chance to examine the status of our old wounds, review the health of our self-esteem, and practice graciousness, forgiveness, and self-love. These self-connected capacities help us move beyond self-justifications or explanations intended to make us feel better.

Our values as service providers will be apparent in how we respond to these situations. Self-connected service entails maintaining a balance of self-respect and compassion while remaining open to another person, no matter how they view you.

This does not mean we try to be neutral. It also does not mean we accept harm or abuse. Service in the world is never neutral, and self-respect requires us to stand against any action that seeks to harm us. We use the energetic force of self-connected service to attend and respond to the needs and information of the moment with all our capacities.

As we're able to ground ourselves in loving energy, these capacities expand. In a state of universal love for others and ourselves, we become less concerned with assigning blame or emerging as a winner. We soften to recognize that we can care even when we don't agree, and connect even when friendship isn't in the cards. We have the power to choose to let down our guard and become willing to embrace our nature even when those around us can't or won't.

When you have decided that someone doesn't like you, what happens to your thinking?

How does that influence the way you show up?

You Have Buttons

When someone pushes my buttons, it is so easy to think the button-pusher is the problem. I hope and pray that whatever they're doing to bug me will stop. If only they would just be different, do different, or go away. Then I remember that our reaction to other people has absolutely nothing to do with them. We choose our response, no matter what someone else does or says.

As we noted in the last chapter, this does not mean we overlook or excuse unacceptable behavior, nor do we stay in relationships that trespass or ignore our limits. Rather, when we put a foot down or draw a line, we do so from a place of self-honor and respect. This doesn't require us to condemn the other person. There's a difference between these things. There is no blame involved. Respect is not a zero-sum game.

Our buttons and triggers belong to us. What drives me around the bend with a particular person may be the very thing that draws other people in. Our lives and experiences are subjective and come down to our own personal interpretations at the end of the day.

When someone behaves in a way that infuriates or irritates you, you have a divine opportunity. If you choose to stay focused on what the person has done to get your goat, this opportunity will be lost on you. Our tendency to focus on the other person and the need for their alteration or enlightenment (or absolute destruction) strips us of any peace we might hope to find. As we noted earlier, these ego projections only fuel the flames of our discontent.

For us to be comfortable and at ease, nobody else has to change. That guy who always seems to set you off is actually doing you a favor. Whether you like it or not, he is consistently showing you precisely where you possess a smoldering grudge or an implicit bias or an untended injury. He is pointing directly at your current opportunity for healing. He is offering you a chance to resolve something once and for all.

It might not feel like it, but this is a gift.

Once these unprotected aspects of our nature come to the light of our awareness, we stand face-to-face with a moment of potential release and resolution. Most of our internal buttons and triggers began as defense mechanisms. Remember that fear is a type of protection. It sounds an alarm intended to keep us safe.

Embrace the intent behind your self-made buttons. Those wounds left scars, but there is no need for you to re-create the injury. When someone's action seems to flip an old familiar switch, it's healing time.

This is likely where you will notice the themes of your life most prominently. The repetition of an emotional experience is what builds the circuit and creates our reactive response. It's not a trigger or a button unless it has been tripped more than once. If you want to, you can trace each button back to the experience that planted it.

You likely have many memories that reinforce your knee-jerk reactions, keep the triggers sensitive, and ensure the buttons are at the ready.

Triggers and buttons often lead to habitual responses of self-abandonment. Becoming aware of a habitual reaction allows you the opportunity to transform it into a chosen one. At some point in the interaction or experience, you can detach from the intensity of your reaction and choose differently. Your point of power occurs at the moment when you embrace your ability to wait just one more second.

We can accept the opportunity to disarm our triggers and render our buttons inoperable. After all, at the end of the day, is it worth losing your peace over? Maintaining a center of peace within will always help navigate rough roads and uncertain journeys.

Our buttons aren't always connected to what others say or do directly to us. Sometimes we react in relation to our beliefs and values as well. This often shows up as we witness other people in action or watch the news, for example.

Each of us has our way of viewing what's "right" and "wrong" in the world. We have our viewpoints and opinions. The social challenges of our world can be triggering. Maybe you have very strong feelings and ideas when it comes to abortion or addiction. Perhaps you have beliefs about single parents or the impact of divorce on children. Examples are endless. Maybe any talk about religious beliefs makes you shudder. You might have heartfelt convictions about punishment or the legal system. Many of these deeply held beliefs are attached to some personal experience. All are deeply infused with emotional energy.

Beliefs can be true or false, helpful or unhelpful (or anywhere in between). What matters most is how they function. Our beliefs impact our actions and choices as we pursue our desires and intentions. Like any element of the personal lens, beliefs can shift and change, expand or narrow.

As service providers, many of us have been instructed to set aside some of our deeply held beliefs in an effort to appear unbiased and nonjudgmental. Instead of exploring our beliefs and how we might remain true to our personal values without imposing them on others, we've been encouraged to embrace and embody neutrality.

This is a doomed attempt.

We might be able to camouflage our beliefs beneath a blanket of acceptable neutrality, but we cannot easily disarm our buttons. As service providers, we need to understand our triggers and buttons—especially as they are attached to our deeply held beliefs and values. When we ignore these powerful parts of ourselves, we will find ourselves repeatedly trapped in reaction and ill-prepared to respond to the realities of the moment. This usually feels bad to us and deeply confusing to others.

Tripped triggers often set off a flood of intense emotional response. They're connected to deep memories as well as strong beliefs. They're usually implanted early in life. When set off, they herald an opportunity for transformation, but first they can catapult us headfirst into an outburst we somehow never saw coming.

Sometimes we really do surprise ourselves. A seemingly innocent remark by someone irks us to no end. What the hell are we so bothered about? With a little digging, we can find what is there to be discovered. We don't need to judge ourselves for having the trigger. We can learn to appreciate the gift of an occasional shake-up, even if it comes with discomfort.

Sometimes we need to be taken off guard to find better balance.

As you develop your self-connection muscles, buttons and triggers become your exercise instructors. They show you precisely where you have a growth opportunity. In service to others, your capacity to recognize your personal triggers and buttons—and how to safely and responsibly disarm them—is a lifeline to remaining present and engaged.

What is the first physical signal you experience when one of your buttons has been pushed?

Spare the Drama

A while back I began to notice a pattern of behavior in some of my long-term friendships. I knew that dynamics had changed. I felt tension where it hadn't existed before. We would make plans to get together, and when the time to meet came near, I didn't feel like it anymore. Anticipating their disappointment or irritation if I canceled, I would see it through, all the while wishing I were somewhere else and angry with myself for not following my own heart.

And of course there was the guilt. What was wrong with me that I didn't feel like spending time with an old friend? Or better yet, let's make a list of what's wrong with *them* so I don't have to feel bad about not wanting to spend time with them.

What a cycle. There's no good answer. I've come to realize that it's just drama. I caught myself one time spewing out a driver's seat monologue in which I had constructed an entire plot around nothing. I had cast the victims and the villains for an event that hadn't even happened yet. "It's just so much drama!" I yelled.

I was alone in the car, muttering and screaming to myself. My friend wasn't the source of drama. I was!

This is where humility and a sense of humor become lifesavers. Use them generously.

If we create the drama, we can dismantle it. Things do not have to be so complex.

The summer my mom was in hospice, I had very little time to spend with anyone beyond my family. Even so, little breaks from the intensity of caring for my mom alongside my siblings were important, and I knew I needed them. I began to notice that when I needed such a break, the perfect friend would somehow show up. There was no need for drawn-out planning sessions or fitting into someone's schedule.

People would also reach out from time to time wanting to get together when I had a spare moment. In those moments, I started to practice listening to the truth of my feelings. Did my heart feel like being with that person right now? If the answer was no, I accepted that without question. I started to realize that I didn't need to justify my not wanting to be with them at that time. I didn't need to manufacture a reason. I practiced respect—for myself and for my friends—by being honest.

You don't have to wait for a family crisis to re-center yourself and your needs in this way. You can use this strategy in relationships that feel disconnected or have run their course. You can use it with the acquaintance who doesn't feel like a fit for you. Employ it with the coworker you cannot stand.

We have opportunities to honor our heart's energetic pull without making a case for it.

This practice allowed me to stay soft and kind. It prevented me from digging for drama where it didn't exist. It gave me the space to be with the people I needed to be with and to be as present as possible to what was happening in my life.

Keep it simple. Each day is the perfect opportunity to practice the self-care of saying no when we need to and yes when we want to. These words can be complete sentences. This doesn't mean we play mind games with the people in our lives. When there is a need for conflict resolution or a heart-to-heart, trust that you will know that too. Honoring the precious reality of our daily lives includes following what we know is best for us in each moment. It means not giving up our peace in the pursuit of making someone else wrong so we can be right. It releases blame and respects people.

Learn and Teach

One of the best ways to learn is to teach. Explaining something to someone requires us to put our thoughts in order and choose specific language to express them. This helps us solidify our own perceptions and understanding. Guiding another through a learning process can illuminate the cracks in our personal comprehension, reveal where we're missing key information, and show us where we require deeper integration.

Even getting confused can help guide us toward clarity.

Speaking what we've learned allows us to hear our own thoughts. Another person may pose questions that urge us to dig more deeply into our novel notions. These alternative perspectives challenge our initial perception, sharpen our thinking, and offer welcome insights and connections.

This can be especially helpful when the information is dense or complicated. As we try to explain intricate material or many-threaded situations or even complex emotions, we are actually talking *ourselves* through a learning process. We become more aware of potential flaws in our understanding that might be leading us toward inaccurate conclusions.

Learning and teaching are intricately connected. We might tend to think of them as opposite ends of the spectrum, activities that require completely different sets of skills, but they're simply two sides to the same precious coin.

What counts is the gold.

When offered the opportunity to learn, we're invited to examine our openness. How attached are we to our beliefs and ideas and the conclusions they supply? Are we capable of allowing these commitments to inhabit our heads and hearts as guests while we consider an expanded range of perspectives and possibilities?

A willingness to suspend preconceived ideas long enough to consider alternative views assists us whether we are teaching or learning. We can't teach anything unless we are open to learning at the same time. In this way, teaching and learning are fundamentally communal activities. We learn about what others think and how they respond to the material we are sharing. We also learn a great deal about how we interact with ideas in both roles.

The distinction between learning and teaching is not always clear. If you're a naturally external processor, like me, your eagerness to share what you're learning can create uncomfortable encounters.

I can recall a time early in my spiritual journey where I was learning at a rapid pace. Like a sponge, I was continually absorbing new ideas and information—even to the point of saturation. Wringing out my proverbial sponge with others from time to time was my attempt at alchemy. Conversations with friends seemed to alchemize new ideas (when I was ready, that is) into integrated parts of my worldview. When someone asked me to explain a comment I had just made, I could hear myself either intimately owning and articulating my newfound knowledge or tripping in my attempts to overcome what turned out to be a superficial understanding. Learning in this way helped me discover what I didn't know yet.

Sometimes the friends in my circle looked at me like I had lost my mind. They weren't necessarily ready to join me in this inquisitive place. Often, they seemed more interested in demanding that I prove what I was saying or making me convince them about some aspect of my insights.

Having to defend ideas that were so new to me was exhausting. With some friends, the conversations felt more like inquisitions than dialogues. The element of judgment shut me down. Confused and a little hurt, I eventually just abandoned those conversation topics with those people.

Many years later, I was able to see how the problem with my friends' response was really about me. Rather than arising from any significant disagreement between us, the disconnect had to do with the way I was processing new ways of thinking and being. I wasn't ready to be tested or challenged; I was just learning out loud.

I have since come to realize that this is a necessary phase of my learning journey, especially when I'm experiencing a radical shift in perspective. Transformative learning often creates an unsettled feeling. As we play with the possibility of letting go of old convictions and expanding our horizons, we can feel exposed and isolated.

I've come to understand that dialogue is not always the first place to go when I am learning new things. Sometimes I need to mull things over for a while before I feel courageous enough to be challenged. Create this safety for yourself as you integrate any new knowledge. Before you rush to share your new inspirations with others, know that you may feel challenged if your conversation partners don't immediately understand or match your level of enthusiasm.

I learned that I needed trusted partners in the process of turning information into knowledge. Learning wasn't about me spouting off my newfound yet-to-be-applied-and-lived ideas. I felt most at home with people who also were curious about the concepts I had been exploring. I sought out and found people who made it safe to say, "I don't really know what that means yet, but I'd like to keep exploring it." These are the types of teaching and learning communities I try to facilitate today.

As your integration deepens, your sharing with others starts to flow naturally in exchanges that feel safe for you and also welcoming to others' input. It can take time to develop the self-trust that makes this possible.

When we're anchored in conviction and fed by community conversation and support, our ability to contribute to learning explorations with a sense of authority begins to bloom. Confident, convicted authority arises from a place of true trust and a willingness to keep learning. The best teachers are committed to and energized by the ongoing challenge of discovery. They know how to keep exploring, and they are open to a variety of teachers. This kind of learning and teaching has little to do with credentials and formal authority structures and everything to do with curiosity, a sense of wonder, and a thirst for growth.

Who or what is your current greatest teacher?

How are you showing up as a resource for others?

What was the last remarkable thing you learned?

Nobody Owes Us Education

As service providers, we cannot expect those we serve to teach us what they need. It's important that we take personal responsibility for our own learning and the expansion of our minds and hearts. When we refuse this responsibility, we too often place the burden of our ignorance on people who are in search of a soft place to land.

Service relationships are partnerships, but there is a big difference between saying "Teach me what I need to know" and "I'm here to learn how to best serve you." The former places the onus on those accessing our service to inform and enlighten us. This is an unfair responsibility. It is up to us to show up with open minds and hearts, prepared to learn and ready to challenge ourselves to expand our perspectives and examine our intentions.

Beyond specific relationships of service, this insight also applies to the learning we need to undertake in other areas of our shared society. Those of us living with racial and socioeconomic privilege are being called to learn, to atone, and to live and behave differently. Racism and discrimination toward Black and Indigenous people and other people of color are unacceptable and violent expressions in our world. They have been for hundreds of years. The coronavirus pandemic has brought these and other ongoing injustices into sharper focus.

At the same time, stereotyping, generalizations, prejudiced attitudes, and discriminatory actions toward people living with health challenges, mental health struggles, developmental disabilities, and addictions must be overcome. In all of these areas, many of us are becoming more keenly aware of what we don't know, even as we desire to address and dismantle the biases that are baked into our systems and structures as well as the ones that live in our hearts.

Learning is a big part of the change we seek. It is time to stretch beyond our comfort zones and show up ready to have difficult conversations. The need for intense internal examination is strong, but that's only the first step in the overhaul of our unbalanced and misdirected systems. We need to learn and teach as we undertake this work.

If you are a person of color or a member of any marginalized group, you may be more than ready to step into the role of teacher with your friends and colleagues. You may also be utterly exhausted by it all. You get to decide how you wish to engage in dialogue that educates others.

For those of us who are white and/or experience privilege in other ways, it is time to seek out and stay in the conversation. It is not acceptable to forfeit our personal responsibility. The fact that we have always retained the ability to choose whether or not to pay attention to how structural injustices benefit us at others' expense is evidence of our privilege. Knowing that, we have a responsibility to act.

As we undertake this transformative education together, be kind to yourself and others. Prepare yourself to always show up in learning mode so you can garner the wisdom of any group you find yourself with. There is always something to learn and something to contribute.

Know that you will make mistakes. Compassion for yourself and others can make the learning process more graceful. None of us learn well in harsh conditions, so ensure that you are caring for your own personal needs. Resist the urge to transfer your responsibility to others, especially those who have borne the impact of an angry and ignorant world for so very long.

And when you find yourself surrounded by others who share the same privilege you have (whether with regard to race, disability, or some other factor), know that you can make a difference in the discourse. Resist the urge to blame or judge others, and instead extend a desire to understand. As you learn what needs transformation in your own heart, you will be able to offer your input from a place of authenticity, transparency, and kindness.

Your Experience Matters

Let's give life a little credit. As a teacher, it's unmatched.

Every day is filled with learning and teachable moments. These come from outside us in the people and events we encounter as we go about our lives. They also come from within us, often provoked or occasioned by what we do and whom we meet during the day. What insights emerge on the commute to work? How does your heart speak to you when you wash the dishes? What messages does your ego urgently deliver when you are mired in frustration or conflict? What do your dreams churn up when you're sleeping? And what does your soul say when you slow down enough to listen?

What if we started fully appreciating our experience as service providers and listening more carefully to the evidence contained in our hearts?

Our service organizations' fund-raising departments often place great value on the lived experience of those we serve. We learn about the battle from the person who's fighting it. We understand the impact of pain when we sit beside the one who is hurting. We recognize growth and healing when we join in celebration with those who have overcome.

Given these commitments, our collective resistance to embracing these experiences in the lives of those who provide service and manage care seems baffling.

We too readily gloss over our own lived experience as service providers. Perhaps this is an attempt to remove ourselves and our stories from the service relationship. If so, it is a tactical mistake. Recognizing the connection between our personal challenges and our greatest discoveries offers a grounding energy to our service. Our own experience of growth allows us to see it in others and deepens our capacity for presence and engagement.

We capitalize on our lived experience when we allow ourselves to sink deeply into what we sense, think, do, and feel, and absorb and integrate all the wisdom it has to offer. Honoring our experience involves recognizing and claiming its value. You will never learn anything in a textbook that surpasses the value of what you have lived.

Imagine your life as a laboratory where everything can be the object of your observation. Watch it. Take notes. Listen to it. Feel it. Take more notes. Peer at it from different angles. Shake it up and see where things land. Do the same thing over and over. Do something completely different. Release control. Hold on tightly. Play with the events of your life like a scientist would manipulate the variables in an experiment.

Life will supply your share of struggle and strife. The first order of business is to live it and live through it. Learning will make itself evident as you make yourself available to it. They say to "write when you are raw and publish when you are healed." I think this sentiment can apply to life as a service provider as well. Learn and grow in your rawness, and serve as you integrate your experience.

Your own quirky personal design as a human being is exactly the beautiful stuff you need to make a difference around and within yourself. Everything that makes you who you are is precisely what's needed at this time in our world. You are here. What you've got to offer has a place to land.

Use what you learn about yourself and this world to fashion anchor points for your journey. An anchor point is an idea, a reframe, a process, or an activity. It is a prayer, a hope, a whisper of gratitude, a good cry, or a soft shoulder. Anchoring ourselves allows us to remain open, even while sheltered, and feel held without feeling frozen. When we are anchored, we are more readily able to recall what matters and why, and to integrate what our life of service is teaching us.

Know yourself, and be willing to be surprised. See your truth, and revel in your mystery. Get comfortable with the perfection of your flawed human experience. Make yourself safe, and become that safe place for other souls on the path of transformation and growth.

What keeps you grounded?

Name three anchor points that help you stay open.

CHAPTER 10

Be Here Now

An Invitation to Presence

This final invitation borrows the phrase Ram Dass used as the title of his bestselling 1971 book. A friend and spiritual guide offered Dass the advice "Be here now." It came at precisely the right moment in his journey. These three words became a crucial insight that expanded to completely change his own life, and then go on to make a difference in countless others'. Inspired by Ram Dass's book and its message, George Harrison wrote a song with the same title in the same year. Ray LaMontagne wrote one thirty years later.

Be. Here. Now.

Whether we use it to shape songs or as a meditation mantra, a slogan on a bumper sticker, or a handwritten note taped to the bathroom mirror, millions of us try to accept this invitation every day.

As a spiritual teaching, as a word of kind counsel, or as a personal reminder, these simple words are an invitation to presence. They invite us to offer all our attention to the current moment and whatever it offers. For service providers, the willingness and ability to accept this invitation and embody its wisdom in our work and our lives can make the difference between conscious, self-connected, focused service and merely checking boxes, completing work, or clearing caseloads.

I fear that too many of us have become accustomed to being elsewhere now. As we're inundated with the suffering and struggle of the world and the inequities and injustice of our society, many of us have conditioned ourselves to look past the plight of individual people in individual moments—including places and circumstances where we are uniquely positioned and equipped to offer something of ourselves.

This can be a particular challenge for service providers who witness and work with human need and immediate pain on a daily basis. Sometimes it can feel as though all of life is an endless pull on our heartstrings and a constant draw on our time, energy, and resources. We seek to escape from the presence of suffering in all kinds of ways. Some of these behaviors, like overwork and competitiveness, are frequently rewarded with promotions and plaudits. Others are seen as failings of character or tragic mistakes.

The truth of this underscores the need, in these times of ongoing crisis and unsettled future, for the self-awareness and self-regard at the heart of conscious service. Only as we connect honorably and lovingly with ourselves will we be able to authentically connect with others. Only as we resist the ongoing urge to abandon ourselves will we be able to support others as they find their way along life's journey.

As we begin to inhabit the present moment with more and more attention, we will find that invitations to serve are abundant. Opportunities for service will arise in your interactions, on your errands, in the line at the grocery store, on your walk in the park. You are not required to take every opportunity. Not every call is meant for you.

There is no limit to the number of good deeds that need doing in the here and now. In fact, opportunities to make a difference in our world are so numerous that many pass unnoticed every day. There is also no quota of good deeds that must be accomplished by any one of us— me and you included. We are invited to simply show up, open and willing, ready to respond based on the energy, time, and resources we have available to us in each moment of each day.

That's it.

Becoming present allows us to focus our energy and ground our giving in gratitude rather than fear. It allows us to know our role and act from its authority. It allows us to embrace our humanity and honor its limits. It allows us to remain engaged, knowing that each moment is too full of possibility and power to ignore.

I believe that those who are able to be here now—to inhabit the present moment with full attention and self-connected peace—are uniquely positioned to be catalysts for the great transformations our world requires today.

■   ■   ■

An Invitation to Accept the Invitations

Like any set of big ideas, conscious service means nothing as an intellectual concept. Ideas—including every concept I've offered in this book—are suggestions. They point to patterns and hint at possibilities. Ideas become useful only as they become real. Just like our values, our ideas become real in the actions and choices by which we demonstrate our priorities and navigate the challenges and opportunities daily life supplies moment by moment.

The invitations that have guided our exploration of conscious service throughout this book offer ways to reframe and focus your life and your work as a service provider. Together, they invite you to consider that your life and your work, so often assumed to be realities best kept separate, really are one thing. Conscious service is based on the understanding that our full presence and self-aware participation in the relationships that form and shape our unique identities are deeply relevant to the relationships through which we offer service that makes a difference.

A life of more sustainable and life-giving service rests on our capacity to integrate what we know and who we are into what we do. The more skillfully and intentionally we are able to bring these elements of our being into alignment, the happier we will be, the easier our lives will feel, and the more effective and sustainable our labors of love and service will become.

So, by way of recap, and as a concluding call to practice responsive presence in all you do, I offer you a handful of invitations gathered from the pages you've traversed. Here they're stamped with a final welcome: make them real in your life by embracing and embodying them in each present moment, day after day, as you continue the sacred journey of conscious service.

Receive them again with my respect, affection, and love.

Know Why You're Here

The invitation to purpose challenges you to pay attention to where you are as well as what you're being called into. It welcomes you to the work of examining your motivations and intentions as well as your most deeply held values and beliefs. Notice how these powerful personal forces are influencing and affecting you today. Even the best-articulated statement of purpose means little when it stays tacked on the wall or appended to your résumé.

Know why you're here now—in this moment. Speak it plain and make it matter. Claim your purpose with courage and commitment.

Why are you here today?

Show Up Fully

The invitation to wholeness welcomes you to become more aware of how amazingly complicated people are, and how the fullness of who *you* are matters in every corner of your life. It invites you to explore the power of your physical, cognitive, emotional, relational, and spiritual channels of being. Open all the channels of your marvelous human system and embrace the depth and breadth of human experience as it's happening, heartbeat by heartbeat. When we show up split, half-assed, or distorted, we miss moments of connection and fail to honor ourselves and others.

Show up fully now—in this moment. Experience your fullness and the magnificence of the people you're with through new eyes and with fuller attention.

How can you show up fully today?

Embrace Full Responsibility

Most of us desire the experience of freedom, even if we don't always know exactly what the freedom we crave feels like or how it can appear in our lives. I suspect what gets in the way is our doubt that true freedom is even possible. The invitation to freedom puts this word right beside *responsibility* and asks you to try holding on to the power that we too often and too easily sign over to others. Rejecting this invitation can lead to bitterness and blame. Remember that embracing responsibility doesn't automatically mean taking on more tasks. We find freedom as we practice responding (rather than reacting) to whatever is going on within us or around us.

Embrace full responsibility now—in this moment. Demonstrate your freedom in ways that honor yourself in all your roles and respect the autonomy of the people you serve.

Where can you use your freedom today?

Connect with Your Self

The invitation to discovery challenges you to resist the urge to avoid your true self. It welcomes you to a lifelong adventure of knowing and caring for yourself in all your mixed-up radiance. As you accept this invitation, you will move away from viewing these choices as selfish or self-indulgent and discover positive self-connection as a foundation for joy and fulfillment and a fundamental part of the ongoing process of personal growth and maturity. These are the qualities of character that can support sustainable service and good health.

If you long for a life that includes self-love, self-compassion, and organic self-care, then this invitation is one you cannot turn down. Stand by your own side in every moment, welcome yourself back when you drift away, and share the best of who you are with the people around you.

Connect with yourself now—in this moment. Discover what you need, and then offer it to yourself with grace.

How can you connect with yourself today?

Communicate with Love

The invitation to enlightenment calls you beyond the tools of effective communication and past feelings of fear to the human-sized place of clarity and connection as you relate to others. By accepting this invitation, you engage in communication that recognizes and respects the nuances of human experience, avoids using personal power to manipulate or control people, and adds greater awareness and focus to the intimate acts of speaking and listening with care. Receive each moment with connected clarity and choose to bring the gifts of enlightened communication to every interaction, no matter how small.

Communicate with love now—in this moment. Expand your capacity to receive every kind of message by listening with your heart. Deliver every message from the same place.

How can you express love today?

Focus on Transformation

It's tempting to see problems and want to fix them. The invitation to vision asks us to wait before we rush in with solutions, and to watch before we make assumptions about what's happening and how we need to be involved. It welcomes us to recognize that relationships are where we will be changed the most, and where our efforts to serve can be aimed and invested in the highest good. Shift your vision from solving problems and fixing people. Instead imagine your work as witnessing and walking beside transformational moments in your own life and in the lives of the people you serve.

Focus on transformation now—in this moment. Look for larger indications of healing and wholeness. Share what you see with somebody close.

What is being transformed in or around you today?

Create Community Together

The invitation to leadership can feel daunting at first. Relax. This call doesn't necessarily mean it's time to start gunning for a promotion. Our organizations are made up of human beings; these systems need people at every level and in every role who can access and engage the humanity beneath the hierarchy and tap the power that so often gets buried in bureaucracy. When the structures that guide and support our work genuinely invite input and value personal expression, they can become communities of unbridled creativity, deep passion, and shared energy. Each of us has the capacity to lead and contribute to this transformation.

Notice the cultures that surround you daily. See these structures through the lens of leadership and claim with confidence your power to co-create communities of partnership that work for everyone.

Create community now—in this moment. Lead from where you are. You are the only one who possesses your unique blend of vision and power, and the only person who can make your contribution.

Where can you join in creating community today?

Seek and Share Support Continuously

The invitation to compassion is a gentle reminder that you are a member of the human race. As such you are worthy of compassionate care, *and* you are an inexhaustible source of hope and healing energy for others. Accepting this invitation welcomes you to embrace the varied expressions of service you will likely experience in your life, as both provider and recipient. If the call to compassion feels scary, you're invited to step back and reevaluate what you assume this response asks of you. You will know that you have accepted this invitation when your well of compassion bathes not only others but also yourself, giving you the courage to seek and accept support when you need it. Experience and enjoy the peace that comes with authentic compassion for self and others.

Seek and share support now—in this moment. Trust that compassion springs from a place deeper than fear. Offer it to yourself.

How can you receive what you need today?

Learn from Your Life

We can live our lives in closed loops, with closed fists and closed minds. In times of crisis and change, when we feel threatened or spent, it's tempting to shut down entirely. The invitation to openness is a call to resist this impulse and instead embrace the ever-evolving world and our constantly shifting place in it with courage and gratitude.

Accepting this invitation can provide you with an arm's-length view of any situation. Openness creates opportunity for illumination. As you commit to learning and accept the challenge of teaching what you have found to be true, you will be changed. Hardness is softened by curiosity. Jaded vision is cleansed by compassion. Clarity comes by way of integration. And the capacity to hold ourselves lightly enough to laugh will ease the inevitable aches and pains that come with the hard-won lessons life offers. Look at the present moment through the eyes of a learner, and trust that the world is wider and more generous than you can yet imagine.

Learn from your life now—in this moment. You don't have to wait to learn the hard way. Use what today offers to discover a new path through an old obstacle.

What will you learn today?

Our culture of achievement and celebrity can make us think we have to do something big in order to make a difference that matters. The truth is that the tiniest acts of internal kindness can move us outward in love. The most subtle alterations in our perspective can transform the whole picture. Every moment is an opportunity for connection and creation. Be here now. This can change the world.

All we have to do is accept the invitation.

Epilogue

On May 25, 2020, George Floyd was killed in Minneapolis, Minnesota, in the United States. Mr. Floyd died beneath the knee of a white police officer. Rage and sorrow about the murder, along with a passionate outcry for justice, were heard and felt around the world, even in my northern nation of Canada.

My friend and writing colleague, Erika, a service provider herself, is an African American woman with a young family. Erika and I were scheduled for our weekly check-in Zoom call the day after Mr. Floyd was killed.

Erika looked exhausted and sad. We spent the hour together just processing what had happened. Watching her expression as we spoke, I realized that my friendship with Erika, one of the first close friendships I've shared with a Black person, made this act of violence—another in a long and awful history of racist hate crimes—feel closer and more terrible to me than any such crime I'd heard about before. It also showed me where I had previously shielded myself from similar realities as a service provider.

In that conversation, the privilege I possess as a white woman was as palpable as the chair I was sitting on. My privilege offers me degrees of separation and distance from Erika's experience. I do not have to think about racial violence or feel it or fear it in the same way as she does.

For Erika and her family and friends of the same race, and for millions of people around the world, violence, racism, and fear for their lives and freedom continue to be very real and very present.

Before our call that day, in many ways and for many reasons, I was afraid. I didn't know if I was equal to the conversation that might be asked of me. I was so aware of not wanting to say the wrong thing or to inflict pain, from what I might say and from what I might not get right.

Gently and with care, we walked the landscape of dialogue that day. Our care and respect for one another made it all right to not know what to say, to cry when the opportunity for release was there, and to express love as well as immeasurable hurt.

Erika told me later that she had been nervous about our conversation too. We had never before discussed race or the differences in our realities.

I knew I needed to listen closely, to ask questions with great care, and to challenge my preconceived notions. Because Erika and I have a solid friendship and we share conceptual frameworks and language that help us communicate well, we were able to navigate this sensitive conversation in ways that deepened our connection and offered us both an opportunity to learn and heal.

In the year that has passed since May 25, 2020, and since our time together the next day broke open our relationship's power, Erika and I have had many more conversations about race, discrimination, violence, and healing. Our comfort with one another has grown. Our trust has deepened. Our talk has become more organic.

Erika has graciously helped me. Through dialogue with my friend, I have learned to challenge my ideas, my ignorance, my personal bias, my privilege, and my power. I've also come to more deeply understand my role in the larger exploration and discussion of racism and white supremacy in our society.

Because of her roles, Erika has found herself in the thick of many interactions, discussions, and conflicts about racialization, violence, and equity. These experiences frequently challenge her deeply. Sometimes she stays silent from fear or courtesy, and sometimes she lashes out in anger and impatience. Now she wants to find a way to navigate these challenges in ways that feel more self-loving and self-honoring.

Where she previously might have let comments slide, Erika knows she will speak up. As opportunities to inspire awareness in others and delve more deeply into her personal wounds come up, Erika is learning how to balance her energy and conserve her resources. She chooses which opportunities to engage and which she lets pass unremarked.

The opportunity to walk with Erika in this journey as I continue to learn and grow and as I keep pushing the edges of my own comfort zone has been an honor. It has allowed us both to practice our commitments with one another and to embody the energy of service that grounds our relationship in grace.

I think now about how easy it would have been to skip our call that day. Excuses to flee from the presence of pain abound. We could have put it off because of the intensity of our emotions and uncertainty about the other's level of interest. We could have avoided the conversation altogether and pushed through with other agenda items. But I see now how that would have been an act of self-abandonment on both our parts. Avoidance or denial would only have added pain to Erika's emotional experience, deepened my own ignorance and sense of personal powerlessness, and wasted our relationship's ability to become a container for the type of transformation that this world so desperately needs.

We may fear connections and conversations for what they might tell us about ourselves. We may fear that by extending ourselves to another in spirit and in action we will lose something. But the risk involved in relationships is the risk of love. It is also the essence of conscious service.

In my own country, we continue to try to face the atrocities of our own colonial past. The reverberation of assimilation, oppression, residential school systems, and cultural genocide continue to be very real in the lives of the Indigenous peoples of Canada, and these concerns are becoming more real for the rest of us as well.

We know that our world needs to change in order to survive, and we're starting to realize that means *we* have to change. Any difference we hope to make in the world around us must begin with a difference in us. The conscious service approach begins and ends with attention to and respect for the internal work that will expand to include and impact the worlds of our relationships, organizations, cultures, and societies.

We recognize that we may not always feel whole, but we show up with all we are, letting our deepest values guide us. We resist taking responsibility for others, even as we embrace our responsibility for creating community and facilitating connections that lead to transformation. We act in faith that people can change and systems can be transformed for the better. We remain present to both ourselves and the people we're with, finding opportunities to serve and support one another naturally and from places of strength and joy. We seek ways to engage and include people who have been pushed away from the table. We do all this with love, trusting in our own worth as well as the abiding value of every person we encounter.

And we do these things together.

NOTES

Note: The number that begins each note indicates the page in this book where the cited material appears.

Introduction

4 **"If your vision of service does not include":** Alan Cohen, *A Deep Breath of Life: Daily Inspiration for Heart-Centered Living* (Carlsbad, CA: Hay House, 1996), 101.

Chapter 1

17 Torey Hayden, *One Child: The True Story of a Tormented Six-Year-Old and the Brilliant Teacher Who Reached Out* (New York: HarperCollins Publishers/William Morrow, 1980, 2016).

33 **"[V]irtues" as values in action:** James E. Loehr and Tony Schwartz, *The Power of Full Engagement: Managing Energy, Not Time, Is the Key to High Performance and Personal Renewal* (New York: Free Press, 2005).

Chapter 2

71 **[S]ocially intelligent people have a keen sense:** Daniel Goleman, *Social Intelligence: The New Science of Human Relationships* (New York: Bantam Books, 2006), 108.

75 **[W]henever I observe behavior:** Debbie Ford, *The Dark Side of the Light Chasers: Reclaiming Your Power, Creativity, Brilliance, and Dreams* (Carlsbad, CA: Hay House, 2012), 25.

76 **Likewise, whenever you admire:** Ford, *Dark Side of the Light Chasers.*

Chapter 3

81 **[A] gift in "ugly wrapping paper":** Iyanla Vanzant, *One Day My Soul Just Opened Up: 40 Days and 40 Nights Toward Spiritual Strength and Personal Growth* (New York: Atria Books, 1998), 283.

Chapter 4

119 **"Wherever you go":** Jon Kabat-Zinn, *Wherever You Go, There You Are: Mindfulness Meditation in Everyday Life* (New York: Hachette Books, 1994, 2005), 137.

Chapter 5

147 **[E]nlightenment is not about adding:** Marianne Williamson, *A Year of Miracles: Daily Devotions and Reflections* (New York: HarperOne, 2013), 8.

168 **Respect is demonstrated:** Carl Rogers, *Client-Centered Therapy: Its Current Practice, Implications and Theory* (Boston: Houghton Mifflin, 1951).

Chapter 6

204 **"There are few presumptions":** Michael Ignatieff, *The Needs of Strangers* (New York: Picador, 1984), 11.

Chapter 7

212 **A young man noticed one day:** Ed Buller, https://www.youtube.com /watch?v=ZB_3augrDqo.

Chapter 8

246 **[C]ompassion has often been misunderstood:** Iyanla Vanzant, *One Day My Soul Just Opened Up: 40 Days and 40 Nights Toward Spiritual Strength and Personal Growth* (New York: Atria Books, 1998), 148.

Chapter 9

280 **[D]ecentralizing leadership in organizations is key:** Peter M. Senge, *The Fifth Discipline: The Art and Practice of the Learning Organization* (New York: Doubleday /Currency, 1990, 2006), 3.

ABOUT THE AUTHOR

Elizabeth Bishop is the creator of The Conscious Service Approach™, a research-based set of principles designed to enhance both the experience of service providers and the quality of service they offer.

Bishop's professional background includes more than forty years in human service. Her experience ranges from facility- to community-based services and from direct service to management and leadership responsibilities. She has specialized in developmental services, brain injury rehabilitation, and mental health programs. She has taught at the post-secondary level for more than thirty years, including within formal academic programs, continuing education, and professional development training. Above all, Bishop is an avid learner from life, with all its depth and wonder.

As the founder of Elizabeth Bishop Consulting, she facilitates an ongoing discussion about what it means to be of service through her regular blogs, social media presence, workshops, and online courses.

ABOUT HAZELDEN PUBLISHING

As part of the Hazelden Betty Ford Foundation, Hazelden Publishing offers both cutting-edge educational resources and inspirational books. Our print and digital works help guide individuals in treatment and recovery, as well as their loved ones.

Professionals who work to prevent and treat addiction also turn to Hazelden Publishing for evidence-based curricula, digital content solutions, and videos for use in schools, treatment and correctional programs, and community settings. We also offer training for implementation of our curricula.

Through published and digital works, Hazelden Publishing extends the reach of healing and hope to individuals, families, and communities affected by addiction and related issues.

For more information about Hazelden publications,
please call **800-328-9000** or visit us online at **hazelden.org/bookstore**.

Other Titles That May Interest You

Take Good Care

Finding Your Joy in Compassionate Caregiving

In this 2017 Nautilus Book Award-winning book, author Cynthia Orange brings together compelling testimonies from a wide range of caregivers, advice from leading experts in the field, and her own hard-won wisdom to capture the subtle differences between care*taking* and care*giving*. With a foreword by Susan Allen Toth, the critically acclaimed author of *No Saints around Here: A Caregiver's Days,* this book shows us *how* and *why* caring for each other can be a mutually rewarding experience. 220 pp.

Order No. 3425

Conquering Shame and Codependency

8 Steps to Freeing the True You

Darlene Lancer sheds new light on shame, revealing how feelings and beliefs about shame affect identity and behavior and how shame can corrode relationships, destroying trust and love. She then provides the eight key steps needed for healing from shame, learning to love yourself, and developing healthy relationships. 248 pp.

Order No. 7554

The Language of Letting Go

Daily Meditations on Codependency

In this favorite daily meditation book, Melody Beattie integrates her own life experiences and fundamental recovery reflections especially for those of us who struggle with the issue of codependency. Each day's meditation provides a guide through the day and encourages us to remember that each day is an opportunity for growth and renewal. 408 pp.

Order No. 5076

For more information about Hazelden publications,
please call **800-328-9000**
or visit us online at **hazelden.org/bookstore.**